BACKROADS & BYWAYS OF

NEW MEXICO

BACKROADS & BYWAYS OF

NEW MEXICO

*Drives, Day Trips &
Weekend Excursions*

FIRST EDITION

SHARON NIEDERMAN

THE COUNTRYMAN PRESS
A division of W. W. Norton & Company
Independent Publishers Since 1923

We welcome your comments and suggestions.
Please contact:
Editor
The Countryman Press
500 Fifth Avenue
New York, NY 10110
or e-mail countrymanpress@wwnorton.com

Maps by Michael Borop (sitesatlas.com)

All photographs taken by the author except for those listed below:
Page 90: ©Wilsilver77/iStockphoto.com; page 106: © brians101/iStockphoto.com;
page 186: © benedek/iStockphoto.com

For information about permission to reproduce selections from this book, write to
Permissions, The Countryman Press, 500 Fifth Avenue, New York, NY 10110

For information about special discounts for bulk purchases, please contact
W. W. Norton Special Sales at specialsales@wwnorton.com or 800-233-4830

Manufacturing by Versa Press
Series design by Chris Welch

The Countryman Press
www.countrymanpress.com

A division of W. W. Norton & Company, Inc.
500 Fifth Avenue, New York, NY 10110
www.wwnorton.com

978-1-68268-362-0 (pbk.)

10 9 8 7 6 5 4 3 2 1

PREVIOUS PAGE: VALLEY OF FIRES RECREATION AREA LAVA FLOW SUPPORTS A RICH VARIETY OF PLANT LIFE

This Road Is Made of Stories

Remember when you came to town, fell in love with
Desert sunlight, Indian drums, discovery itself
Placed a pawned turquoise ring on your finger
Promised you'd never leave, and you haven't

But today you left the museum
Walked downtown Route 66
Met the toothless beggar in torn black lace
Offered her your last dollar bill
"What for?" she asked
Then spun you around

Central Avenue crumbled away
As the road came into focus
AcomaLagunaBudvilleSanFidelCubero
Where Hemingway never wrote
"The Old Man and the Sea"

This road is made of stories
Told in café whispers and 3 am motel darkness
Clues scattered at White's Garage and left behind
Where waters flow both east and west
Fragments are all you get, cheap curio ashtrays of the aunts
A map that will fall to pieces
If you open it one more time

Just look ahead, keep going, accept what comes
All the way to the edge of beyond
Your home is in the thunderclouds, the next abandoned pile of rust
Too beautiful to pass without a photo.

—Sharon Niederman, June 2019

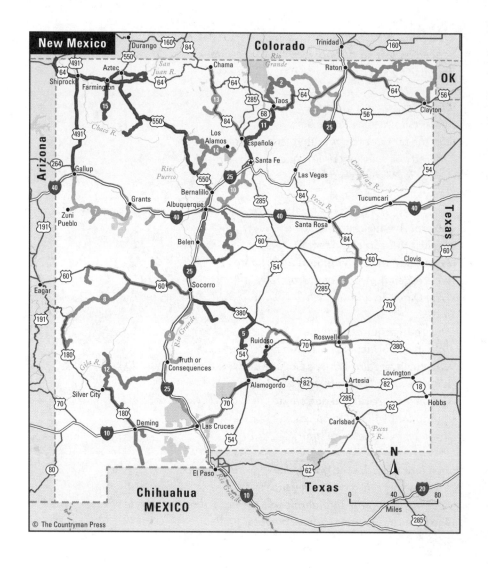

Contents

Introduction

Many people who visit New Mexico are initially drawn to Taos, Santa Fe, and Albuquerque. The blend of culture, history, art, cuisine, and natural beauty is practically irresistible. Even those who live here find themselves visiting these cities over and over.

But once you fall in love with New Mexico, you want more. You've been to the Santa Fe Opera. You've been to Indian Market. You've been to the Albuquerque International Balloon Fiesta. You've visited Taos Pueblo. These places and events are fantastic, even life-changing.

But there comes a time when you want to venture outside the well-known sites and events to find your New Mexico. You want the quiet villages, slow roads, local museums, mom-and-pop cafés where people take time to visit, share stories, and where memories are long. You want to make discoveries that are exciting because you made them, not necessarily because they are safe, popular tourist destinations that get a lot of ink.

You may have been to Chaco Culture National Historical Park, but have you been to Four Corners outliers like Salmon Ruins and Aztec Ruins National Monument? These are smaller and less grand in scale, but it may be that accessibility that gives them the power to inspire a deeper, more intense experience of the Ancestral Puebloan culture.

Whether you are a visitor or a long-time resident, the good news is that in New Mexico, there is plenty of room to roam. As the fifth-largest state by land area with a population of only slightly over 2 million, traffic slows down and disperses once you leave the main highways. New Mexico has many miles of backroads—so many we can't travel them all in the pages of this book. But we will travel enough of them that they will take you to the

LEFT: FOLLOW HISTORIC ROUTE 66 AS IT SWOOPS WESTBOUND

real New Mexico, add depth to your knowledge of the place, and reveal the state's heart to you, the openhearted traveler.

As for the well-traveled roads, interstates, and busy highways, sometimes it is necessary to drive them partway to get to where we really want to journey and find that authentic sense of place that is waiting beyond the next bend in the road.

We may be remote—much of our history is rooted in our remoteness, and the travel across long, deserted roads to reach us—and we may appear foreign—people still ask if they need a passport to come here and if we accept US currency—but New Mexico offers so much of the national psyche to explore: Billy the Kid, Route 66, UFOs, Harvey Girls and railroads, the Wild West and cowboys, Native Americans, Georgia O'Keeffe, the Manhattan Project—each a topic worth many books by themselves. My hope is to whet your appetite for more, but also to spike your curiosity with information that sustains the desire for the next trip. I like to say New Mexico is my muse: Stories rise up from out of the landscape to continually pique my imagination.

New Mexico signage is sometimes sparse and can be confusing. This book curates several well-identified byways, such as the Jemez Scenic Byway, the Turquoise Trail, and the Enchanted Circle, for the sake of thoroughness and organized passage, I have created some new routes by linking roads and towns in a way that makes driving sense. And I suggest, through the organization of the table of contents, which trips may be linked together.

Exploration, discovery, surprise—that's what fuels our road trips. I've been traveling these roads over two decades, and I always find intriguing new sights and experiences in the most unexpected places. And isn't that what travel is really all about?

Practical Stuff

A FEW OF MY PERSONAL TRAVEL TIPS

- When you see something that catches your eye, stop, spend time looking, snap that photo. Don't think you will come back later. That never happens, and you miss the shot.
- Don't be afraid to ask people in a restaurant what they are eating. They are likely to tell you they have been eating here since they were kids with their grandparents. You will get a lot more than just a report of the red chile enchiladas.
- Always wear a hat.
- Always wear sturdy, comfortable shoes.
- Always carry water, snacks, a flashlight, a blanket, a spare battery charger, basic first aid kit, including peroxide, healing ointment, Afrin for nosebleeds, and bandages.
- Make sure your spare tire is at proper pressure before you set out.
- Keep in mind this is the land of *mañana*—that doesn't literally mean tomorrow, it just means "not now." This is New Mexico, not New York. Little is done in a New York minute. Should you, for example, arrive at a motel at 4 p.m., having been told your room would be ready then, and your room is not ready, getting angry or even annoyed will get you nowhere. Maintain complete politeness and understanding. Take a breath, accept it, and go check your emails.
- Don't attempt to advise anyone that it's not done the way they are doing it where you come from. The attitude is: go back where you came from if you don't like it. That's how we do it here. Subject closed.

THE OLD WEST MAY BE ASLEEP, BUT IT IS STILL ALIVE ON FOLSOM'S MAIN STREET

- New Mexico is virtually non-smoking.
- Talking or texting while driving is frowned upon. If you are stopped, you will be slapped with a $100 fee.
- Strictly obey speed limits on outskirts of and within small towns. I guarantee you will get a ticket if you do 45 in a 35-mph zone in Eagle Nest or Cimarron. And you don't have time to come back to talk to the judge.
- Make no disparaging remarks about any group of people. New Mexico is a big small town, and everybody is related.
- Respect posted rules. If a museum, church, shop, or Indian pueblo says no photographs, do not attempt to sneak one in.
- Always call ahead to your destination to be sure it is open. Hours posted on websites are not always accurate, and they are not always adhered to.
- Check road conditions. Visit NMroads.com or call the hotline at 511 or 800-432-4269.

WEATHER AND ALTITUDE

- Stay out of arroyos or running ditches.
- Temperatures vary greatly—as much as 40° or 50°F in a day. Dress in layers and be prepared.
- Hydrate. Even if you are not thirsty, it's important to keep drinking water.

- Alcohol and caffeine can pack a greater punch at a high altitude. Moderation in all things. Ibuprofen and dark chocolate help with symptoms of altitude sickness.

PHONES

- Cell: In remote areas, such as along the High Road, there may not be cell service. Backroads by their nature go through remote areas.
- Area codes: New Mexico has two area codes, 505 or 575. If one does not work, try the other.

MAPS AND DIRECTIONS

- Do not rely on GPS. GPS directions may be misleading here.
- Invest in up-to-date paper maps and the New Mexico Road & Recreation Atlas

INDIAN PUEBLO ETIQUETTE

There are 19 Indian Pueblos in New Mexico, plus the Navajo and Jicarilla and Mescalero Reservations. If you are a guest at an Indian Pueblo, please remember:

- Do not venture outside of the gathering area, usually around the plaza.
- Do not attempt to cross or walk in the dance area.
- Do not clap between dance rounds.
- Maintain a respectful silence, including silencing your cell phone.
- Do not photograph churches, cemeteries, kivas, or sacred spaces, even if you have purchased a photo permit.
- Do not sit in seats reserved for families.
- Contact the Indian Pueblo Cultural Center at indianpueblo.com or call 505-843-7270.

NEW MEXICO FUN FACTS

- State plant: yucca
- State tree: pinon

- State Gem: turquoise
- State Tie: bolo
- State cookie: biscochito
- State pastry: sopapilla
- State bird: roadrunner
- State motto: *Cresciteundo* (It grows as it goes)
- State fish: Rio Grande cutthroat trout
- State animal: black bear
- State question: red or green?
- State flag: orange Zia sun sign on gold background. The actual emblem of the Zia Pueblo, it announces the four directions.
- New Mexico has 33 counties and 102 towns.

HELPFUL BOOKS

- *The Place Names of New Mexico* by Robert Julyan
- *Roadside New Mexico: A Guide to Historic Markers* by David Pike
- *A Brief History of New Mexico* by Myra Ellen Jenkins and Albert H. Schroeder
- *New Mexico: A New Guide to the Colorful State* by Chilton, Chilton, et. al.

EMERGENCIES

- Call 911 for immediate help, or contact the New Mexico State Police (505-827-9300; 505-827-3476) or Search and Rescue Resource Officer, 4491 Cerrillos Road, Santa Fe (505-827-9228)
- Drunk Busters DWI Hotline (877-DWI-HALT or 877-394-4258) is a toll-free hotline; #394 (or keypad letters DWI) is the convenience key for cell phones.

PRICE CODES

In keeping with the curated nature of this book, which attempts to describe the most authentic experience possible, recommendations for dining and lodging avoid chain establishments and emphasize locally owned restaurants and motels.

Dining

Dining costs are estimated per single entrée.

$	Inexpensive	Up to $20
$$	Moderate	$20–50
$$$	Expensive	$50–75
$$$$	Very Expensive	Over $75

Lodging

$	Inexpensive	Up to $75
$$	Moderate	Up to $130
$$$	Expensive	Up to $200
$$$$	Very Expensive	Over $200

OLD JAIL →

JESSE JAMES SPENT THE NIGHT IN CIMARRON'S OLD
JAILHOUSE—SEE FOR YOURSELF ON THE WALKING
TOUR BEHIND THE ST. JAMES HOTEL

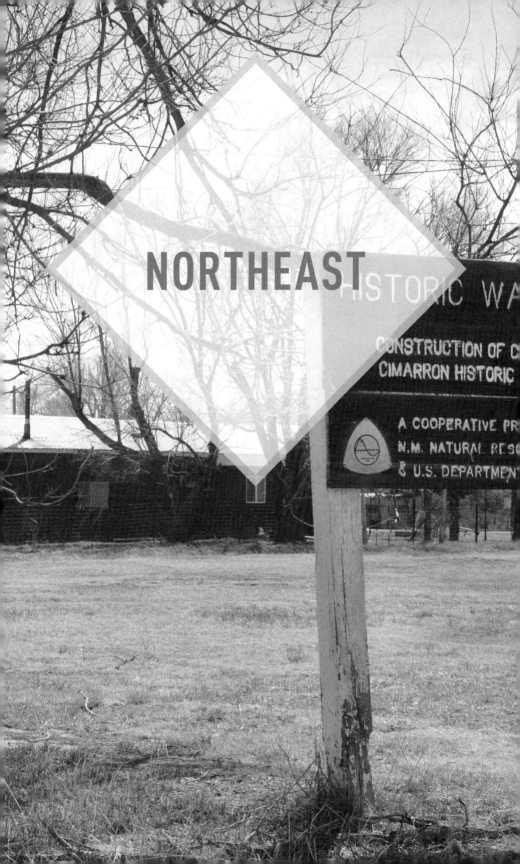

NORTHEAST

1

ALONG THE DRY CIMARRON

THE BACKROADER'S BACKROAD: HOW SWITCHBOARD
OPERATOR SARAH ROOKE SAVED FOLSOM AND BUFFALO
SOLDIER GEORGE McJUNKIN CHANGED HISTORY BY
DISCOVERING THE FOLSOM POINTS

ESTIMATED LENGTH: 90 miles Raton to Clayton; 217 miles on Dry Cimarron Route

ESTIMATED TIME: One day to a weekend

GETTING THERE: Go north on 2nd Street in Raton, bear right, and go 6 miles to
the junction of NM 72 and NM 526. Go right on NM 72 toward Yankee, once
a homesteader settlement, while keeping an eye out for deer, wild turkey,
bear, and the occasional mountain lion. Altogether, the trip is 41 miles from
Raton to Folsom along NM 72. Climb 500 feet toward Johnson Mesa, impas-
sible and unplowed in winter. The flat, lava-topped Mesa is 14 miles long and
about 5 miles wide. Once on the mesa top, look west from this 8,000-foot
elevation for an incomparable panoramic view of the Sangre de Cristo Mountains. The mesa was named for one of the first settlers in Colfax County,
Elijah Johnson, a cattleman drawn to the rich grasslands of this open range.
Tough Mesa dwellers farmed potatoes, oats, and wheat, grazed their cattle,
and harvested the lush grass. The women made and sold prized butter. Coal
miners from Blossburg moved up here and staked homesteads. Although
local ranchers still turn their herds out on summer pasture here, Mesa
dwellers soon learned the harsh winter blizzards that swept across made it
all but uninhabitable. Sad little graveyards with infants' headstones mark the
struggle for survival. Deserted homesteader cabins are scattered along the
Mesa, and the hand-built little Methodist rock church, always open, where
Sunday services are still held during the summer, testifies to the community
that once dwelled here. In summer, the mesa is covered in white flowers, and
meadowlarks call; fall is a festival of yellow blossoms.

HIGHLIGHTS: Sugarite Canyon State Park, Capulin Volcano National Monument,
Clayton Lake Dinosaur Trackway

LEFT: VIEW THE MOUNTAINS AND MESAS OF THE HILL COUNTRY FROM CAPULIN VOLCANO NATIONAL MOUNUMENT

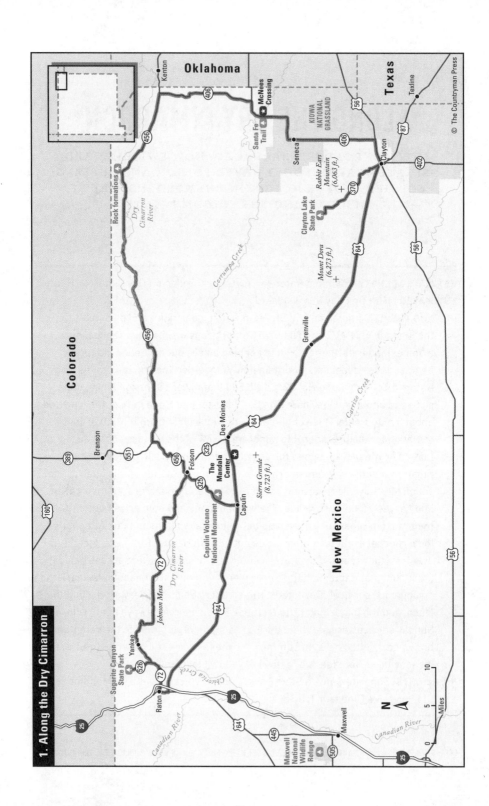

1. Along the Dry Cimarron

Colorado

Oklahoma

Texas

New Mexico

Kenton

McNees Crossing

Santa Fe Trail

KIOWA NATIONAL GRASSLAND

Texline

Seneca

Clayton

Rabbit Ears Mountain (6,063 ft.)

Clayton Lake State Park

Rock formations

Dry Cimarron River

Corrumpa Creek

Mount Dora (6,273 ft.)

Grenville

Carrizo Creek

Branson

Des Moines

Folsom

The Mandala Center

Sierra Grande (8,723 ft.)

Capulin Volcano National Monument

Capulin

Johnson Mesa

Dry Cimarron River

Yankee

Sugarite Canyon State Park

Raton

Chicorica Creek

Maxwell National Wildlife Refuge

Maxwell

Canadian River

Canadian River

N

Miles

© The Countryman Press

RATON

At an altitude of 6,680 feet, the jumping-off point for this journey through northeast New Mexico is at the northernmost exit on I-25 before crossing over Raton Pass to Colorado.

With beginnings as a watering station on the Santa Fe Trail called Willow Springs, the town sprang up in 1879 with the purchase of acreage from the Maxwell Land Grant. With the coming of the Atchison, Topeka & Santa Fe Railway over the 7,835-foot pass, it was the highest point on the line. It was crossed by the Indians and the Spanish for centuries. The AT&SF triumphed over the Denver & Rio Grande Railway in a bitter battle for right-of-way to the pass. So important was coal mining there that Raton took on the nickname the Pittsburgh of the West. For years, the town ran on railroading, ranching, and coal mining; however, Main Street is largely deserted now, and this small town seems not just quiet, but in decline, with too many boarded-up storefronts and houses in disrepair. Here is where the Rocky Mountains roll out to meet the Great Plains; here is the journey into the wide-open grasslands where antelope roam. A century ago, this place suffered "the worst hard time," as author Tim Egan called Dust Bowl days. But this is a place to experience mountain biking, hiking, kayaking, fishing, and camping in the summer; and in the winter, there's ice fishing and snowshoeing. At other times, you can avoid crowds and have mountain meadows of wildflowers and starry dark skies all to yourself.

Descending from the mesa for 12 miles leads to **Folsom**, population 54, at the junction of NM 72, 325, and 456, and 38 miles east of **Raton** off NM 72, named for Frances Folsom, future wife of President Grover Cleveland, who visited here. Go right on NM 456. This sleepy not-quite-ghost-town with its remains of a hotel and general store was once a bustling stockyard and railroad shipping point that had its beginnings in 1887, when the Colorado & Southern Railroad came through. However, in 1908, the town suffered a disastrous flood. No one expected a flood from the **Dry Cimarron,** a river so named because it runs underground for miles. The town was washed away and 17 people died. Many were saved through the efforts of telephone operator Sarah J. Rooke, who gave her life to notify villagers of the impending disaster. A historic marker in her honor stands beside the Folsom Museum, (once the 1896 Doherty Mercantile), a hodgepodge of western gear, vintage costumes, household goods, photos, and rusty farm equipment. Folsom's other famous citizen was George McJunkin, the African American freed slave cowboy who became foreman at the Crowfoot Ranch, who, just after the big flood, discovered 19 chipped bone arrowheads in a Pleistocene bison bone, now known as the Folsom Points. In 1926, this discovery ultimately helped rewrite archaeology, as it showed that this land was inhabited as far

THE FOLSOM MUSEUM, CURATED CIRCA 1928, IS CROWDED WITH VINTAGE TREASURES

back as 15,000 years ago. The points are on display at the Denver Museum of Nature and Science. Four miles northeast of **Folsom** on NM 456 are spring-fed waterfalls known as Folsom Falls, now closed to the public, on the **Dry Cimarron**. The town is also known as the place of Black Jack Ketchum's (of the Hole in the Wall Gang) last train robbery, where he was captured. Ketchum was taken to **Clayton** and hanged on Main Street; he was decapitated in the process.

At **Folsom**, choose between two very different routes. Either one will take the rest of the day: The Dry Cimarron, the purest stretch of lonesome road you are likely to encounter anywhere in the West, or traveling to **Clayton** via **Capulin** along US 64/US 87 will both last 54 miles. It is also possible to make a loop by heading out along the Dry Cimarron and back along NM 72; however, to see and do everything along the way, it would be best to over-night in **Clayton**.

DRY CIMARRON ROUTE

Take NM 456 east to NM 406 40 miles north of **Clayton**.

At Tollgate Canyon, Charles Goodnight trailed many cattle from Texas to Wyoming between 1866 and 1869. He thought the toll was too high to go through Raton Pass, and he found another pass to travel. It came north from the Canadian River toward Capulin Crater, then it went west and dropped down to the Dry Cimarron about 1.5 miles west of **Folsom**, the Picketwire

(Purgatoire) River in Colorado and on to Wyoming. Trinchera Pass was an easier grade than Raton Pass and free of tolls. This became known as the **Goodnight Trail**, or the Goodnight Loving Trail (1867–76). This era and the men of this time were celebrated in Larry McMurtry's classic book *Lonesome Dove*. Return from the museum to the right to find Folsom Falls. It is located 4 miles northeast of Folsom, New Mexico, on NM 456. Pass a cemetery on the right, and take NM 456 to the **Dry Cimarron**, so named because the river flows underground, fed by springs, for much of its course, which ends atop Johnson Mesa. It is very dry, dusty, and covered with scrub vegetation. The road turns to dirt and gravel in stretches. Local lore maintains this deserted roadway was a bootlegging route during Prohibition; indeed, it is difficult to imagine a better place to smuggle rum.

This is a backroader's backroad dream; there is very little if any traffic, save the occasional ranch truck. Take extreme caution during summer thunderstorms, because the roadway becomes hazardous. Allow a half-day to travel the 215 miles east toward **Clayton** on the rough asphalt two-lane road. The desert vegetation of sage and yucca, apache plume, and salt bush is broken by the occasional windmill and ranch sign or spot a jack rabbit or coyote. The scenery, with its buttes, red cliffs, and black lava-topped mesas, is isolated and wild, quintessentially western. Continue east on NM 456, crossing the Dry Cimarron River several times. At Travessier, there is a picturesque overlook which is the entrance into the Dry Cimarron Valley. On the north side, you will see a colored sandstone formation that has the appearance of a battleship. On the north side of the route, you will see Wedding Cake, a round mound rising about 300 feet above the valley floor, with its grass-covered slope and red, white, and brown layers of sandy rock, aptly named because it appears to be a large layered cake. In early days, many couples exchanged wedding vows atop this geographic formation. The Dry Cimarron Valley contains many natural features such as Battleship. Instead of turning

WINDMILLS STILL WORK ALONG THE DRY CIMARRON

toward **Clayton**, counter-intuitively turn toward Oklahoma. Just before the Oklahoma border, turn right (south) on Highway 406 toward McNees Crossing. A state historic sign sits in the actual "ruts" of the Cimarron Cutoff of the **Santa Fe Trail,** still visible. A short distance to the north is a gate (close it). To the east is a windmill and nearby is a small marker erected in 1921 on the 90th anniversary of the first celebration of the Fourth of July in what is now New Mexico. The trail crosses the North Canadian River, which is also called Corrumpa Creek by locals. The crossing is named for a young scout of an east-bound caravan who was killed in 1828.

From McNees Crossing, it is 23 miles to **Clayton**. Turn right at US 56.

CAPULIN ROUTE THROUGH RATON-CLAYTON VOLCANIC FIELD

From **Folsom** go 7 miles on NM 325 South to **Capulin Volcano National Monument**. A visitor center with videos, a well-stocked bookstore, and informative exhibits provides a worthwhile introduction to this relatively young, 58,000- to 62,000-year-old volcano. Behind the Visitor Center is a short nature walk, a 10-minute-long, easy, paved, accessible, pet-friendly trail. Capulin, meaning wild plum or chokecherry, was once a hunting ground for Plains Indians. It is still considered a sacred site by Jicarilla Apache people who continue making ceremonial visits here. Drive up to the trailhead of a moderate-to-difficult mile-long trail around the 8,125-foot-high volcano rim that allows views of five states: New Mexico, Colorado, Kansas, Texas, and Oklahoma. Best of all, the views of the Raton-Clayton Volcanic field are panoramic, 360 degrees. And it is easy to imagine the caravans of prairie schooners of the **Santa Fe Trail** pioneers crossing the country below. This is the country New Mexico author Max Evans dubbed "the Hi-Lo Country," and it is easy to see why, with all the up-and-down of the landscape. **Capulin Monument** is a Gold Tier Dark Sky State Park, named by the International Dark-Sky Association. Summer evening programs with rangers and high-powered telescopes give visitors dazzling starry night experiences. Alternatively, hike into the 415-foot-deep cinder cone on the Crater Vent Trail of the volcano. Go left at the park exit in 3 miles, where you will see **Capulin Country Store,** a spot to pick up cold beverages and snacks as well as browse local crafts. Upon exiting the monument, go left (east) at the junction with US 64/87, a well-paved highway, for 51 miles to **Clayton**.

Capulin lies 28 miles southeast of Raton on US 64/87, a settlement of Hispanic farmers founded sometime after the Civil War. Pass many abandoned homesteads—which will beckon to photographers—as the journey spins through the still-inhabited village of **Des Moines** (pronounced as it is spelled). Just west of Des Moines, 38 miles southeast of **Raton**, on the north side of US 64/87 between MM 384 and 385, is a historic marker for the New Goodnight Trail blazed by Charles Goodnight. The arrival of the railroad in New Mexico in the 1880s, as well as the fencing of the West in 1877, ended the great cattle drives. On the right, 10 miles beyond Capulin, see Sierra Grande, at 8,720 feet, the largest stand-alone mountain with a circumference of 40 miles in the United States. At 6.4 miles beyond Capulin, pass the Mandala Center, an ecumenical spiritual retreat located between the **Capulin** and **Sierra Grande** volcanos. Along the way, herds of pronghorn antelope graze near **Mt. Dora**, named for the daughter of Senator Stephen Dorsey, a crony of Albert Bacon Fall of Teapot Dome notoriety, involved with selling public lands for personal gain. About 30 miles west of **Clayton**, you will see to the left **Rabbit Ears Mountain**, named not for its resemblance to the ears of a hare, but for Chief Rabbit Ears. The landform is a 2.5-million-year-old cinder cone volcano. A Comanche or Cheyenne chief, depending upon which version of the story is told, was killed here. The chief's name was Orejas de Conejo, which means "rabbit ears." The mountain is notable for being a landmark for travelers along the Cimarron Cutoff route of the Santa Fe Trail. The **Cimarron Cutoff** was an alternative to the **Mountain Branch** of the Santa Fe Trail, which climbed steep Raton Pass, the highest point on the trail; it was faster but more dangerous because it lacked water and was more vulnerable to Indian attack.

Just at the edge of Clayton, make a slight right before the bridge at the Clayton Lake sign. Stay on NM 370 for 10 miles; look for sign indicating a left turn. Travel 2 miles to the park entrance. The Dinosaur Trackway site is 0.25-mile walk from the parking area. See the sign on the left for **Clayton Lake State Park,** 15 miles along NM 370 North. This gem of a fishing lake (where the state record walleye was caught) stocked with catfish, trout, and bass, is actually a 170-acre recreational reservoir. The park has the Lake Observatory, and it is an excellent dark place to view night skies. But the outstanding feature is the **Dinosaur Trackway**, in the dam spillway, an accessible boardwalk through 500 fossilized dinosaur footprints left by eight kinds of dinosaurs in the mud of a seabed of the shoreline of the Gulf of Mexico 100 million years ago, during the Cretaceous era. It is actually the second-largest such trackway in the Western Hemisphere.

Clayton, founded in 1887, named for Senator Stephen Dorsey's son, is a quiet town of 3,200 that feels like it is still in the 1950s, on the state's eastern border with the Texas and Oklahoma panhandles only 9 miles west. In many ways, it is more kin to those states than to New Mexico. It got its start with the railroad and became a major cattle shipping point. It is considered the gateway to New Mexico's section of the Cimarron Branch of the **Santa Fe Trail**. The trail was opened in 1821 by William Becknell, when, after Mexico achieved independence from Spain, he brought a wagon load of goods 900

CLAYTON LAKE STATE PARK HAS GOOD FISHING, AN OBSERVATORY, AND THE HEMISPHERE'S SECOND LARGEST DINOSAUR TRACKWAY

miles from Independence, Missouri, to **Santa Fe** and sold out immediately. Spain forbade trade with its colonies, but Mexico was open to commerce, as was the United States; New Mexico became a US territory in 1848 with the signing of the Treaty of Guadalupe Hidalgo. It was largely a military and mercantile trade route until the coming of the railroad in 1879. It remains a hub for ranchers and, today, is a resting spot for Texans traveling through to Colorado and the ski resorts of New Mexico. Railroads and cattle have been its mainstays. The town's center of activity may be found in the three-story **Eklund Hotel**, built by Swedish immigrant Carl Eklund in the 1890s, a restored western inn with a bar, a period dining room with plush rose upholstery that serves tasty Mexican food, burgers, and homemade daily specials, a popular Thursday night open mic, and some darn fine traveling musicians. The **Herzstein Memorial Museum** around the corner from the hotel on 2nd and Walnut Streets has a surprisingly good collection of western memorabilia, WPA artifacts, dolls saddles, wedding dresses, and information on the Dust Bowl and **Santa Fe Trail**. It has been rated as highly haunted as well, with sightings of orbs and spirits supposedly confirmed. Across the street from the Eklund is the **Luna Theater**, dating back to 1916 and known for its restored neon winking moon; it shows recent releases. Mock's Crossroads Coffee Mill at 2 South Front Street is a café with Wi-Fi that serves a respectable cup of joe and decent lunches. Nearby are Santa Fe Trail markers at approximately 19 miles north of Clayton off NM 406. A portion of the

Cimarron Route crosses the **Kiowa National Grasslands**, a 2-mile section of trail and interpretive site, planted to restore the earth after the Dustbowl, with Santa Fe Trail swales. There are 137,000 miles of unspoiled short grass prairie in this section of the grasslands.

About 17 miles north of Clayton is a 3-mile section of the Santa Fe Trail, open for walking and horseback riding. The trail is marked by rock posts. The ruts from the wheels of the wagons that made this trek in the 19th century are still visible.

Travel 90 miles back to Raton along US 64/87. An alternative shorter route to Clayton, or one you might wish to return on to complete the loop, is to travel out Clayton Road across **Chicorica Creek,** 1 mile east of Raton. At 11 miles, see the TO Ranch on the north, one of the oldest and largest ranches in the region. Still looking to the north, the profile of **Capulin Volcano** emerges, while straight ahead is the rather spread-out volcano known as **Sierra Grande**. Along the way, pronghorn actually do roam, as cattle graze on rich grasslands that untold eons ago were the bottoms of inland seas.

Raton has a history museum at 108 South 2nd Street and several blocks of a historic downtown that parallels the railroad tracks. The Southwest Chief stops twice a day at the 1903 classic Atchison, Topeka & Santa Fe Railway Mission Revival station. The 1915 **Shuler Theater,** a century-old European Rococo jewel box, offers live music and theater productions as

THE 1892 EKLUND HOTEL IN CLAYTON HAS OLD WEST ATMOSPHERE, CONTEMPORARY CONVENIENCE, AND AN OPEN MIC ON THURSDAY NIGHTS

well as tours of its century old stage and fittings. It also has state-of-the-art movie sound and projection. The best way to find a tour is to stop in at the theater and ask to see it; a fine WPA and New Deal art collection in the **Arthur Johnson Memorial Library** and **Sugarite Canyon State Park**, with camping, kayaking, hiking, mountain biking and fishing, with 3,600 acres and 20 miles of trails. From the north end of town on 2nd Street, go under the underpass, bear right, and travel NM 72 to NM 526 to get there, about 10 miles NE. The trail around **Lake Maloya** is 4 miles, or you can take the 2.5-mile Lake Maloya trail one way from the trailhead at the west end of the dam over onto the Colorado side of the park. It is a moderate hike, and the birding is magnificent, with everything from bluebirds to blue heron; or, you can just do the trail along the lake. There are three lakes altogether: Lake Dorothey, Lake Alice, and Lake Maloya, each with

TWICE A DAY, THE SOUTHWEST CHIEF STILL WHISTLES THROUGH CLASSIC AT&SF MISSION RATON TRAIN STATION

trails. Black bear and mountain lions call this place home. With sufficient moisture, wildflowers are abundant; this is one of the prettiest places to find wildflowers in summer. The Visitor's Center displays vintage photos from the days when Sugarite, a corruption of the word *chicorica*, meaning place of many birds, was a coal camp, and there is a well-signed hiking trail in back of the center that takes you through the remains of the coal camp where, at its height, 1000 people lived and worked between 1910 and 1941. It's an easy, approximately 1-mile hike one way to the entrance of Mine 2 and the same distance to the Cable Wheel House on an unpaved surface. Pick up self-guided tour brochures at the Visitor Center.

Back in town, find the 3-mile **Climax Canyon Park** hike at Apache Avenue and South 6th Street, 3.25 miles round trip from the parking lot, a moderate to strenuous hike through pinon and juniper to excellent views of Raton and nearby mesas.

Enchanted Grounds Coffee Shop is the place to connect with Raton folks, and if you are after Frito pie, the **Art of Snacks** serves a spicy one. Barbecue is available at the Ice House, and Mexican food can be had at El Matador and Casas Lemus Restaurant & Inn. **Colfax Ale Cellar** offers live music from time to time, plus some more than respectable local brews. Patchwork Phoenix is a gathering spot for quilters and crafters and a friendly spot for newcomers to drop in.

Only 32 miles south of Raton on I-25 is the **Maxwell National Wildlife Refuge**, on the Central Flyway, home to more than 289 species of birds, including bald and golden eagles, cranes and herons, wintering grounds for snow geese and a bonanza of watchable wildlife. Trails along Lakes 14 and 15 are eminently walkable and uncrowded. This is truly one of the most peaceful outdoor adventures in northeast NM.

IN THE AREA

Accommodations

HEART'S DESIRE BED & BREAKFAST, 301 South 3rd Street, Raton. Call 575-445-0000. $$.

HOTEL EKLUND, 15 Main Street, Clayton. Call 575-374-2551. $$.

Attractions and Recreation

ARTHUR JOHNSON MEMORIAL LIBRARY, 244 Cook Avenue, Raton.

CAPULIN-VOLCANO NATIONAL MONUMENT, 44 Volcano Road, Capulin. Call 575-278-2201.

CLAYTON LAKE STATE PARK, 141 Clayton Lake Road, Clayton. Call 575-374-8808.

CLAYTON-UNION COUNTY CHAMBER OF COMMERCE AND TOURIST INFORMATION CENTER, 1103 South 1st Street, Clayton. Call 575-374-9253.

HERZSTEIN MEMORIAL MUSEUM, 22 South 2nd Street, Clayton. Call 575-374-2977.

LUNA THEATER, 4 Main Street, Clayton. Call 575-374-2712.

THE MANDALA CENTER, 96 Mandala Road, Des Moines. Call 575-278-3002.

MAXWELL NATIONAL WILDLIFE REFUGE, Maxwell. Call 575-375-2331.

RATON MUSEUM, 108 South 2nd Street, Raton.

RATON REGIONAL AQUATIC CENTER, Roundhouse Road and Memorial Lane, Raton. Call 575-445-4271.

RATON VISITOR INFORMATION CENTER, 100 Clayton Road, Raton. Call 575-445-3689.

SANTE FE TRAIL ASSOCIATION. CALL 620-285-2054, Website: www .santafetrail.org.

SUGARITE CANYON STATE PARK, NM 526, Raton. Call 575-445-5607.

Dining and Drinks

ART OF SNACKS, 1117 South 2nd Street, Raton. Call 575-707-8020. $.

BRUNO'S PIZZA AND WINGS, 133 Cook Avenue, Raton. Call 575-445-9512. $–$$.

ENCHANTED GROUNDS COFFEE SHOP AND CAFÉ, 111 Park Avenue, Raton. Call 575-445-2219. $.

MOCK'S CROSSROADS COFFEE MILL, 2 South Front Street, Clayton. Call 575-374-5282. $.

Events

CHRISTMAS ON THE CHICORICA, December.

INTERNATIONAL SANTE FE TRAIL BALLOON RALLY, July.

2

ENCHANTED CIRCLE

STRIKING GOLD IN HIGH PLACES WHERE THE WEST WAS ONCE REALLY WILD

ESTIMATED LENGTH: 84 miles

ESTIMATED TIME: One day

GETTING THERE: Setting out from Taos, the 84-mile Enchanted Circle Scenic Byway makes a loop through Taos. The two-lane circle is easy to navigate. Starting from Taos, on the southern end, turn off Paseo del Pueblo Sur at the Visitor Center, 2 miles south of the Plaza at 1139 Paseo Del Pueblo Sur, and go through the series of roundabouts to US 64; alternatively, depart Taos via Kit Carson Road, and drive directly out of town 3 miles east toward US 64. It's a 24-mile drive through winding Taos Canyon, following the Rio Pueblo de Taos through Carson National Forest, passing the community of Shady Brook to Angel Fire. The drive takes around 40 minutes, mainly due to the series of hairpin, elevation-gaining turns as you approach Angel Fire.

HIGHLIGHTS: Vietnam Veterans Memorial State Park; Eagle Nest Lake State Park; D. H. Lawrence Ranch

---

The enchantment of the **Enchanted Circle Scenic Byway** is a serendipitous combination of nature, high mountain scenery, the Wild West, and mining history, with opportunities to sample fine food and drink for good measure. The height of the road is exhilarating without being dangerous, the history is informative without being overwhelming, and the pace is lively without being exhausting. With two ski areas and a cross-country snow area, it's a place to celebrate winter sports, and it includes two state parks. The best time to drive the **Enchanted Circle** is fall, usually the last weekend in September, when aspen forests lining the roadway are at their peak of shimmering gold. However, the road makes a fine excursion regardless of the season, and it is

LEFT: GO FOR THE GOLD ALONG THE ENCHANTED CIRCLE, ONE OF NEW MEXICO'S MOST COLORFUL FALL DRIVES

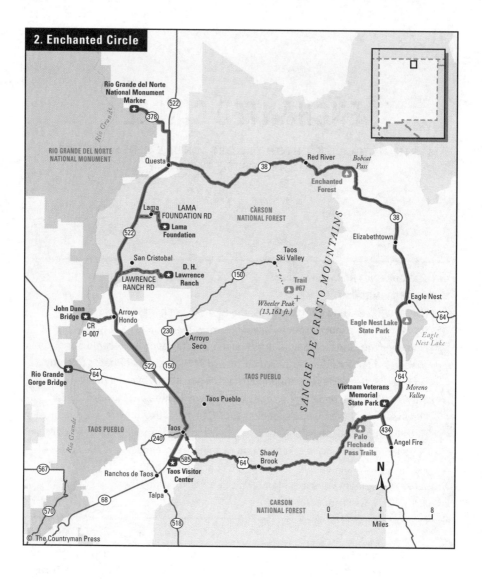

just long and varied enough to provide the fresh perspective and fresh air a quick road trip can bring. When heading out in cold weather, be prepared for winter driving conditions. Roads, particularly through Taos Canyon, can be icy. While the trip can be made comfortably in a day, even with time outs for exploring the sights close-up, if plans include overnighting at any of the hospitable towns along the way, this road trip becomes a mini-vacation. Pack a picnic, binoculars, camera, fishing boots, and multiple layers—the weather can change in a flash. This area was once all part of the 1.7-million-acre Maxwell Land Grant, the largest parcel in the Western Hemisphere, held by mountain man Lucien Bonaparte Maxwell. One advantage here is that the roads are smooth, and even high mountain portions are not difficult to drive.

US 64 was originally an Indian highway traveled by Plains Indians such as Apaches, Comanches, and Kiowas, who followed the Cimarron River. They journeyed through a 9,107-foot pass called Palo Flechado (tree pierced with arrows), named for the Flecha de Palo Indians. Shooting remaining arrows into a tree was a custom marking a successful buffalo hunt. The Elliot Barker Trail, a 7.6-mile loop, is rated moderate and leads to a pond and then a dense spruce-fir forest. It is graced with abundant wildflowers. The La Jara Trail at Forest Road 5 parallels a stream in the Rio Grande Valley. It is also possible to access the trail by parking at the Palo Flechado historic marker at the top of the pass on US 64 and crossing the road to pass through the gate. An alternate approach is to hike from the trailhead through the first meadow and turn left to cross the small creek. This route begins with a moderately steep climb over log steps, until it reaches a flatter section through the forest. At the first major trail intersection, turn left and follow a 0.75-mile loop that returns to the trailhead, for a total hike of just under 1.5 miles.

At the intersection of US 64 and NM 434, go right 2 miles into **Angel Fire**. The name Angel Fire is associated with the Ute Indians. As one story goes, while making camp here, a group of Ute experienced a lightning-caused fire; just as they were about to evacuate, the wind shifted, and a rainstorm extinguished the fire. Another story says the name comes from the reddish alpenglow on the Angel Fire Mountain Peak at dawn and dusk. Formerly the Monte Verde Ranch, in 1964 the resort of Angel Fire began when the ranch owner laid out a golf course. The town has many second home condominiums and rentals, but it also retains a small, involved community of full-time citizens. There you will find a brewpub, a grocery store, a barbecue restaurant, a couple of cafés, and an RV camp. **Angel Fire Resort** offers skiing, ski school, Nordic Center, snowshoeing, snowboarding, rentals, and a family snow play hill for sledding, plus a terrain park, considered the best in the state, zipline, tubing, and more. The resort has a high percentage of beginner and intermediate slopes. Snow Bear Camp Child Care tends to children aged 6 weeks to 11 years old, and the Little Chiles program teaches skiing to children age 4 to 6 and more. Plus, there's the state's only night skiing. Summertime is gorgeous, with golfing, hiking, and zip line.

Exiting Angel Fire, go right on US 64 and immediately see **Vietnam Veterans Memorial State Park** at 34 Country Club Road. In 4 miles, come to Mountain View Boulevard. Go left up the hill. Established in 1968 and hand-built by Dr. Victor Westphall and his wife, Jeanne, this stark structure honors their son David, killed in Vietnam in 1968. Records of all US military members who gave their lives in Vietnam are assembled here. Be prepared for a deeply moving experience and the realization of this national tragedy on a personal level. On Memorial Day weekend, hundreds of motorcyclists from all over the country assemble here to honor Vietnam Veterans in the

DR. VICTOR WESTPHALL'S MEMORIAL TO HIS SON DAVID, WHO WAS KILLED IN THE VIETNAM WAR, GIVES VISITORS A DEEPLY MOVING EXPERIENCE OF GRIEF AND HEALING

annual Run for the Wall as they make their way to the Vietnam Memorial in **Washington, DC**.

Leave Angel Fire and arrive at the Moreno ("dark") Valley, a glorious expanse of wild grasses studded with wildflower meadows. **Wheeler Peak**, the state's tallest peak, is visible on the west side of the Moreno Valley. Located 21.4 miles from Taos on NM 150, Wheeler Peak, at 13,161 feet, is the state's highest mountain. It is composed of Precambrian granite and metamorphic rocks. The trail to the summit (Trail #67) may be reached via the Williams Lake Trail from the Bavarian Lodge in Taos Ski Valley.

The **Moreno Valley** was created with the uplift of the Rocky Mountains between 70 and 40 million years ago. The Sangre de Cristo Mountain Range is just as old. The Range is 130 miles long and 32 miles wide between **Santa Fe** and **Las Vegas**, New Mexico. After the Rocky Mountain uplift, the earth's crust in New Mexico began to spread, causing faults along the base of the Sangre de Cristo Range.

Starting in 1866, a gold rush on **Baldy** transformed this area into a population center. By 1907, over $6 million in gold was mined from these mountains. **Eagle Nest Dam**, constructed 1916–18, in its day, was the largest privately-owned dam in the country. It preserved Cimarron River water, providing a stable source of water for agriculture while fostering farming and ranching.

Although wild iris are not favored by ranchers, for practical reasons, this area has one of the most beautiful displays of this flower in the state, peaking around Memorial Day Weekend.

Eagle Nest, at 8,200 feet, ringed by the Sangre de Cristo Mountains (named the Blood of Christ Mountains because they would turn red at sunset when capped with snow), is as cute a mountain town as you will find. With a boardwalk on Main Street, fly shops, knick-knack shops, and burger and ice cream emporiums, it exudes a small-town vibe as it invites fishers, hunters, and vacationers in search of a peaceful escape. Its past as a wild party town during the 1920s, when it was named **Therma** (after the daughter of the postal inspector) has vanished, along with the slot machines reputedly tossed in the lake to get them out of sight of The Law. Fourth of July fireworks over the lake are worth the trip. **Enchanted Circle Gateway Museum** on the north end of the Drive gives a good introduction to the area, offering exhibits on local Moreno Valley history, arranging tours, and providing information.

WHEELER PEAK, THE STATE'S HIGHEST POINT, STANDS WITHIN THE SANGRE DE CRISTO RANGE

Eagle Nest Lake State Park, located in the Moreno Valley 2.7 miles east on US 64 from Eagle Nest, has a crystal blue 2,400-square-foot lake stocked with kokanee salmon and trout. Boating, wildlife viewing, walking along the lake, and camping are all fine at this cool alpine refuge ringed by mountains.

At the summit of **Bobcat Pass**, 9,820 feet up, 14 miles from Eagle Nest, 13 miles east to **Red River** on NM 38, is the **Enchanted Forest**, 10 miles of groomed and rough trails on 600 acres of alpine forest. The place is pet-friendly, with dog-friendly trails where you can ski with your dog, and prime ski terrain for classical, freestyle, and Telemark, with warming huts, instructors, rentals, yurt rental, snowshoeing on 15 kilometers of runs, and special events. Overall, this is NM's prime XC ski spot.

Elizabethtown

Located 4 miles north of Eagle Nest on NM 38, Elizabethtown was the first incorporated town in New Mexico, in 1868. E-town, as it was known, was named for the founder's daughter and was a boom-and-bust gold mining settlement and a hideout for notorious characters running from the law. The ruins of several buildings and the cemetery still linger. At one time, the population was upwards of 7,000, and there was a movement to make it the state capital. Now it is a ghost town, with abandoned mining relics scattered about.

Red River is 17.4 miles up Bobcat Pass, named for the wild cats that inhabit this area, if you go north from Eagle Nest on NM 38. This friendly, lively resort town is made for fun, especially the family kind. The ski area is super family-friendly, and there's plenty of lodging, cafés, and shopping to make a it a four-season escape. Red River has been working on upping its summer resort game. At 8,750 feet, it is the highest town in the state. It was founded in 1892 by homesteaders. Gold, silver, and copper prospectors followed shortly, bringing the population to 5,000. When the mines played out, the town began its self-renovation as a tourist destination. The river runs red after rains due to high mineral content, hence the name. **Bull 'o'**

BOBCAT PASS IS KNOWN FOR CROSS-COUNTRY SKIING AND SNOWMOBILING

the **Woods Saloon** is the social and entertainment center of town, with live entertainment nightly and an immense selection of brews. **Mallette Park,** at the west end of town, three blocks from Main Street, is a climbing area of a granite face with six bolted routes. The park also has a disc golf course. Shotgun Willie's is the place for barbecue and burritos.

Red River Ski Area specializes in family fun, starting with Buckaroo Day Care for children aged six months to four years. The Youth Ski Center has group and private lessons for ages 3 to 12 and snowboarders ages 7 to 12. Red River boasts of being the best value Rocky Mountain ski area, with 4,500 beds available. The mountain is 10,350 feet. Red River started in 1969 when Texas oilman John Bolton built the first lift using derricks and cables imported from Texas oil fields. The big annual event is Mardi Gras on the Mountain. There's a moonlight ski and snowshoe event, a spring break torchlight and fireworks show, and a calendar packed with events.

From **Red River** to **Questa**, it's approximately 12 miles through the **Carson National Forest** on NM 38. If you look to your right and are lucky, you may see the elusive, sure-footed Rocky Mountain bighorn sheep on the ridge above; I was fortunate recently and found the herd down on the road, grazing on early spring greens. The males have massive, curling horns, and their ability to navigate the narrow ridges and forage is even more impressive when you realize they weigh 300 pounds or more!

Questa means "slope," or "ridge," and it is here the missionary Don Francisco Laforet settled when he was driven from settling on the Red River by Indians in 1829. The village, established in 1883, is a tight-knit traditional farming and trading spot; many of its residents took jobs with the Chevron molybdenum mine, and the fortunes of land, water, and people have risen and fallen with the mine, now closed. The isolated history of Questa made for many self-taught craftsmen. and the town has a tradition of carving, weaving, and painting. Questa honey is a delicacy; there are beekeepers on the road just north of town where you may purchase this local treat. As the Gateway to the Rio Grande del Norte Monument, visitors can drive to an overlook where the Red River meets the Rio Grande in the depth of the Gorge. Drive north through town to find a sign 4 miles up. Turn left and drive slowly through the village to the entry of the **Rio Grande del Norte Monument**, one of the nation's newer national monuments. In March 2013, President Barack Obama declared these 27 million acres of Rio Grande Rift and Taos Plateau a significant landscape to be preserved. Encompassing several Native American pueblos, rock art, wildlife, native grasslands, and geologic features formed over 70 million years ago and much more, this cultural and natural treasure is a haven for all who love the outdoors.

From Questa, it is about 20 miles to Costilla and 36 miles to the Latir Lakes. It is 55 miles to Ft. Garland, at the Colorado border.

ACCESS TO THE VAST RIO GRANDE DEL NORTE NATIONAL MONUMENT MAY BE FOUND NORTH OF QUESTA

From Questa, head back to Taos on NM 522. The road is not long, only 24 miles, but there are plenty of swooping hills en route. On the way, pass Lama Mountain at 8.5 miles, site of the ecumenical **Lama Foundation**, a half-century-old spiritual retreat center where Ram Dass originally created the New Age mantra: "Be Here Now." The community continues, with visiting spiritual teachers and workshops on permaculture, gender, and other contemporary issues, as well as providing hermitage, or private retreats high on the mountain. All are invited to Visitor Day Sundays during the summer, to experience a vegetarian feast and the Sufi Dances of Universal Peace in the Lama dome. It is said the Kiowa peace path travels up Lama Mountain. Anyone traveling this path was said to be protected from attack and without enemies.

Just below **Lama** on NM 522, pass the marker for **San Cristobal**, the location of the **D. H. Lawrence Ranch.** Here in 1934, British author Lawrence's widow Frieda built a shrine for his ashes. Aldous Huxley was a guest here. The property, known as Kiowa Ranch, was given to the Lawrences in 1925 by Taos salonista Mabel Dodge Luhan. It is a 4.2-mile drive from the historic marker and turnoff on route NM 522 to the gate of the ranch. Originally a guest of Mabel Dodge Luhan in Taos, Lawrence, who challenged Victorian mores with novels such as *Sons and Lovers* and *Lady Chatterley's*

Lover, lived and wrote on this ranch during the 1920s. Although he died and was cremated in Venice, Frieda Lawrence buried his ashes on the property; the room where his ashes are entombed definitely does have the aura of a shrine. "*I* think New Mexico was the greatest experience I ever had from the outside world. It certainly changed me forever," Lawrence said of his time in New Mexico.

Twenty miles south of Questa, see the village of **Arroyo Hondo**. This was the location of **Turley's Mill**, known for its Taos Lightning brew, 188 proof and flavored with gunpowder, chile, and tobacco. Turley's Mill was burned, and Turley killed, in the Taos Uprising of 1947.

Below it is the one-lane **John Dunn Bridge** across the Rio Grande, built in 1908. Turn off NM 522 at the bar, Midtown Market, in Arroyo Hondo and go 3 miles west on CR B-007, a dirt and gravel rough road down to the bridge. This will take you to the bridge at the confluence of the Rio Grande and the Rio Hondo. The Black Rock Hot Springs are nearby. Taos was connected with the outside world to the west in 1965 with the construction of the **Rio Grande Gorge Bridge**, at 600 feet, the second-highest suspension bridge in the US highway system.

IN THE AREA

Accommodations

ALPINE LODGE, 417 West Main Street, Red River. Call 575-754-2952. Email info@alpinelodgeredriver.com. $$.

ANGEL FIRE RESORT, 10 Miller Lane, Angel Fire. Call 575-377-6401 or 855-990-0194. Website: angelfireresort.com. $$–$$$.

ARROWHEAD LODGE, 405 Pioneer Road, Red River. Call 575-754-2255. Email arrowhead@newmex.com. $$.

EXPRESS ST. JAMES HOTEL, 617 South Collinson, Cimarron. Call 575-376-2664. $$–$$$.

GOLDEN EAGLE PARK CAMPGROUND, 540 West Therma Drive, Eagle Nest. Call 575-377-3188. $.

Attractions and Recreation

ANGEL FIRE CONVENTION AND VISITORS BUREAU, 3365 Mountain View Boulevard, Angel Fire. Call 575-377-6555. Website: www.angelfirefun .com.

ARTESANOS DE QUESTA, 41 NM 38. Call 575-586-9302.

BOBCAT PASS WILDERNESS ADVENTURES, 1670 NM 38, Red River. Call 575-754-2769. Website: bobcatpass.com.

D. H. LAWRENCE RANCH, San Cristobal. Call 505-277-5572.

EAGLE NEST CHAMBER OF COMMERCE, 284 East Therma Drive, Eagle Nest. Call 575-377-2420.

EAGLE NEST LAKE STATE PARK, 42 Marina Lane, Eagle Nest. Call 575-377-1594.

ENCHANTED CIRCLE GATEWAY MUSEUM & VISITOR CENTER, 580 East Therma Drive, Eagle Nest. Call 575-613-3468.

ENCHANTED FOREST XC SKI AND SNOWSHOE AREA, 29 Sangre de Cristo Drive, Red River. Call 575-754-6112. Website: enchantedforestxc.com.

E-TOWN TOURS, Eagle Nest. Call 575-377-2286.

NANCY BURCH'S ROADRUNNER TOURS. Call 575-377-6416. Website: nancyburch.com.

RED RIVER SKI AND SUMMER AREA, 400 Pioneer Road, Red River. Call 575-754-2223. Website: redriverskiarea.com.

RED RIVER STABLES, 800 East Main, Red River. Call 575-754-1700. Website: redriverstables.com.

RED RIVER VISITOR CENTER, 101 River Street, Red River. Call 575-754-3030. Website: www.redriver.org.

RIO GRANDE DEL NORTE NATIONAL MONUMENT. The Del Norte Visitor Center is located at 1120 Cerro Road. Go north from Questa on NM 522 and turn left on State Road 378; the visitor center is about 17 miles from the turnoff. The Río Grande Gorge Visitor Center is in Pilar at the intersection of NM 570 and US 68. Call 575-751-4899 or 575-758-8851 (the Taos Field Office).

VIETNAM VETERANS MEMORIAL STATE PARK, 34 Country Club Road, Angel Fire. Call 575-377-2293. Website: www.angelfirememorial.com.

Dining and Drinks

BRETT'S BISTRO, 201 West Main, Red River. Call 575-754-9959. $$–$$$.

BULL-O' THE WOODS SALOON, 401 East Main Street, Red River. Call 575-754-2593. $$.

COMANCHE CREEK BREWERY, County Road B-24, Eagle Nest. Call 575-377-2337. $$.

ENCHANTED CIRCLE BREWING CO., 20 Sage Lane, Angel Fire. Call 505-507-8687. $$.

HAIL'S HOLY SMOKED BBQ, 3400 Highway 434, Suite F, Angel Fire. Call 575-377-9938. $.

PAT'S PLACE, 2422 NM-522, Questa. Call 575-586-0111. $.

RED RIVER BREWING CO., 217 West Main, Red River. Call 575-754-4422. $$.

SHOTGUN WILLIE'S, 403 West Main Street, Red River. Call 575-754-6505. $.

Events

MARDI GRAS IN THE MOUNTAIN, Red River, February.

MEMORIAL DAY MOTORCYCLE RALLY, Red River, May.

Santa Fe Trail

SANTA FE TRAIL
NATIONAL HISTORIC TRAIL

Original Route

← New Franklin,
Missouri
805 miles

Santa Fe,
New Mexico
137 miles →

3

CIMARRON CIRCLE

MEANDERING ALONG THE SANTA FE TRAIL: FINDING
COWBOYS, OUTLAWS, BOY SCOUTS, AND THE HEMISPHERE'S
MOST POWERFUL LAND BARON

ESTIMATED LENGTH: 127 miles

ESTIMATED TIME: Half-day to weekend, depending on schedule and interests

GETTING THERE: Raton is approximately three-and-a-half hours or 232 miles north of Albuquerque on I-25. It is the northernmost town in New Mexico before Raton Pass into Colorado. Three miles south of Raton, take I-25 exit 446 to US 64 west to Cimarron and Taos.

HIGHLIGHTS: St. James Hotel, Santa Fe Trail, NRA Whittington Center, National Scouting Museum, Maxwell National Wildlife Refuge

---

The tour combines Wild West history with **Santa Fe Trail** history, with peace and quiet on slow roads and the potential for discovery and enrichment of your concepts of the Old West. This path highlights, in natural and built environments, the independent spirit of the people, hands-on living, and the values of treasuring land, water, animals, and freedom that are still alive in Colfax County. Cowboy culture flourishes here, and the road feels like a trip back in time. But don't be fooled. The folks who live out here are savvy survivors who choose to live alongside contemporary culture, rather than joining it and giving up what they and their families have treasured for generations.

Depart **Raton** on I-25 south. After 3 miles, go right (west) on US 64. On the right is the historic marker for the **Clifton House,** a significant resting spot on the Mountain Branch of the Santa Fe Trail and a stop for the Barlow and Sanderson stagecoach line. Built by rancher Tom Stockton, hailing from Tennessee, a southerner who came to these parts following the Civil War, it was quite grand in its day and originally stood two stories high and was made mostly of adobe. Here, outlaw Clay Allison shot another notorious

LEFT: TO APPRECIATE THE PIONEERS' ARDUOUS JOURNEY, PUT YOUR FEET ON THE PATH OF THE SANTA FE TRAIL AND OBSERVE THE STILL VISIBLE WAGON RUTS THAT PRAIRIE SCHOONERS LEFT IN THE EARTH

outlaw, Chunk Colbert, but only after he had finished dinner, because, as Allison said, "I didn't want to send him to Hell on an empty stomach." In 14 miles, see the **NRA Whittington Center**. Here are top shooting ranges plus the Frank Brownell Museum of the Southwest. On this facility is the Van Houten coal mine, and it is possible to tour the coal camp there. See the Raton Airport on the left. The ride to Cimarron is straight ahead through flat rangeland, where elk and pronghorn regularly roam. Cholla cactuses sprout spiky branches in the dry grass. Hills hover at the horizon, and arroyos carve the landscape, while vintage windmills and weathered corrals testify to a long history of ranching. See the junction of US 64 with NM 445 to the left (south). Go through it, remaining on US 64 West. It is possible to see buffalo from Ted Turner's **Vermejo Ranch** on US 64. Ahead rise the Sangre de Cristos, part of the Rocky Mountain range. Motor on and come to **Cold Beer** in 24 miles on US 64, usually with Dodge and Ford pickups and Harleys parked out front. We're saving this fine cowboy-biker bar for the last stop on the tour. It is located in what was the town of Colfax, now a ghost town, just west of the Vermejo River. Near two railroads, Colfax City was promoted

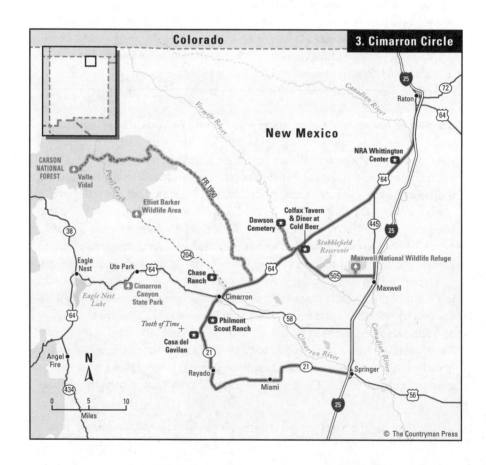

THERE'S BEEN A BAR HERE SINCE PROHIBITION—COLD BEER IS A FAVORITE NORTHEASTERN WATERING HOLE

by developers in 1908, but after a 24-year struggle, it faded. The ruins of a hotel still stand. The name Colfax is for Schuyler Colfax, Vice President under President Ulysses S. Grant, a figure in the Credit Mobilier of America scandal in 1873. Colfax County was created in 1869.

Immediately after Cold Beer, see a small sign for **Dawson Cemetery** on the right, as well as an historic marker. A visit to this cemetery, only a mile or so off the main road, is one of the most haunting things you are likely to experience in all New Mexico, and it may stay with you the rest of your life. Rows and rows of identical iron crosses mark two of the most devastating coal mining accidents in the West: 263 people died in 1913 and 124 people lost their lives almost a decade later in 1923. The names reflect the many nationalities of miners, from Mexico, Greece, Italy, and Eastern Europe, who came to work in this bustling coal camp of 9,000 that had schools, a hospital, a golf course, a baseball team, and more. Phelps-Dodge created an idyllic mining town named for the original settler of the area, John Dawson, a friend of Lucien B. Maxwell who ranched on the Vermejo River. In 1950, when the demand for coal was gone, Phelps-Dodge shut down the mine, residents were given 30 days to leave, and the town was dismantled and razed.

Returning to US 64, at 7 miles further west, see a sign for the turnoff to the **Valle Vidal**, Valley of Life, on the right. While this is an incomparable drive of 46 miles through forests and high mountain meadows, from the **Carson National Forest** to **Costilla** which, true to its name, is known for its high mountain fishing of native Rio Grande cutthroat trout, elk herds of 2,000, the largest in the state, mule deer, mountain lion, black bear, bird and wildlife, if you choose to take this predominantly dirt 4WD road, be sure you have a spare tire and be prepared to use it. The road is rough, containing jagged rocks and other sharp materials perilous to tires. I speak from personal experience—I have had a flat tire every time I have traveled here. Perhaps I am jinxed. The first 17 miles are public access through Ted Turner's **Vermejo Ranch**. Be prepared with food and water if you head this way, because there are no facilities of any kind. With the exception of the **Shuree Ponds**, with its two-trout limit, all fishing here is catch and release. To plan your trip, please go to the US Forest Service website: www.fs.usda.gov/carson.

Three miles beyond the Valle Vidal exit, on the right, you will see a sign for a Santa Fe Trail crossing. This area is rich with Santa Fe Trail markings, including ruts and swales. The life of the trail, primarily a military and mercantile trail, lasted from 1821, with the victory of Mexico over Spain that opened the territory up to trade, to 1879, with the coming of the railroad, which brought better transportation of goods. The land is also stenciled by the hundreds of wagons that traveled over it. Ruts are the wheel marks left by individual wagons traveling in a line; swales are the markings made by several wagons traveling abreast. A guide to ruts and swales visible in this area is available at the Visitor's Center in **Cimarron**. To the left, 5 miles southwest from Cimarron, is a distinctive thumb-shaped 22- to 40-million-year-old igneous formation in the mountains above Cimarron known as the **Tooth of Time**. This landmark told travelers that from here was only 7 days to Santa Fe.

Just before reaching Cimarron on US 64, see a sign for the **Elliot Barker Wildlife Area,** 14 miles to the right on NM 204. Restricted visiting days and hours are indicated on the sign. Remote and lovely, this is a special place where wildness still abounds. I was greeted by a huge black bear on my first visit. The area was named for a former director of the New Mexico Department of Game and Fish who was also a poet and author. It was purchased in 1966 to protect prime habitat for deer and elk. A long high mesa with canyon slopes, rocky outcrops, and side canyons with Ponil Creek flowing through the middle, this is the perfect habitat for deer, elk, bear, and turkey. Motorized vehicles are not allowed beyond the parking lot, and bicycling is permitted only on designated trails.

Immediately on the right is shady **Ponil Campground & RV Park,** located on **Ponil Creek,** a quiet campground open year-round for RVs and from May through September for tent campers. (Ponil is a name for apache plume shrub.)

In 2 miles, enter the village of Cimarron, which means "wild." Back in the day, this place was one of the wildest, most lawless spots on the map. To paraphrase the Las Vegas Optic: "It was a quiet week in Cimarron. Only three men died." It was, in the words of one old-timer, a gambler named Doc, a place where "it was really easy to get killed. Buckets of blood flowed in the streets." The Cimarron River flows west to east through the town on its way to join the Canadian River. Beyond Cimarron on US 64 lies **Cimarron Canyon State Park**, a prime brown trout fishing and camping destination. Cimarron has a well-deserved reputation as one of the most authentic Old West towns still existing, and the past comes alive in the architecture, the natural setting, the ranching way of life, and the memories of the inhabitants. Two pertinent items: speed limits are strictly enforced here; and, as you enter town, if it is the right time of day, you may have to wait for the resident deer or elk herd to cross Main Street. In 2018, the town was hit hard by the Ute Park Fire, causing many already-struggling businesses to close up shop. Things are just starting to return to normal. However, it is always possible to find a burger, a brew, and plenty of interesting Old West exploration. The town comes to life in summer when up to 23,000 Boy Scouts and leaders from all over the country arrive at **Philmont Scout Ranch** to experience backcountry adventure and practice outdoor skills. Along the main street is a display of portraits of the historic figures who lived in the area and influenced the era. A walk through this display provides a capsule history of the place.

Founded in 1841 with the filing of the Beaubien-Miranda Land Grant, later known as the Maxwell grant, Cimarron was, between 1862 and 1876, the base of the agency of Utes and Apaches, who were furnished supplies weekly from Lucien Maxwell's **Aztec Mill**. Find it by going just past the hotel and turning right on 17th Street. Now a museum run by the CS Ranch, it is well worth touring, offering three floors of history on the Maxwell Grant, Native Americans of the area, ranchers, and scouting. It was built by Maxwell in

DEER ABIDE PEACEFULLY ON THE PHILMONT SCOUT RANCH

1864 to grind wheat and corn for nearby Indians as well as Fort Union, to fulfill his government contracts. Maxwell's government contract to provide for the local Indians was but one of his many wealth streams. Cimarron was a significant stop on the Taos branch of the Santa Fe Trail, and Maxwell's house, which burned long ago, was a main stop for gamblers and travelers of all stripes.

Go east on NM 21, then cross the **Cimarron River** to find one of the most interesting sights of Cimarron, the landmark **St. James Hotel**, featured on *Unsolved Mysteries*. The scent of roses in a certain room, the bottle of whisky consumed at night left behind in an empty room with a locked door, and the unexplained flickering of candles in the window all point to supernatural activity within this 1872 building. Founded by Henri Lambert, the French-trained cook some say was chef to Abraham Lincoln, and who was invited to Cimarron by Lucien Maxwell to open Lambert's Inn, the hybrid Victorian Western lobby décor contributes to the romantic ambience. The hotel has been the scene of wild gunfights, to which the 27 bullet holes in the bar ceiling give testimony, and every single Wild West personality stayed here, from Annie Oakley to Butch Cassidy. Today, Lambert's restaurant is the most elegant in the area, but the menu offers casual dining as well. The hotel was given a serious update when it was purchased a dozen years ago by Express Ranches.

Behind the St. James Hotel is the start of the self-guided **Old Town Walking Tour,** which takes you through Cimarron of the 1880s to the old Colfax

THE ST. JAMES BAR AND RESTAURANT IS THE PLACE TO MEET UP AND DINE IN CIMARRON

County jail, where Jesse James once stayed, the well, the campground of the Santa Fe Trail travelers, and several other well-marked stops.

Before you leave Cimarron, you may want to retrace your path across US 64 to the **Visitor Center** located in the park and the street of shops bordering it. Here you can find ice cream, coffee, barbecue, and brews.

From the St. James, continue east on NM 21 5 miles to the **Philmont Scout Ranch**. On this stretch of NM 21, it is possible to see Santa Fe Trail road markings. This immense tract of land, 140,000 acres, was donated by Oklahoma oil tycoon Waite Phillips to the Boy Scouts of America for their headquarters. His summer residence, **Villa Philmonte**, 10 miles south of Cimarron, an elegant 20,000 square foot Mediterranean home built in 1927 with art and furnishings intact, has been preserved and is open for tours during summer. The **Chase Ranch**, one of the area's oldest ranching operations, has recently been acquired by the Boy Scouts, and the old ranch house is preserved and open for tours during summer as well. Please call the Philmont for hours and directions.

On the left, just past Philmont Ranch Headquarters, the **National Scouting Museum** offers free admission. Here you can learn the story of Philmont Scout Ranch and of scouting. The Seton Memorial Library houses the personal library and artwork of Ernest Thompson Seton, founder of the Boy Scouts. There is a superb collection of southwest jewelry and art as well as an excellent western bookshop here.

Tooth of Time Traders, a Scout enterprise, offers top quality gear for high country adventure, as well as souvenirs.

Just underneath the Tooth of Time is the **Casa del Gavilan** (House of the Hawk), a white adobe structure built in 1911 for Jack and Gertrude Nairn. It is recognized as one of earliest and best examples of Pueblo Revival architectural style, and it displays original art by Frederic Remington and Charles Russell. The courtyard is a tranquil place, and to stay here is to travel back in time to an era that prized graciousness and good conversation, with good whiskey, of course. It is open seasonally, but the property is for sale and there is no telling when and for how long it will be receiving guests.

Lucien Maxwell and Kit Carson were such good friends that they decided to settle down together and build houses beside each other on the Rayado River, 11 miles south of Cimarron. They would raise their children here. They also married their respective spouses in a double ceremony. Today, **Rayado** is an historic district administered by the Philmont. During the summer, Kit Carson's house is open as a museum, with candlelight storytelling on certain evenings. Down to the flour sacks in the storehouse, this museum is historically authentic. It was the original **Fort Union**, built to protect the frontier from Indian raids. At this interpretive site, staff dress in period clothing and demonstrate frontier skills such as blacksmithing and cooking.

MOUNTAIN MEN KIT CARSON AND LUCIEN B. MAXWELL AGREED TO SETTLE DOWN AND BUILD NEIGHBORING HOMES IN RAYADO; TODAY KIT CARSON'S HOME IS A MUSEUM

NM 21 follows the original Trail 11.4 miles as far as the turn to the left toward **Miami**.

An early 20th-century farming development, founded in 1908, Miami was settled by German Dunkards, Baptists who cultivated fruit trees and crops on what was an old stage route between Springer and Elizabethtown. The Dunkards believe in a particular form of Baptism and an ascetic way of life related to that of the Mennonites.

Miami is named for the town in Ohio, but it is originally an Indian name. Today it is a quiet, picturesque ranching and residential community that often struggles with water issues. A private lake on the west edge of town is known for its northern pike.

Thirteen miles beyond Miami is **Springer**, named for brothers from Iowa, Frank and Charles, founder of the vast CS Ranch, the 13th-oldest ranch in

DETOUR

The Chase Ranch

The Chase Ranch may be seen on guided tours. This historic adobe ranch house and its post–Civil War-era apple orchard in process of restoration show ranch life from the Colfax County War era through territorial and statehood periods and into the 20th century. (Contact the Philmont for directions and hours.)

the United States. It remains in the hands of the founder's family. Frank Springer, lawyer for the Maxwell Land Grant Company, and his brother were two of the most influential people in the development of northeast NM, including Eagle Nest Dam. Springer was earlier known as **Dorsey**, named for Senator Stephen W. Dorsey of Arkansas. A town originated here in 1879 with the coming of the railroad. Springer Lake is 3 miles northwest of Springer. Springer is the site of the Colfax County Fair held in early August. The former Colfax County Courthouse in Springer, the previous county seat before it was relocated to Raton in 1897, is now a visitor center and museum, the **Santa Fe Trail Interpretive Center**. The town is located near the Cimarron Cutoff of the Santa Fe Trail. It is also the home of a detention facility, the town's major employer. One of the most interesting buildings in town is the elaborate Victorian Gothic **Mills Mansion**, built by attorney Melvin W. Mills, located on the southern end. The three-story, 32-room adobe structure on the Cimarron River faces the Mountain Branch on one side and the Cimarron Cutoff of the Santa Fe Trail on the other. Mills was implicated as a member of the notorious Santa Fe Ring, a secretive group of powerful men, including Territorial governor Samuel B. Axtell. During the Territorial era, the

Lucien B. Maxwell and the Maxwell Land Grant

Lucien Bonaparte Maxwell, of French-Canadian descent, came from his home in Illinois at age 15 to hunt beaver for the fur trade along the rivers of the West. Along with Kit Carson, who went as a guide, he joined the exploratory John Fremont Expedition as a hunter in 1842. In 1844, he married Luz Baubien, the 14-year-old daughter of Carlos Beaubien, and put himself on the way to acquiring the Beaubien-Miranda Land Grant. Maxwell eventually became the largest landholder in the hemisphere; the vast Maxwell Land Grant of 1,700,000 acres was headquartered in Cimarron. The Land Grant sold, and so commenced what became known as the Colfax County War, as the Maxwell Land Grant Company tried to evict homesteaders and squatters who had settled there. Gold was discovered on Baldy in 1867. The sale of the grant to an English company in 1869 triggered the Colfax County War. While Maxwell had allowed homesteaders to live on the land he owned, once the company took over, the attempt to evict the "squatters" who believed they had rights to the land resulted in skirmishes lasting twenty years. It is said that the Santa Fe Ring, a secretive organization of powerful Territorial politicians and lawyers, including Territorial Gov. Samuel Axtell, had control of the grant. They orchestrated the shooting of Rev. Tolby, a squatter ally, that triggered the Colfax County War. Local outlaw Clay Allison sided with the settlers.

group promoted their own political and economic interests and controlled the Maxwell Land Grant. (They were also influential in the Lincoln County War.) Mills is said to have played a part in what was known as the **Colfax County War**, a battle between the Maxwell Land Grant Co. and homesteaders who laid claim to their holdings on the grant. The war was triggered by the murder of Reverend Thomas Tolby, a Methodist circuit-rider, in 1875, an ally who sided with the homesteaders. He was found shot in the back beside the Cimarron River. Mills, along with the Santa Fe Ring, was said to be behind Tolby's murder. Mills ultimately lost everything, including his fruit and stagecoach empire in Mills Canyon. His one-time partner, Thomas B. Catron, another powerful Ring member, foreclosed on his mansion. In the end, Mills begged to be allowed to return to his great house to die, which he did, of old age and heartbreak, on a cot.

At the north end of Springer, exit on to I-25 for 13 miles north to **Maxwell**. Take the Maxwell exit left and go to stoplight at the third street. Go right, following the signs to the **Maxwell Wildlife Refuge**, at NM 505. There, go left for 8 miles to **Stubblefield Reservoir**, known for good fishing for bass,

---

DETOUR

Maxwell National Wildlife Refuge

While Native American tribes including Ute, Kiowa, Apache, and Comanche traversed this area for hunting and trading, the Santa Fe Trail crossed near the western border of the Refuge. The land for the Refuge has a history as part of the 2-million-acre Maxwell Land Grant held by frontiersman Lucien B. Maxwell. Homesteaders, farmers, and ranchers lived here during the 19th century until the mid-20th century.

With 3,700 acres of open space, the Refuge is a winter birder's paradise; chances of observing wildlife like wild turkey and deer "at home" in their natural habitat are good to excellent.

Take the Maxwell exit off I-25. Go two blocks and turn right at the Refuge sign. Follow directions to the Visitor Center. With over 278 bird species through the seasons, this wide-open prairie of short grass and wetlands is bordered by horizons of high mesas and the Sangre de Cristo Mountains. While a paved path of about 2 miles borders Lake 13 and the Refuge is laced with gravel roads that invite exploration by vehicle, so long as an undeveloped trail or roadway does not have a KEEP OUT sign or a closed gate, hikers are welcome to divert on foot from the main roads.

And there certainly are many birds to be spotted here any time of day: golden eagles, trumpeter and tundra swans, great blue herons, and other waterfowl, including Merganser ducks. On a recent Sunday morning drive, I spotted six bald eagles. The Refuge is listed by *Audubon Magazine* as a New Mexico Birding Hotspot.

walleye, pike, catfish, and perch. The road is paved the whole way. Cross the dam and continue 4 miles to arrive at **Cold Beer**, located in the ghost town of **Colfax**. It is said there has been a bar at this location since Prohibition. This is a lively social center of the area, with good selection of beer and spirits, live music on weekends, and all sorts of special events. This is a cowboy bar extraordinaire, a biker destination, the place to stop in for a cold one and watch the game during football season, and the site of local pool tournaments. The current owners have expanded the menu and the green chile cheeseburger with fries never disappoints. From here, continue on US 64 to Taos or back to Raton.

IN THE AREA

Accommodations

BLUE DRAGONFLY INN, 600 West 18th Street, Cimarron. Call 575 425-0005. $$.

BROKEN ARROW MOTEL, 811 Maxwell Avenue, Springer. Call 575-483-3021. $.

CASA DE GAVILAN, Cimarron, NM 21. Call 575-376-3346. $$$.

EXPRESS ST. JAMES HOTEL, 617 Collison Avenue, Cimarron. Call 888-376-2664. $$–$$$.

Attractions and Recreation

AZTEC MILL MUSEUM, 220 West 17th Street, Cimarron. Call 575-376-2417.

CIMARRON ART GALLERY, 337 9th Street, Cimarron. Call 575-376-2614.

CIMARRON CHAMBER OF COMMERCE, 104 North Lincoln Avenue, Cimarron. Call 575-376-2417.

ELLIOT BARKER WILDLIFE AREA, 14 miles northwest of Cimarron. Call 505-476-8000.

KIT CARSON MUSEUM, Philmont Scout Ranch, Rayado. Call 575-376-2281.

MAXWELL NATIONAL WILDLIFE REFUGE. Call 575-375-2331.

THE VILLAGE OF CIMARRON IS MADE FOR BROWSING

NATIONAL SCOUTING MUSEUM, 17 Deer Run Road, Cimarron. Call 575-376-2281.

PHILMONT SCOUT RANCH. Call 575-376-2281.

SANTE FE TRAIL INTERPRETIVE CENTER AND MUSEUM, 606 Maxwell Avenue, Springer. Call 575-483-5554.

VALLE VIDAL. Call 575-758-6200.

VILLA PHILMONTE, Philmont Scout Ranch, Rayado. Call 575-376-1136.

Dining and Drinks

BLU DRAGONFLY BREWING & SMOKEHOUSE, 301 9th Street, Cimarron. Call 575-376-1110. $$.

COLFAX TAVERN & DINER AT COLD BEER, 32230 US 64, Colfax. Call 575-376-2229. $–$$.

ELIDA'S CAFÉ, 801 Railroad Avenue, Springer. Call 575-483-2985. $.

ZAYRA'S CAFÉ, 42 US 56, Springer. Call 575-483-2813. $.

SOCORRO'S SHADY PLAZA IS THE PERFECT SPOT
FOR A PICNIC OR STROLL ON A JULY DAY

SOUTHEAST

4

AVOIDING THE INTERSTATE

BOSQUE DEL APACHE TO MESILLA: FOLLOWING THE RIO
GRANDE THROUGH CHILE FIELDS AND PECAN ORCHARDS
INTO THE MESILLA VALLEY

ESTIMATED LENGTH: 146 miles

ESTIMATED TIME: One day

GETTING THERE: Rather than speeding down I-25 at 75 mph, meander the backroads and linger in the small communities along the way, following the Rio
Grande south. Stop in cafés, enjoy the native fare, talk to the locals, bird-
watch, observe the heartland of New Mexico's agricultural life, and experience the richness of a pace coordinated with the seasons.

HIGHLIGHTS: Bosque del Apache National Wildlife Refuge; New Mexico Farm &
Ranch Heritage Museum

Start this trip in **Socorro,** 72 miles south of **Albuquerque,** home of highly
rated New Mexico Tech. On I-25, grab a cappuccino for the road at M Mountain Coffee or take a spin around the plaza, lively on summer Saturdays with
the **Farmers' Market.** If time allows, visit the **Mineral Museum** on the New
Mexico Tech campus to see a mesmerizing display of precious metals, fossils, gems, and mineral specimens from all over the state.

The headwaters of the **Rio Grande,** the high desert river that runs
through the west all the way to the Gulf of Mexico, forming a natural part
of the border between the United States and Mexico, and supporting life in
this land, begins with a gathering of trickles in gravel beds above Creede,
Colorado, and flows down through the 800-foot-deep Rio Grande Gorge
at Taos, a remarkable viewpoint on the Rio Grande Rift. The river did not
carve this canyon. Rather, friction between the planet's tectonic plates created it. Snowmelt from the San Juan Mountains feeds it, also watering farmers' fields 1,896 miles downstream. In dry years, and during dry seasons,
it is referred to as the Rio Sand because of the islands that emerge in the

LEFT: MESILLA VALLEY PECAN ORCHARDS ARE NURTURED IN THE SHADE OF THE ORGAN MOUNTAINS

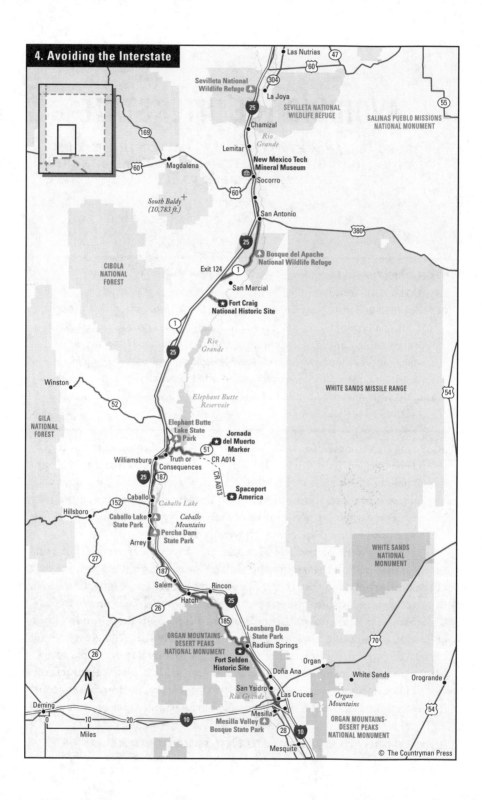

4. Avoiding the Interstate

riverbed. Drought, overuse, and lack of proper management have placed this river—supporting vegetation, wildlife, and the way of life that defines the western United States—in a precarious position. So far, New Mexico's agricultural traditions have held their own against the ever-pressing needs of water for urban development, but the battle is continuous and contentious.

For millennia, the Rio Grande meandered. As it changed course, indigenous people learned to adapt, shifting locations to make best use of the rich soil flooding brought. The bosque, the world's largest cottonwood forest, stretching much of the length of New Mexico, thrived as the cottonwood co-evolved with the river, releasing its seeds when the river was at its height. Now, as the state dams the river for flood control and repurposes its waters for agriculture, the Rio Grande no longer floods, and the bosque is dying. Its cottonwoods, which have a lifespan of 75 to 100 years, are unable to reproduce.

In 2018, the Lower Rio Grande in Texas was named one of America's "most endangered rivers." The Lower Rio Grande is #4 on the list, threatened by border wall construction that would cut the river off from its floodplain, potentially exacerbating flooding and erosion and blocking access to this life-giving resource for people and wildlife.

To follow the river south is the best way to understand and get to know the people, landscapes, and multiplicity of life forms that depend on it. For many living in villages, farms, and ranches along the way, life changes very little from decade to decade. Travel through the land of Rio Abajo, the south, the lowland, and you will feel a palpable change of pace from the Rio Arriba, the high ground above La Bajada Pass. You are likely to see red chile drying in the fields or the flood irrigation of pecan orchards.

The agricultural way of life predominates in southern New Mexico, and there is a sense of honor in living by the seasons and a power in facing whatever Mother Nature may send your way. Continuity of values, love of faith and family, and community strength are where people focus their energies.

Conquistador Juan de Onate named Socorro in 1598 because he and his party were given help and aid, or "succor," by native Piro Indians. To begin the backroad journey, it is necessary to travel 11 miles south on the interstate to **San Antonio**. Turn right, east, on Exit 139 to get to San Antonio, birthplace of hotelier Conrad Hilton. His father, Gus Hilton, established a stagecoach line to **White Oaks** and was known as the "merchant king of San Antonio." The town is home of the **Owl Bar & Café**, 0.025 mile from the highway exit, which serves a legendary green chile cheeseburger and homemade fries. The Owl has been around since the Manhattan Project days, when scientists came from Los Alamos, the Secret City, to this area to test the atomic bomb on the **Trinity Site.**

Turn right on NM 1 and head south 9 miles through the village, noting Rio Abajo Antiques, the old Crystal Palace, and a photogenic deserted wooden train station, toward **Bosque del Apache National Wildlife Refuge** (forest of the Apache, who camped and hunted here), New Mexico's premier birding site, beside the Chupadera Mountains. The heart of the refuge, founded in 1939, is made up of 3,800 acres of wetlands and fields that yield food for birds and other creatures who visit and dwell here. The excellent Visitor Center can answer questions and offer you books and educational materials. Mid-November through mid-February is the peak time to view snow geese and sandhill cranes that migrate along the Rio Grande Flyway, as well as owls and bald eagles. During the spring and fall, migrant warblers and flycatchers may be seen. In summer, you can spot waders, nesting songbirds, shorebirds, and more are visible along the 15-mile auto tour loop. **The Festival of the Cranes** occurs annually in late November. The event includes speakers, special tours, and wildlife displays. The most spectacular sights are the dawn liftoff of thousands of cranes and their sunset fly-in, as photographers line the waterways to catch the sight. Many miles of level roads invite bicyclists. Return to I-25 via San Antonio or take the 16-mile partially paved backroad, continuing on NM 1, to **San Marcial**, once a thriving railroad town with a Harvey House, until it was flooded out in the 1920s. Nothing remains from those good old days. From San Marcial, exit onto I-25 and continue south.

Continue south to **Truth or Consequences** in 64.2 miles. Originally named Hot Springs, the town got its name when it was selected in a national contest on a 1950s TV program hosted by Ralph Edwards called *Truth or Consequences*, in an offer to change its name. And every year, as part of the

THOUSANDS OF SANDHILL CRANES MAKE BOSQUE DEL APACHE THEIR WINTERING GROUND; RECENTLY, A BANDED CRANE FLEW IN FROM SIBERIA TO JOIN THE FLOCK

Sevilleta National Wildlife Refuge

Exit 169 off I-25 (approximately one hour south of Albuquerque). The state's largest refuge at 360 square miles, or 230,000 acres, the Sevilleta melds four life zones: the Chihuahuan desert, the shortgrass prairie, the Colorado Plateau shrub steppe, and the pinon-juniper woodland. In addition, the Rio Grande runs through it, offering its deep bosque forest to shelter birds and wildlife, while creating 5 miles of riparian setting for marsh and water birds. The incomparable diversity of this refuge provides home to more than 1,200 species of plants, 251 species of birds, and 89 species of mammals, with 8.5 miles of hiking trails, from the 0.5-mile walk from the visitor's center to more challenging trails with views of mountains, mesas, and desert terrain. It extends from the Sierra Ladrones in the west to the Los Pinos Mountains in the east.

Fort Craig

Thirteen miles south of San Marcial, with the San Mateo Mountains to the west and the Jornado del Muerto Mountains to the south, find the Fort Craig Rest Area on the west side of the highway between MM 113 and 114. The 19th-century military installation is 9 miles to the north.

From the San Marcial I-25 exit, go east over the Interstate and south on old Highway 1, about 11 miles. Then follow the signs to Fort Craig. Established in 1854, it was used in the Civil War and thereafter to control local Apaches. It was home to the Buffalo Soldiers of the 9th Cavalry and the 38th and 12th Infantry from 1866–76. The area was previously home to indigenous Piro, before the Apache came to trade. The Piro joined with the Spanish as they fled south during the Pueblo Revolt of 1680 or integrated with other tribes, leaving the land in control of the Apache. Northbound travelers on the Camino Real stopped for rest and water at Fort Craig. By 1861, with 2,000 soldiers stationed there, Fort Craig was the largest fort in the Southwest. In 1862, with General Henry Hopkins Sibley leading Confederate troops up the Rio Grande, occupants of Fort Craig staged "Quaker Guns," or fake wooden cannons, with empty caps alongside real cannons and some Union soldiers, deferring the Confederate attack. Following the Civil War, the Army returned to controlling the Apache and raiding the Navajo, as they pursued Indian warriors Geronimo, Victorio, and Nana. After Geronimo and Nana surrendered in 1885, the Army abandoned Fort Craig. Through its donation by the Oppenheimer family, the property eventually went to the Bureau of Land Management and is now a BLM Special Management Area. The massive earthworks have been partially reconstructed.

deal, Mr. Edwards returned to celebrate the annual May fiesta, for over 50 years. Sitting on a 110-degree aquifer, the town calls itself the Hot Springs Capital of the World, with dozens of spas where travelers seek health and relaxation by soaking in the geothermal mineral pools. **Geronimo Springs Museum** celebrates Sierra County's cultures, from prehistoric times to the present. The **Spaceport America Visitor Center**, near the site of planning for tourist travel to space led by Virgin Galactic's Sir Richard Branson, is 35 miles southeast of Truth or Consequences and tours are available. Tickets may be purchased here at the Visitor Center. Galleries, artist studios, offbeat boutiques, import stores, and second-hand shops line the streets. Renegades from Santa Fe have moved here to find affordable housing, as have people of modest means. The town has a distinctly blue-collar vibe.

To get to nearby **Elephant Butte Lake State Park**, take NM 52 east out of Truth or Consequences. At this park, a 40-mile lake with 200 miles of shoreline came about with the construction of **Elephant Butte Dam**, an engineering marvel of its day, in 1912–16. Originally intended for irrigation, it's now a popular place for boating, water skiing, fishing, picnicking, and hanging out on the beach. If the light is right and you hold your gaze in the proper direction, it is possible to discern the elephant profile rock formation for which the site is named.

Leaving Truth or Consequences through the village of **Williamsburg**, go left on NM 187 to follow the Rio Grande on its southerly course. Travel on the two-lane asphalt road through olive green stretches of creosote and wild grasses, as well as many tumbledown home sites in various state of

Jornado del Muerto ("Journey of the Dead One")

The 90-mile slice of Chihuahuan desert that stretches from **Las Cruces** to Socorro was a brutal challenge for travelers. It is located far from the Rio Grande, but passage along the river, with water access, was even more difficult. The crossing took three days, but travelers mostly moved by night. Today, the western half is occupied by ranchers, while the eastern half is part of the White Sands Missile Range. From the Truth or Consequences turnoff, follow the road to the Sierra County Court House, taking NM 51 16.5 miles toward **Engle**. A marker is located at the crossing of the road with the **Camino Real,** the 1600-mile journey from Durango, Mexico, to Santa Fe forged by Onate, on a pullout on the south side of NM 51 at mile marker 15. This is the only place on the auto route where the actual roadbed of the Camino can still be seen. While the Jornada saved travel time, water was (and still is) scarce to nonexistent, and Indians were hostile to travelers who dared cross this way.

HOT SPRINGS BATHERS IN TRUTH OR CONSEQUENCES RELAX AS THE RIO GRANDE FLOWS BY

disrepair. In 4 miles, cross Paloma Creek. At 10 miles, come to **Caballo Lake State Park**, a peaceful getaway spot against the rugged **Caballo Mountains**, offering water recreation, such as boating, kayaking, canoeing, sailing, swimming, and fishing. Choose from 170 campsites, with plenty of sites with utility hookups for RVs. There is just as much to do off the water: hiking, horseback riding, birding on a New Mexico Birding Trail, and picnicking. The geologically complex rock formations reveal sedimentary remains of a tropical Paleozoic sea and granite Prezoic surface rocks 2 billion years old, all shaped by tectonic activity to form the Head of the Horse (hence the word *Caballo*).

Continue south, past several private RV parks. This peaceful area is appealing to snowbirds and campers. At 17 miles south of Truth or Consequences, cross over I-25. Here you will begin to see the expansive green fields of the fertile Hatch Valley. In 1 mile, go left on East Grand Percha Drive, and 2 miles farther, you will arrive at **Percha Dam State Park**, one of the state's premier birding spots, boasting the fine New Mexico Birding Trail. Percha has a reputation as a dwelling place for bald eagles; however, in the height of summer, it is a superb place to observe and hear a large variety of songbirds.

Beyond Percha Lake State Park, expanses of cultivated fields of beans, chile, onions, and cotton stretch out to the horizon. Here the culture centers on farming, and many, if not most, of the people hail from multigenerational growing traditions. They are mostly bilingual and, in their way,

HATCH LIVES UP TO ITS MONIKER AS "CHILE CAPITAL OF THE WORLD"

bicultural, in a part of the country integrated with Mexican people and customs. Hope you're ready for lunch, because the **Arrey Café** in the heart of southern New Mexico's agricultural country is ready to serve you. This is the kind of roadside café, hidden away in a faded blue doublewide, that many dream of finding. Relying on Hatch beans and chile, the café serves some of the most delicious salsa and the biggest, plumpest chile rellenos. The green chile cheeseburgers are legendary, and the price is beyond reasonable. The clientele is strictly local, composed of farmers and farm workers. **Arrey** is named for the first postmaster, Urbano Arrey, one of the first homesteaders; his descendants continue to live here. Continuing south on NM 187, you will see pistachio orchards, warehouses of pecan growers, chile-packing plants, and chile pickers working the fields. In the distance to the

Hatch

This town is named for General Edward Hatch, Commander of nearby Fort Thorn. Technically, there is no chile variety designated "Hatch." The chile grown here and branded "Hatch" is considered tastier and more authentic than the chile from elsewhere. Chile is the state's largest agricultural crop. The chile varieties developed at New Mexico State University, such as Big Jim, that give NM cuisine its reputation for flavor, are grown here. Hatch grew from an AT&SF train stop in the 1880s to a crossroads town of 1700 at the junction of NM 185, 187, 26, and 154. It is 33 miles northwest of Las Cruces. It is known for the Hatch Chile Fiesta, held during Labor Day weekend, and it is the place to buy dried red chile and fresh or frozen green chile year-round. You can wander among the shops to find chile-themed clothing, home décor, and souvenirs. Today farmers struggle with drought and compete with imported Mexican chile. Red chile is the ripened version of green chile—it's the same fruit. Hatch is a good place to ponder the state question: red or green?

south, the jagged **Organ Mountains** come into view. Largely composed of igneous rock, the Spanish named them Los Organos because they resemble the pipes of an organ. The highest point is Organ Needle, at 9,012 feet, then Organ Peak at 8,872 feet. Throughout history, they have attracted miners. The mountains include a cave where Geronimo supposedly hid as well as a training ground for astronauts on the moon mission. This range is visible for 100 miles in every direction. You may have to dodge a few tumbleweeds, depending on the season.

Twenty-two miles south of Arrey, you will arrive at Hatch, the Chile Capital of the World.

Depending on the season and the rainfall, see the Rio Grande curving along as you motor south on NM 185 past farms and pecan orchards.

Leasburg Dam State Park, 15 miles north of Las Cruces on NM 185, is popular for fishing, canoeing, and kayaking. There is also a cactus garden, as well as a trail to the historic dam built in 1908 to channel water from the Rio Grande to irrigate the Upper Mesilla Valley.

Radium Springs, 15 miles north of Las Cruces, once had free-flowing hot springs, and soldiers from Fort Selden visited there. The amount of radium in the water is miniscule.

Fort Selden State Monument, 12 miles north of Las Cruces, was an active military base during the Civil War and during the Indian Wars. Douglas MacArthur, it is said, was born here. The Monument offers living history programs and Dutch oven cooking demonstrations. Plenty of antique cannons and military wagons are on display.

FORT SELDEN IS REPLETE WITH CIVIL WAR–ERA RELICS

Dona Ana, 2 miles east on NM 185 and 5 miles north of Las Cruces, settled in 1843, is today a bedroom community of Las Cruces, although it was once the county seat. Dona Ana County was one of nine original counties created by the Territorial Legislature in 1852, which at that time spanned the entire width of New Mexico. The town's plaza was reconstructed recently. Dona Ana Robledo was a 17th-century ranch owner. This was the first county seat.

Continue on NM 187 and drive into Las Cruces, easily recognizable with its plethora of restaurants, motels, and strip malls on Avenida de Mesilla, a street which leads 4 miles directly to quiet, historic **Mesilla**.

Mesilla, 1 mile south of Las Cruces, retains its Old Mexico charm with quaint Territorial style adobe homes, streets wide enough for a burro cart, *acequias* running through town, a historic plaza over which flags of six nations have flown, including the American flag first flown in 1854 to mark the signing of the Gadsden Purchase, and an abundance of galleries, boutiques, snack shops, a bookstore, the historic **Fountain Theater,** gourmet shops, and cafés lining the plaza and surrounding streets. Standing over the plaza like a sentry is the **Basilica San Albino**, dating to 1855. The brick church, dedicated in 1906, was built around the original adobe church, which was torn down and carried away as the new one was built. Time virtually stands still here, in the place that was at one time the Arizona capital of the Confederacy and on the path of the Butterfield Overland Stage Company.

SIX FLAGS HAVE FLOWN OVER THE PLAZA AT OLD MESILLA

DETOUR

Mesilla Valley Bosque State Park

A lovely walking area is Mesilla Valley Bosque State Park, the banks of the southern Rio Grande, with trails for walking, jogging, and biking. There is an easy 2-mile loop through the riparian habitat along the bank. This is a designated New Mexico Birding Trail, with a clear panorama of the Organ Mountains with the Rio Grande in the foreground. Take Avenida de Mesilla (NM 28) southwest out of Mesilla. Turn right on Calle del Norte (NM 359) and head west. Cross the bridge over the Rio Grande and turn left onto the park entry road. Turn right into the Visitor Center parking lot. Be aware: This park tends to close early, around 4 p.m., and dawn is the best time for bird watching.

La Posta Restaurant sits in a 175-year-old building that served as a stage stop. Life takes place behind the adobe walls, in charming courtyards originally built to protect households from invading tribes. Markets and special events are held in the plaza throughout the year; one of the most memorable is November 2, Dia de los Muertos, better known as Day of the Dead, representing a Meso-American custom of honoring the dead with food, drink, and celebration, particularly those who have passed during the previous year, that has taken hold in New Mexico, with memorial altars, vendors, and a procession to the cemetery.

The word *mesilla* means "little table," referring to the geographic spot where the town is located, in the Mesilla Valley of the Rio Grande. Directly to the south on NM 28 is a string of wineries laced between little farming villages, but begin the wine tasting tour in town, on Avenida de Mesilla at St. Clair Winery, Luna Rossi, or Blue Teal.

Las Cruces, home of New Mexico State University, the state's agricultural land grant college, is a relaxed, friendly college town attractive to retirees and snowbirds. It is a comfortable mix of traditional and contemporary ideas. It was founded in 1849, but the name *Las Cruces* appears in Spanish documents as early as 1682. In 1853 it became the county seat. The city gets its name from a group of crosses marking the graves of travelers on the Camino Real. Three iron crosses were erected in 1959 at the intersection of North Main Street and Solano Drive to commemorate the site. This town has so many excellent New Mexican restaurants that it's hard to name a favorite. It also has a couple of good bookstores, a reviving downtown, a thriving food co-op, live theater, museums, and Aggies college sports. The 400,000-acre **Organ Mountains-Desert Peaks National Monument** offers high desert hiking at all levels, as well as biking and plenty of desert beauty. The town's proximity to the border influences its flavor; there is a year-round calendar of family-friendly festivities, including a Renaissance Faire and a mariachi festival. The **Bataan Memorial March**, held annually in March since 1990, is a full marathon with a shorter 15-mile length that now attracts close to 10,000 participants. **Matachine** dances are held in Tortugas, on the south end of Las Cruces following Main Street, during the Feast of Our Lady of Guadalupe, December 10–12. This distinct multicultural event includes a procession up Tortugas Mountain, also known as A Mountain. The Saturday morning farmers and crafts market held on the Downtown Mall ranks as one of the best in the country. Las Cruces is distinctly urban. It is the state's third-largest city, with the shopping malls, chain stores, and restaurants that would populate any medium-sized American city. One stellar attraction is the **New Mexico Farm & Ranch Heritage Museum,** which displays farm animals, the agricultural history of the state, cultural artifacts (such as farm implements), quilts, and fine Western art and photography. The museum also offers a Heritage Garden; a Children's Discovery Garden; a working blacksmithing shop; pony rides; and demonstrations of wool spinning and weaving, Dutch oven cooking, dowsing, and more.

From Las Cruces, head east or west on I-10. El Paso, Texas is less than an hour south on I-25.

IN THE AREA

Accommodations

BLACKSTONE LODGE, 410 Austin Street, Truth or Consequences. Call 575-894-0894. $$$.

HOTEL ENCANTO DE LAS CRUCES, 705 South Telshor Boulevard, Las Cruces. Call 575-522-4300. $$–$$$.

RIVERBEND HOT SPRINGS, 100 Austin Street, Truth or Consequences. Call 575-894-7625. $$–$$$.

Attractions and Recreation

BOSQUE DEL APACHE NATIONAL WILDLIFE REFUGE, 1001 NM 1. Call 505-835-1828.

DRIPPING SPRINGS NATURAL AREA, 10 miles east of Las Cruces on Dripping Springs Road. Call 575-522-1219.

FORT CRAIG, Fort Craig Road, San Antonio. Call 575-835-0412.

FORT SELDEN, 1280 Fort Selden Road, Radium Springs. Call 575-526-8911.

GERONIMO SPRINGS MUSEUM, 211 Main Street, Truth or Consequences. Call 575-894-6600.

HATCH VALLEY CHAMBER OF COMMERCE, 210 West Hall Street, Hatch. Call 575-267-5050.

LAS CRUCES CONVENTION AND VISITOR CENTER, 211 North Walter Street, Las Cruces. Call 575-541-2444.

LAS CRUCES FARMERS' & CRAFTS MARKET, 125 North Main Street, Downtown Mall, Las Cruces. Call 575-201-3853.

MESILLA VALLEY BOSQUE STATE PARK, 5000 Bosque del Norte, Mesilla. Call 575-523-4398.

MINERAL MUSEUM, New Mexico Tech, 801 Leroy Place, Socorro. Call 575-835-5420.

NEW MEXICO FARM & RANCH HERITAGE MUSEUM, 4100 Dripping Springs Road, Las Cruces. Call 575-522-4100.

AN ABUNDANCE OF UNIQUE CRAFTS MAKES THE SATURDAY-MORNING LAS CRUCES FARMERS' AND CRAFT MARKET ONE OF THE COUNTRY'S FINEST

YOU CAN'T LEAVE HATCH WITHOUT TAKING HOME SOME CHILES

ORGAN MOUNTAINS-DESERT PEAKS NATIONAL, 571 Walton Boulevard, Las Cruces. Call 575-525-4300.

SEVILLETA VISITOR CENTER, Website: www.fws.gov/refuge/sevilleta.

SOCORRO COUNTY HERITAGE AND VISITOR CENTER, Fisher Avenue, Socorro. Call 575-835-8927.

SPACEPORT AMERICA VISITOR CENTER, 301 South Foch Street, Truth or Consequences. Call 844-727-7223.

Dining and Drinks

ARREY CAFE, Arrey. Call 575-267-4436. $.

THE BEAN OF MESILLA, 2011 Avenida de Mesilla, Mesilla. Call 575-527-5155. $–$$.

CAFÉ DE MESILLA, 2190 Avenida de Mesilla, Mesilla. Call 575-524-0000. $$.

CHOPE'S BAR & CAFE, 16145 South NM 28, La Mesa. Call 575-233-3420. $$.

LA NUEVA CASITA, 195 North Mesquite Street, Las Cruces. Call 575-523-5434. $.

LA POSTA DE MESILLA, 2410 Calle de San Albino, Mesilla Plaza. Call 575-524-3524. $$–$$$.

LA VINA, 4201 South NM 28. Call 575-882-7632. $$.

LOS ARCOS STEAK & LOBSTER HOUSE, 1400 North Date Street, Truth or Consequences. Call 575-894-6200. $$–$$$.

PACIFIC GRILL, 800 North Date Street, Truth or Consequences. Call 575-894-7687. $$.

SPARKY'S IN HATCH: COME FOR THE BBQ, STAY FOR THE GREEN CHILE LEMONADE

SI SENOR, 1551 East Amador Avenue, Las Cruces. Call 575-527-0817. $$.

SPARKY'S BURGERS, BBQ & ESPRESSO, 115 Franklin Street, Hatch. Call 575-267-4222. $$.

Events

DIA DE LOS MUERTOS, November 2.

FESTIVAL OF THE CRANES, weekend before Thanksgiving.

HATCH CHILE FIESTA, Labor Day Weekend.

5

VALLEY OF THE FIRES TO THREE RIVERS TO CLOUDCROFT

LAVA FLOWS, PETROGLYPHS, AND THE
CLOUD-CLIMBING RAILROAD

ESTIMATED LENGTH: 171 miles

ESTIMATED TIME: One-day driving (without stops); one weekend to allow
for visiting

GETTING THERE: San Antonio is located 11 miles south of Socorro on I-25 or 82
miles south of Albuquerque on I-25. Take San Antonio exit 380 east toward
Carrizozo, which is 65 miles or approximately one hour's drive.

HIGHLIGHTS: Valley of Fires Recreational Area, Three Rivers Petroglyph National
Recreation Site, Tularosa, Cloudcroft, White Sands National Monument

From **San Antonio,** heading east on US 380, cross the intersection with NM 1 and almost immediately cross the **Rio Grande.** This arrow-straight two-lane highway provides the essence of a road trip—the perfect escape from the daily grind, the repetitions of your mind, the daily clamor, or whatever else you'd like to get away from. This is the grand, glorious, gorgeous big empty, the open road, all sky, horizons too far to measure, desert vegetation punctuated by spiky century plants, yucca, mint green creosote, juniper, cedar, and weathered wooden fence posts. The road has enough up-and-down elevation to keep you awake. Here you can see weather coming from any direction; distant summer storm clouds let loose fountains of smoky virga, or rain that falls without hitting the ground. Pillars of white thunderheads form and transform as you drive the 65 miles to **Carrizozo.** Along the way, cross the northern edge of the Jornada del Muerto, the arid stretch of the Camino Real, between the Rio Grande and the ghost town of Bingham.

Seven miles east of San Antonio, pass the **Fite Ranch,** a longtime working ranch that is now a rustic but comfortable B&B. Twelve miles east of San

LEFT: IT'S HARD TO BELIEVE TRAINS TRAVELED ACROSS CLOUDCROFT'S PRECARIOUS-LOOKING MEXICAN TRESTLE
BACK IN THE DAY; TODAY THE AREA IS A HAVEN FOR HIKERS

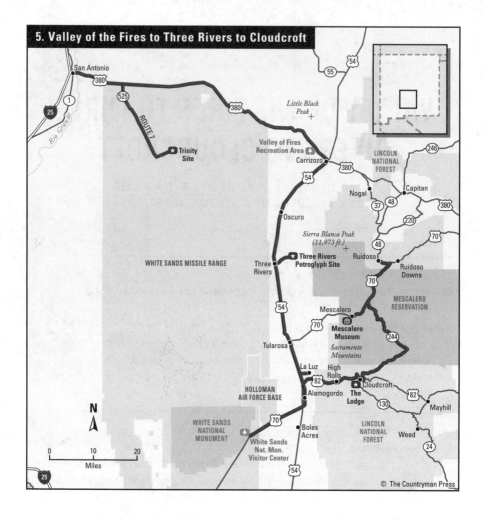

San Antonio
380
525
ROUTE 7
Trinity Site
Rio Grande
25
1
380
Little Black Peak
55
54
Valley of Fires Recreation Area
Carrizozo
380
54
Nogal
48
37
Capitan
380
220
LINCOLN NATIONAL FOREST
246
Oscuro
Sierra Blanca Peak
(11,973 ft.)
48
70
Three Rivers Petroglyph Site
Ruidoso
Three Rivers
WHITE SANDS MISSILE RANGE
Ruidoso Downs
70
54
Mescalero
MESCALERO RESERVATION
70
Mescalero Museum
244
Tularosa
Sacramento Mountains
La Luz
High Rolls
HOLLOMAN AIR FORCE BASE
82
Cloudcroft
Alamogordo
The Lodge
82
Mayhill
130
N
WHITE SANDS NATIONAL MONUMENT
70
Boles Acres
LINCOLN NATIONAL FOREST
Weed
0   10   20
Miles
White Sands Nat. Mon. Visitor Center
54
24
25

© The Countryman Press

Antonio on US 380 is the gate that is 5 miles south of Stallion Range Center, the entry point to the **Trinity Site**, where the first atom bomb was tested in 1945, immediately prior to being dropped on Hiroshima and Nagasaki. It's open two days a year, in April and October.

Believed to be the youngest lava flow in the continental US, Little Black Peak, 9 miles north of Carrizozo, spewed lava a mere 1,500 to 5,000 years ago, well within ancestral memory, to create a valley 44 miles long and 5 miles wide. It formed the **Valley of Fires Recreational Area**. This *malpais*, or badlands, supports extensive Northern Chihuahan plant and animal life. Banana yucca, cane cholla, mesquite, sumac, and creosote abound, decorating the dramatic landscape of twisted, ropey lava. Because the lava here is similar to that found in Hawaii, Hawaiian words are used to describe the formations. For example, the more fluid lava that covers most of the field is called "pahoehoe." Across from the park's visitor center, find the trailhead of the 0.75-mile Malpais Nature Trail loop. The Recreation Area has 19 camp-sites, some electricity, drinking water, and shelters, and it is adjacent to the Malpais. Five miles west is the railroad town of Carrizozo, established in 1899, named for the area's native carrizo grass. It was at one time a busy supply and shipping center for mines near Oscura, White Oaks, and the Nogal-Lincoln area to the east. With tremendous effort, the town, languishing at the crossroads of US 54 and US 380, is in the process of reinventing itself as something of an artist's haven, and at least a half-dozen galleries, including a sizable photo gallery, the **Tularosa Basin Gallery of Photography**, which boasts of being the largest photo gallery in New Mexico at 7,500 square feet, hang on here, as do Gallery 408 and a few secondhand shops. One shop with a great deal of personality is the Soul of the West Bootique. You can grab a good cup of coffee at the 12th Street Coffee Shop. Neon-colored life size burro sculptures decorate the town's main street, 12th Street, in a Burro Trail; you will often find burros in surprising places, like on rooftops. Like other small towns in New Mexico, such as **Truth or Consequences**, there is a deserted air here, characterized by a paradoxical feeling of abandonment and possibility. You could surmise there is nothing going on, or, there could be a lively creative pulse beating somewhere just beyond the surface, should you care to hang out long enough to search for it. This place is perhaps waiting to be discovered; perhaps it will be abandoned once again as the core group of 30 or so artists who have moved in depart for the next promising venue. A drive around town will show the practiced

WELCOME TO CARRIZOZO, WHERE COLORFUL BURROS RESIDE ALL OVER TOWN

eye several interesting historic buildings, both commercial and residential. Open March through November is the **Carrizozo Heritage Museum** celebrating railroading and local ranching.

On the south end of town, take US 54 toward **Three Rivers**. US 54 parallels the railroad track. Pass the Oscuro (dark) Bombing Range, where, only 45 miles from here, the first atomic bomb was exploded at the Trinity Site on July 16, 1945.

In 31 miles, come to **Three Rivers Trading Post and Art Gallery**, a treasure trove packed with Western and Indian art and jewelry as well as books, tee shirts, and more. Cold drinks are available here, too, as well as information about the area. Three Rivers Ranch is loaded with New Mexico history, some of it still in dispute. For one thing, it was the hideout of Billy the Kid, who sheltered his stolen cattle here. By 1915, Senator Albert B. Fall of Teapot Dome scandal notoriety had acquired it. Fall was convicted of accepting a bribe while serving as Secretary of the Interior under President Warren G. Harding in 1921. Fall was one of the first two men who represented New Mexico in the US Senate. Here he built an empire of over a million acres.

But the primary reason to visit this spot is to see the **Three Rivers Petroglyph Site**, maintained by the Bureau of Land Management, with 21,000 petroglyphs on the basaltic ridge that rises above the Three Rivers Valley,

THREE RIVERS TRADING POST

one of the largest rock art sites in the Southwest. Here you can take in panoramic views of the Tularosa Basin to the west and the 11,981-foot Sierra Blanca to the east. Many of the sunbursts, handprints, masks, and geometric designs are visible from the 1-mile winding trail. The cosmic spiral, believed to represent journeying, is evident here, as is Kokopelli, the hump-backed flute player believed to represent fertility. It is believed these images date from 900 to 1300 CE and were left by the Jornada Mogollon people. Dogs are not allowed on the trail. By all means, stay on the 1-mile round-trip trail and beware of rattlesnakes. One slithered along beside me as I made my way up the trail. Snakes here do not seem to crave the privacy rattlers usually do; they seem more accustomed to people than most snakes.

Some people believe petroglyphs are picture writing, and certainly, they contain universal symbols, whether or not the meanings are universal. However, their literal meaning remains mysterious. They may indicate the presence of water or wildlife, or they may serve as a kind of map. Some were made by scratching the rock's outer coating, while others were created by chipping through the rock patina with rocks, as if with a hammer and chisel. Scholars continue to debate whether the Jornada Mogollon people were influenced by, and are therefore related to, Mesoamerican culture, or if they developed independently.

It's another 27 miles to **Tularosa**, a New Mexico village unlike any other. Two miles north of Tularosa on US 54 is **Tularosa Winery**, with premium wines made from New Mexico grapes as well as a good selection of New Mexico craft beer. You can bring your own picnic to savor on the covered patio overlooking the vineyard. There are tours by appointment.

In 1862, 100 farmers left **Mesilla** for this area when their fields were flooded out; when they arrived, they dug the *acequias*, or ditches, that still course around the "49" blocks of the historic district, providing the cooling sound of flowing water during the summer and an extraordinary water source for the giant trees that grace the town. Pomegranate trees, Lombardy poplar trees, and sycamore trees have inserted their roots deeply here, and they grow to great size; they provide habitats for songbirds who just can't stop trilling about what a piece of heaven on Earth this is. The original 49 blocks make up a State and National Historic District. Historic Territorial homes were built by soldiers from the California Column of Union soldiers from California, who, after the Civil War, tended to settle down and marry local women. Walking the 49, even better, getting lost in it, to the sound of water from **Sierra Blanca** (home of **Ski Apache)** running in the ditches is otherworldly. When you crave refreshment, there's **Tulie Freeze** for a chocolate dipped custard cone, and for more than a snack, head for **Yum Yum's Donut Shop,** with barbecue beef, Mexican food, and donuts baked fresh every morning. Tularosa gets its name from the cattails (tulies) that grew here when it was a marshland. Tularosa is celebrated in the novels of Eugene

Manlove Rhodes, known as the Cowboy Chronicler, who called Tularosa "Oasis." The author ranched in the San Andres Mountains.

Sierra Blanca, a peak sacred to the Mescalero Apache, measures almost 12,000 feet and rises 7,000 feet up from the Tularosa Basin. It is the highest mountain in the White Mountains. It is a "complex volcano" composed of multiple flows, ash layers, and two or more vents. It last erupted 35 million years ago. As a valley lacking drainage, the Tularosa valley would be better described as a basin. It is 100 miles long, beginning at the southern end of Three Rivers, and it lies between the San Andres Mountains on the west and the Sacramentos on the east.

South of Tularosa on US 54 is **La Luz**, at the intersection with NM 545 at the traffic light. Go east 2.5 miles. This is the oldest ongoing settlement in the Tularosa Basin and dates to 1719. It feels like a lost village from a Gabriel García Márquez tale of magical realism, as if everyone had fallen into a deep sleep that lasted at least a century and was waiting to be woken up. It was settled by emigrants from Tome and Belen in 1860. *Luz* means "light," and the legend of the name tells how the original settlers camped at Tularosa, where a fire, la luz, was lit each night to signal to the pioneers to the south that all was well. It also once had a sizable pottery plant, built by a Rhode Islander. Adobe walls surround **El Presidio Park**, perhaps the most lost-in-time spot in town, and one of New Mexico's most evocative nooks and crannies, dated 1863. Take the La Luz exit and drive straight into town. The park is at the end of the road.

Back on US 54, **McGinn's Pistachios** is easily recognized by its roadside attraction: The World's Largest Pistachio in the parking lot. Inside the shop await all things pistachio, including souvenirs, samples of flavored pistachios, and wine tastings.

Following US 54 13.5 miles east from Tularosa, arrive at **Alamogordo** at the junction of US 54/70 and US 82. Along the drive between Tularosa and Alamogordo, it is possible to glimpse views of White Sands to the right. Alamogordo, meaning "big cottonwood tree," got its name from the large trees that grew around the spring in Alamo Canyon. As the home of Holloman Air Force Base, Alamogordo has a population of 30,000, a shopping mall, chain motels, and restaurants. Alamogordo is perhaps the most convenient base for exploring **White Sands**, and the **Toy Train Depot** will appeal to children. The depot is actually 100 years old, with more than 1,200 miles of model train track and toy trains on display. Train buffs will enjoy the historic railroad artifacts. The 2.5-mile-long toy train track is adjacent to Kid's Kingdom Park, a playground where kids can let off steam. To get to the **Alameda Park and Zoo**, turn left at 10th Street. This is the oldest zoo in New Mexico, established in 1898 by the railroad. It has 300 animals and 90 different species. On Scenic Drive off Indian Wells Road is the **New Mexico Museum of Space History,** five stories of informative displays as well as the **New**

Horizons Dome Theater and Planetarium, a total immersion experience in the starry heavens, along with a replica of the International Space Station. Ham, the first hominid (a chimpanzee) launched into and recovered from space, is buried beneath the museum flagpoles. The growth of Alamogordo, which began as a planned community following the Railroad Era, is linked to military and federal installations. Wartime activity at Holloman Air Force Base brought growth, and then, during the 1950s, the base was re-activated, and the **White Sands Missile Range** quadrupled the population.

The **White Sands National Monument** is 15 miles west of Alamogordo on US 70. Dunes Drive extends 17 miles into 275 square miles of pure gypsum. Thanks largely to the efforts of New Mexico Senator Martin Heinrich, White Sands recently recieved National Park status. This is the largest of only three sites of its kind in the world. The forces of wind and water have eroded the Sacramento and San Andres Mountains, which frame the Tularosa Basin and both have high gypsum content, into **Lake Lucero.** From there, winds blow the crystals toward the northeast at up to 20 feet a year, continuing the evolution of the White Sands. Some dunes are stable enough to support vegetation such as yucca and saltbush, while others do not yet support plant life. The White Sands are a virtual laboratory of evolution, with the development of the earless white lizard and other similar creatures who have learned to survive here. You can hike the dunes, bike a little, or surf the sand on a saucer. Monthly Full Moon nights require reservations, as do monthly three-hour guided tours of Lake Lucero.

One of the most dramatic drives in New Mexico is the 26 miles on US 82 between Alamogordo and **Cloudcroft.** As the road winds toward the Sacramento Mountains, leave the desert flatlands to find valleys filled with orchards leading to mountain meadows and peaks of tall pines, along with mind-blowing expansive views. Pass **High Rolls**, site of the High Rolls Cherry Festival. The village of Cloudcroft, at 9,100 feet, was originally founded as a railroad town and quickly became a resort for El Paso residents seeking relief from summer heat. This town makes a good base for hiking the **Lincoln National Forest,** mountain biking on the Rim Trail, winter snow sports at the local snow play area or the James Sewell ice skating rink, or just a cool summer getaway. **Burro Street** is the "downtown," packed with cute boutiques, ice cream and snack stands, bakeries, and souvenir shops. The **Sacramento Mountains Museum & Pioneer Village** comprise restored buildings and a museum of artifacts. Motels and B&B's abound, but the most outstanding place to stay is the **Lodge Resort & Spa,** a gracious small inn with an elegant traditional American restaurant and superb service at **Rebecca's,** a good place for celebratory dinners and Sunday brunch, along with a high altitude nine-hole golf course that follows Scottish rules of play. The **Lodge,** with its two-story rock fireplace, was originally constructed in 1899 by the Alamogordo and Sacramento Mountain Railway in its quest for timber and railway ties. Climb up the bell tower and see the signatures of Clark Gable, Judy Garland, and other celebrities who visited here. Every governor of New Mexico has stayed in the Governor's Suite. There is also supposedly a resident ghost of a red-headed housekeeper, Rebecca, who disappeared after her logger lover found her with another man. The Victorian-style Lodge is especially charming during the holidays, with its vintage Christmas decorations. Cloudcroft also offers a system of hiking trails, the **Cloud Climbing Trestle Trails**, created along overgrown railroad beds by the Rails-to-Trails Association. Depart from the Depot on the Overlook Trail for 0.2 mile. After enjoying the view from the Devil's Elbow visiting deck, continue to merge into the Cloud Climbing Trestle Trail. Go right on T-5001. See the remains of the S trestle to the left. In 0.8 mile, reach the Mexican Canyon Trestle that spans 300 feet and stands 130 feet above the bottom of the canyon. The precarious wooden trestle looks far too fragile to support the weight of a train. To return, retrace your steps to the Depot to complete a 2-mile hike. The **Sacramento Rim National Recreation Trail** follows the rim of the Sacramento Mountains in a moderate 14-mile hike, yielding sprawling views of Tularosa Basin 5,000 feet below. To get to the trailheads from Cloudcroft, head west on US 82 toward Alamogordo. Just beyond the US 82/NM130 junction, turn left into the **Trestle Recreation Area**. This day

IF YOU CLIMB UP TO THE TOWER AT THE LODGE AT CLOUDCROFT, YOU WILL FIND THE SIGNATURES OF CLARK GABLE AND JUDY GARLAND

use area houses a replica of the Historic Cloudcroft Train Depot. Here find parking restrooms, water, picnic tables, and trail access.

The Alamogordo and Sacramento Railroad, better known as the **Cloud-Climbing Railroad**, was an ambitious dream of entrepreneur Charles B. Eddy, who arrived in New Mexico from New York with his brother John A. Eddy in the late 19th century. His El Paso and Northeastern Railroad chugged through the Tularosa Valley to Santa Rosa in the late 1890s, stopping at Carrizozo and Three Rivers. His railroad needed wood for ties, and so the Cloud-Climbing spur pushed from 4,322 feet up to 9,069 feet into the forest for timber, making hair-raising turns as it crossed the Sacramento Mountains. The 52-foot-high wooden railroad trestle across Mexican Canyon (see description above), which still stands, was one of 58 such crossings. Eddy's spur into the clouds carried passengers into the cool, fresh mountain air, stopping at the site the crew had established: Cloudcroft. The last train came through the Sacramento Mountains in 1947.

Lincoln National Forest offers a million acres of hiking, backpacking, trail riding and camping, with good cross-country skiing through the

Mescalero Apache Tribe

Called Mescalero because they depended on the mescal plant for sustenance, these fierce hunter-gatherers terrorized those who encroached on their traditional homelands, including Spanish, Mexican, and American settlers. Among their great warriors were Geronimo, Victorio, Lozen, and Cochise. The Mescalero now live on their 463,000-acre reservation, although along with the Lipan and Chiricahua Apaches, they once inhabited the entire Southwest. The Mescalero Reservation was established with 400 members in 1873, after their population had been decimated. They were forced to **Bosque Redondo** where they were held with captive Navajo in 1863–64. Today they number around 4,000 and manage successful tourist operations of Inn of the Mountain Gods and Ski Apache. A visit to **Mescalero Apache Cultural Museum**, which you reach by going right on Central Mescalero Road toward the Tribal Administrative Office and then taking the first left into Chiricahua Plaza, gives the story of the tribe from a tribal perspective. Kenalda, the puberty ceremony for young women, is a 4-day ceremonial rite of passage that affirms her connection to White Painted Woman, the tribe's model of virtuous and heroic womanhood, who saved her people. During the ceremony, the young woman dances for many hours as tribal elders recite the history of the tribe. **Ski Apache** has 55 trails, and **Wind Rider Zip Tour**, a 9,000-foot-long zip line, glides above the Sacramento Mountains.

Sacramento Mountains near Cloudcroft. Many camping facilities are located within a 4-mile radius of Cloudcroft in the Sacramento Ranger District. These sites may be accessed by Highways 82, 130, 244, and 6563.

Ruidoso means "noisy water." This place was known as Dowlin's Mill until 1885, when it was named for the Rio Ruidoso that runs through it. Captains Paul and William Dowlin were drawn to the river to build a sawmill and then a grist mill. This popular tourist town lies 47 miles from Cloudcroft north on NM 244; or, alternatively, 32 miles northeast of Tularosa on US 70. It is the home of **Ruidoso Downs**, best known for the All-American Futurity, the nation's richest Quarter horse race. Horse racing began here in a cornfield in the 1930s. Expect crowds and challenging parking—or difficulty even getting into a restaurant—during high summer season. The crowds are likely to be gathered on **Sudderth Street**, the main drag, packed with bars, cafés, housewares, clothing, jewelry, souvenir stores, and western shops. During quieter times of the year, there is much to appreciate. Golfing, hiking, and horseback riding are some of the most popular pastimes, but shopping seems to be the favorite. A favorite café on the main drag is the Village Buttery, which serves homemade soups and desserts as well as satisfying fresh salads and sandwiches. The **Hubbard Museum of the American West** in Ruidoso Downs originated as the Museum of the Horse and has expanded into a rich Western history museum.

IN THE AREA

Accommodations

FITE RANCH BED & BREAKFAST, P.O. Box 205, San Antonio, 7.5 miles east of San Antonio on US 360. Call 575-838-0958. $$$.

INN OF THE MOUNTAIN GODS RESORT AND CASINO, 287 Carrizo Canyon Road, Mescalero. Call 575-464-7777. $$–$$$.

LODGE AT CLOUDCROFT, 601 Corona Place, Cloudcroft. Call 575-682-2089. $$–$$$.

STORY BOOK CABINS, 410 Main Road, Ruidoso. Call 888-257-2115. $$.

Attractions and Recreation

HUBBARD MUSEUM OF THE AMERICAN WEST, 26301 US 70, Ruidoso Downs. Call 575-378-4142.

LINCOLN NATIONAL FOREST, 3463 Las Palomas Road, Alamogordo. Call 575-434-7200.

OLIVER LEE MEMORIAL STATE PARK, 409 Dog Canyon Road, Alamogordo. Call 575-437-8284.

SPENCER THEATER FOR THE PERFORMING ARTS, 108 Spencer Drive, Alto. Call 575-336-4800.

WHITE SANDS NATIONAL MONUMENT, 15 miles west of Alamogordo on US 70. Call 575-679-2599.

Dining and Drinks

CASA DE SUENOS, 35 St. Francis Drive, Tularosa. Call 575-585-3494. $$.

GATHERING OF NATIONS BUFFET, Inn of the Mountain Gods Resort and Casino, Mescalero. Call 800-545-9011. $–$$.

REBECCA'S, The Lodge, 1 Corona Place, Cloudcroft. Call 575-682-2566. $$$.

SACRED GROUNDS COFFEE & TEA HOUSE, 2704 Sudderth Drive, Ruidoso. Call 575-257-2273. $.

VILLAGE BUTTERY, 2701 Sudderth Drive, Ruidoso. Call 575-585-3457. $.

YUM YUM'S DONUT SHOP, 460 Central Avenue, Tularosa. Call 575-585-2529. $.

6

TRACKING BILLY THE KID INTO HISTORY'S HIDEAWAY

CAPITAN, LINCOLN, FORT SUMNER

ESTIMATED LENGTH: 200 miles

ESTIMATED TIME: Weekend-plus

GETTING THERE: Two suggested routes: From Las Cruces, go to White Sands, then to Alamogordo on I-70, take US 70 north to Tularosa, continue up past Blazer's Mill, toward Bent, Mescalero, and through Ruidoso to Capitan and Lincoln. We will follow this route. The other suggested route is covered in Chapter 5, Valley of Fires. A second suggested route: from Albuquerque or Socorro, heading east then south, take US 380 East 11 miles south of Socorro at the San Antonio exit off I-25. Continue east on US 380 through the Valley of Fires to Carrizozo and on to Capitan and Lincoln, and then travel via the directions specified in this chapter into the Hondo Valley to Roswell and Fort Sumner.

HIGHLIGHTS: Lincoln, where the entire mile-long town is a well-preserved historic district, including the Lincoln County Jail and Courthouse where Billy the Kid escaped, with the shootout reenacted on Old Lincoln Days, held annually the first weekend in August; Billy the Kid's grave in Fort Sumner, with the epitaph, HE DIED AS HE HAD LIVED; the UFO Museum and Research Center, Roswell; tours of the 1947 UFO Crash Site, which were held in 2019, for the first time, during the annual Roswell UFO Festival, first week in July.

If time is limited, take the **Billy the Kid National Scenic Highway,** Highway 70 West. Orient the trip and make the most of it with a visit to the **Byway Visitor Center,** next to the Hubbard Museum of the American West in **Ruidoso Downs,** actually a mini-museum, with in-depth information on the area and its prehistory as well as exhibits. The Byway links **Ruidoso, Lincoln, Fort**

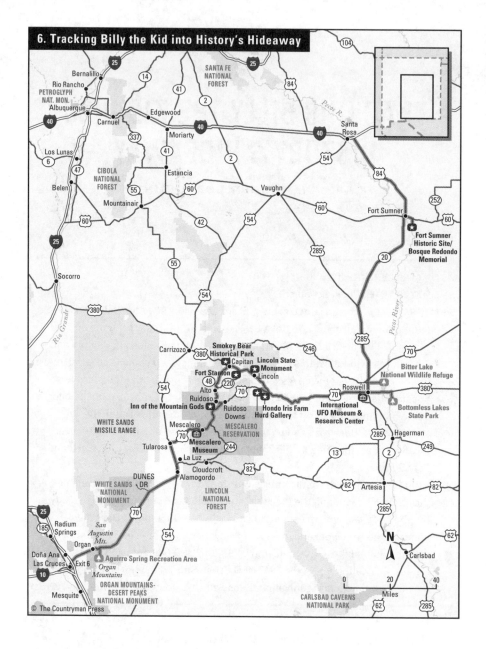

© The Countryman Press

Stanton, and the **Hondo Valley,** all Billy's stomping grounds. Technically, the Byway follows NM 48; NM 220; US 70/380 for 84.2 miles.

Leave **Las Cruces** on I-25 north to Exit 6 to US 70 toward **Alamogordo.** Bataan Veterans Memorial Highway is the designation of US 70 between Las Cruces and Alamogordo, in honor of New Mexico National Guard units from the Las Cruces area who perished in the Bataan Death March of WWII.

This seemingly mundane drive actually has several points of interest.

First, and most arresting as the road climbs, is the stunning view of the backside of the primarily igneous **Organ Mountains**, named for their resemblance to organ pipes on the right. The highest peak of this range is Organ Needle at 9,012, rising from the Chihuahuan Desert floor.

Fifteen miles up the road is **Organ**, a gold and silver mining town dating to the 1850s, today inhabited by about 300 souls.

Beyond Organ lies **Augustin Pass**, between Organ and the San Augustin Mountains, at 5,719 feet.

Continuing the drive, 3 miles past Organ find **Aguirre Springs Recreation Area,** offering camping, hiking, and picnicking, with mostly seasonal streams and creeks. Some of Las Cruces' favorite hikes and a favorite campground are on this site, much of which was constructed by the Civilian Conservation Corps during the 1930s. Now it is included in the **Organ Mountains-Desert Peaks National Monument**, established in 2014.

Thirteen miles further is an historical marker on the right for Colonel Albert Jennings Fountain and his eight-year-old son Henry, most likely murdered here, a murder that to this day remains one of New Mexico's greatest unsolved mysteries. Their bodies were never found. Fountain, resident of Mesilla, newspaper publisher, and lawyer, knew he was in danger, and he brought his son for protection, thinking no one would harm a young child. He was on his way home from Lincoln, where he had spoken out about cattle rustling. Suspects Oliver Lee and Jim Gilliland, rustlers implicated by Fountain, were acquitted in the murder trial that was moved to **Hillsboro**, after being defended by Albert Fall, who went on to participate in the notorious Teapot Dome Scandal. Fountain had defended, and lost, one of Billy the Kid's trials. Two pools of blood and bloodstained buggy were found in the wake of Fountain and his son.

It's only 19 miles further to the entrance to **White Sands National Monument**. Take a left to the monument entrance. The way to see White Sands National Monument is along **Dunes Drive,** 17 miles of paved road through 275 square miles of pure white gypsum dunes, the largest gypsum dune field in the world, which originated over 12,000 years ago at the end of the last ice age.

It's an otherworldly moonscape within the **Tularosa Basin.** Fascinating, too, are the plants and wildlife, such as the bleached earless lizard, that have evolved to exist within this particular environment. The West African oryx was imported for hunting in the 1960s. Reservations are required for such monthly special events as the Full Moon Nights and the monthly ranger-led trip to Lake Lucero, 18 miles to the north, the origin of the white sands. Also: there are full moon bike rides, sunset strolls, and MothaPalooza. From here, it's 12 miles to Alamogordo on US 70.

For information on **Alamogordo,** please see Chapter 5. It's 16 miles on US 54/70 from **Alamogordo** to **Tularosa**. For information on **Tularosa,** please see Chapter 5.

After leaving Tularosa, keep climbing into forests of Ponderosa pine. In 24 miles of gently curving, ascending roads through mountain forest, arrive at **Bent**, on Nogal Canyon Road. It was named for George B. Bent, who established a mine and mill in the early 1900's. Then, in 3 miles, you will come to **Apache Summit** and see **Sierra Blanca,** the mountain that dominates this part of the world and is home to **Ski Apache.** You are now driving through the **Mescalero Apache Reservation.**

Originally for southern Plains Indians, the Mescalero Apache Reservation was established by President Ulysses S. Grant in 1883 as home to about 4,000 tribal members. To reach the **Mescalero Museum**, go right on Central Mescalero Road toward the Tribal Administrative Offices, first left into Chiricahua Plaza. Here you will get a look at the history and culture of the Apache, from their point of view. They received their name because of their association with the mescal plant, which they used for food and fiber. The church at Exit 245 is **St. Joseph's Apache Mission**, constructed through the efforts of Franciscan friar Father Albert Braun, who served as chaplain in WWI and wanted this church to remember those who died.

THE LEGEND OF SMOKEY BEAR LIVES ON IN CAPITAN

Fourteen miles beyond, reach the **Inn of the Mountain Gods,** Carrizo Canyon Road, **Mescalero.** Here you will find four restaurants, an 18-hole golf course, gaming, elegance beyond compare, a complete dream resort, and a great favorite place to get away and play in this part of the world. It is owned and operated by the Mescalero Apache Tribe, and it has 250 luxurious rooms.

Four miles further, cross the Lincoln county line at the Ruidoso Village Limit. Continue driving through the Village of Ruidoso, on **Sudderth Street**, the main shopping and entertainment district. It will be quite crowded and slow going during the high season of summer, a change of pace from high mountain driving.

At the end of Sudderth Street, go right to **Alto** on NM 48. Out here on **Mecham Drive,** there are many places to stay, such as cabins and motels, a bit quieter and more removed from crowded downtown Ruidoso. NM 48 continues to **Alto Lake**, in about 16 miles. Stay on two-lane

NM 48 for about 14 miles to Capitan, best known as the original home of Smokey Bear, the orphan cub whose paws were burnt in a 1950 forest fire in the Capitan Mountains. Here you can learn his story first-hand at **Smokey Bear Historical Park**. Following a long life in the National Zoo in Washington, DC, Smokey was returned here to his final resting place. Presentations on ecology, forest health, and fire prevention become more relevant each year. This quiet village offers a stopping point for lunch at the **Oso Grill** or you can pick up picnic supplies at **Smokey's Country Market,** which has a deli serving burgers, sandwiches, and barbecue chicken and ribs that sell out early. The **Smoky Bear Café and Motel** has rustic, basic clean and

Billy the Kid

Billy the Kid's presence pervades southern New Mexico; he is literally everywhere. He had a presence from Mesilla to Silver City to Lincoln and even up north in **Santa Fe**. During his short life he was said to have killed one man for every one of his twenty-one years. The number of men he shot ranges from only eight all the way to 22. Virtually all New Mexico historical personages whose time overlapped with his encountered him, from Sister Blandina, a teacher invited to Santa Fe by Archbishop Lamy, to Santa Fe's first First Lady, Flora Spiegelberg, wife of Santa Fe merchant Willi Spiegelberg. Regardless of whether these are real-life events or tall tales, the truth is that the story of William H. Bonney (his alias) has triggered the US imagination, where he continues to hang out like a jumping cholla needle that gets stuck in your finger and won't let go.

Wherever the truth of these tales lies, Billy the Kid, born Henry McCarty in the Irish slums of New York in 1859, orphaned at age 14, and shot by Sheriff Pat Garrett at Fort Sumner in 1881, has the enduring power to fascinate. His legend includes stories of his likeable side. For example, local ladies would dress the gunslinger in female attire and let him help them hang out the laundry when the law was about. New Mexico Governor Bill Richardson considered, but eventually refused, the outlaw a posthumous pardon, to make up for the pardon he was promised then denied by Governor Lew Wallace. In addition, Governor Richardson had a plan to exhume Billy's bones for DNA testing to prove he was actually buried in **Fort Sumner** and fortify Billy's presence in New Mexico, in opposition to various unsubstantiated Texas claims. This never happened. Meanwhile, Billy reigns as New Mexico's Number One outlaw and legend. And at the **Bonito Valley Brewing Company** in **Lincoln,** Billy's short and epic life still inspires spirited arguments until the wee hours between friends, amateur historians, and visitors seeking this truth of this character who remains as elusive in death as he was during his heyday.

comfortable rooms. The café on the premises has vintage photos of Smokey and serves simple homey fare for breakfast, lunch, and dinner, seven days a week.

Seven miles beyond Capitan along US 380, turning onto NM 220, arrive at **Fort Stanton**. This preserved military complex has a long and complex history: From 1855–96, it was a military fort, and during that time it played an important role in the Lincoln County War. In 1886 it became the Mescalero Apache Indian base, and subsequently it became the first federal tubercular hospital in 1899. A Civilian Conservation Corps Camp was located here in 1931. The war brought German and Japanese internment in 1945, became a state hospital from 1953–63, and then it housed mental health, drug rehab, and correctional facilities. Living History Garrison day is held the third Saturday of the month; bi-monthly after dark tours, historic house tours, and ranger-led tours are available daily.

Lincoln County, at the time of its formation in 1869, was huge, one-fourth

Lincoln County War

To understand and appreciate southern New Mexico, a bit of background on the Lincoln County War is helpful.

In the big picture, this bloodshed was a mercantile war between the Murphy-Dolan faction, backed by the Santa Fe Ring; cattle baron John Chisum; merchant John Tunstall, Billy the Kid's employer; and Alexander McSween, who formed a rival mercantile company to challenge Murphy-Dolan's economic control. Tunstall's death triggered the Lincoln County War.

While Billy had earned notoriety before the Lincoln County War (1878–81), it was when he and the Regulators defended the Tunstall-McSween interests against the Murphy-Dolan Boys that he began to go on killing sprees and was eventually convicted for the murder of Sheriff William Brady.

If Billy the Kid returned today and walked the main street of Lincoln, he would recognize the stone and adobe buildings. The town, once blood-soaked, exudes an indescribable air of peace. Many of the buildings, in fact the entire town, are said to be highly haunted, with records of specific encounters.

Georgia B. Redfield, a writer who collected local lore during the WPA era of the 1930s, reported: "It is not at all surprising that some of the more superstitious natives of Lincoln, New Mexico believe that 'El espiritu malign,' [spirits of evil] meaning the five men of Billy the Kid's outlaw band, who were killed as they ran from the blazing building [the McSween home], return on dark nights to the scene of the final battle of the Lincoln County

War of 1877-1881. . . Still carrying guns, it is believed they stalk the narrow streets, around El Torreon in the spooky old town, near the old courthouse at Lincoln, now a state monument and popular tourist attraction."

The **Lincoln State Monument** museum is the place to visit first to soak up the story and purchase tickets for the town's other attractions. Old Lincoln Days are celebrated annually the first weekend in August, with a pageant re-enactment of Billy's slipping the cuffs and escaping the Lincoln County Courthouse and Jail, then shooting deputy Bob Olinger with his own gun as well as deputy J.W. Bell. The Kid also supposedly had a hideout at Susan McSween Barber's Three Rivers Ranch (see Chapter 5), from whose burning house Billy fled in Lincoln. Her second marriage to George Barber, an employee of John Chisum, made her the "cattle queen of New Mexico" when Chisum gave her a small herd. Her first husband, Alexander McSween, was killed in the Battle of Lincoln in the Lincoln County War.

LINCOLN'S SETTLERS SOUGHT SHELTER IN ITS STAUNCH TORREON

of New Mexico Territory, or 29,000 square miles. A half-dozen counties were carved from it subsequently.

Along the Rio Bonito, the site of Lincoln was occupied originally by Mogollon and Mimbres tribes from 1200 CE. The area was the western edge of the Comanche hunting grounds and the northern edge of the Mescalero Apache hunting grounds. Mexicans settled here in the 1700s. The town was founded in 1859 as La Placita del Rio Bonito, but it was renamed for President Abraham Lincoln in 1869. Especially interesting is the 20-foot Torreon where settlers took shelter from Indian raids. It was a violent area of six-shooters and whiskey early on, the wildest and most lawless place in the Wild West. Enter Billy the Kid, who came to Lincoln in 1877 to work for Tunstall. Billy's legend grew with his many prison escapes. When he escaped the Lincoln County Jail, it is said that friendly locals removed his leg irons and provided him with a fresh horse.

OLD LINCOLN JAIL WHERE BILLY THE KID SLIPPED HIS HANDCUFFS AND SHOT BOB OLINGER WITH HIS OWN GUN BEFORE HE ESCAPED

A stroll down Lincoln's main street leads to the **Wortley Hotel**, a historic bed and breakfast. This is the place to stay in Lincoln. Hosts Troy Nelson and Katharine Marsh have created a delightfully creaky, small inn right out of the Old West in an 1874 lodging once owned by Pat Garrett, with morning coffee served on the front porch and an exquisite home-cooked breakfast in the dining room. Here history comes alive and lives on.

Across the street from the **Wortley** is **Bonito Valley Brewing Company**. Local brews go with the local history and lore recounted here, as well as the occasional live music, all while hanging out in the big friendly heart of New Mexico.

Annie's Little Sure Shot Coffee Shop, Lincoln, provides the caffeine to keep you going. Proprietor Annmarie LaMay serves her distinct blend in a coffee bar that could rival any coffee house anywhere. Surrounded by pottery and art from the hands of over 50 local New Mexico artists in Old Lincoln Gallery, LaMay's establishment has a delightful patio and is open year-round. By the way, Annmarie is barista to the stars—she caters for films and served her elixir to the *Breaking Bad* cast and crew in Albuquerque from her "mobile coffee house." Annmarie is the force behind the annual **Lincoln Dia de Muertos Festival**, held November 2, with mariachis, historical presentations, altars and more.

At the **Lincoln State Monument,** Lincoln, the Old Lincoln County Courthouse Museum gives context, with thoughtful information on Hispanic settlers, Buffalo soldiers, and the politics of the time.

Leaving Lincoln, journey 10 miles on US 380 to junction 380/70. Go right on US 70, the **Billy the Kid Byway**, and bear right to **San Patricio**.

Here find **Hurd-La Rinconada Gallery, Guest Homes and Winery**, east on US 70 at MM 281. After studying with artist Andrew Wyeth in Pennsylvania, wooing and winning his daughter, artist Henriette, New Mexico native artist Peter Hurd wanted to come home. His Sentinel Ranch, where he painted his neighbors and local ranching scenes, is now the residence of Hurd-Wyeth son and artist Michael Hurd, who also designed the attached Hurd gallery. Five adobe guest cottages are available to rent, including the Wyeth House, the historic home of the Hurd family. Go right on US 70 when exiting Hurd Gallery.

On US 70, at MM 284 between Roswell and Ruidoso, come to **Hondo Iris Farm & Gallery**. Alice Seeley's little bit of paradise bursts forth with blooms of hundreds of varieties of iris that peak in May, followed by peonies and lilies. The gallery of her handmade jewelry features petroglyph designs and offers flowing, colorful, imported, and handmade apparel and accessories. The Faery Garden enchants young and old.

Exit the **Iris Farm**, go right and cross the Rio Bonito. Stay on US 70, continuing through Hondo, for a nondescript drive of 47 miles to **Roswell.**

TALES OF BILLY THE KID ARE EXCHANGED INTO THE WEE HOURS IN LINCOLN'S ONLY PUB

Come for the aliens. Stay for the art and dragonflies. Roswell has glommed on to the 1947 UFO crash that did or did not happen, or was possibly a weather balloon, and the town has ridden it all the way to urban prosperity while maintaining its small-town aura. Downtown Roswell is virtually wall-to-wall UFO tee shirt and trinket shops. Starting out as a stop on the Goodnight-Loving and Chisum cattle trails, Roswell's Old West roots have endured in the farms, dairies, and ranches that surround the city. Located at the crossroads of US 285, US 70, and US 380, Roswell is a master of community re-invention. When Walker Air Force Base closed in 1967, the town diversified into a thriving hub of business, education—it is the home of the highly respected New Mexico Military Institute—and tourism. While tourists may be found thronging the streets year-round, tourist business peaks during the first week of July, when thousands from

WILL YOU BECOME A BELIEVER AT ROSWELL'S UFO MUSEUM AND RESEARCH CENTER?

around the world come for the annual UFO Festival, and true believers attend seminars on the latest testimonies and evidence of "abductions" and "hybrids" walking amongst us.

The **International UFO Museum & Research Center** does its best to convince malingering doubters. Eyewitness reports, the Roswell Incident Timeline, evidence of contact within ancient societies, and the largest and most comprehensive collection of UFO-related information in the world, including accounts of those who have experienced actual contact, fill this warehouse-like space.

This small, booming city boasts a beautiful historic district and the

Bottomless Lakes State Park

Turn east on US 380 for 12 miles. Then turn onto NM 409 South 3 miles to Bottomless Lakes State Park. These eight small lakes are actually sinkholes in the Pecos River Valley, bordered by high red bluffs, with walking trails, swimming, fishing, and rental paddleboats at the larger Lea Lake. Fees are $5 per day vehicle use; $10–18 camping. One of the hikes includes a boardwalk over a wetlands with blinds for bird and wildlife observation. When cowboys arrived, they attached rocks to their lariats and tossed them into the lake, and since they could not hear the rock touch bottom, they conjured the current name. Established in 1933, this was the first state park in New Mexico.

Bitter Lake National Wildlife Refuge

North on US 285 to Pine Lodge Road, then east 11 miles to the visitor center. One of my favorite outdoor spots in New Mexico, this wetlands along the Pecos River is home to over a hundred species of dragonflies and damselflies and has abundant butterfly populations. Several short, easy hikes make this a peaceful place to become enraptured by nature. Over 357 bird species live here; some are endangered species. An 8-mile auto tour will allow for wildlife spotting; and bike riding is available on the 8-mile gravel drive leading to the paved 4-mile round trip trail.

Spring River Recreation Trail, with 5.5 miles of paved, gentle, and scenic hiking and biking.

The **Roswell Museum and Art Center** is as fine a regional museum as may be found. Permanent exhibits of Peter Hurd and Henriette Wyeth are breathtaking, while artists of the stature of Fritz Scholder and Georgia O'Keeffe appear frequently.

Next door to the museum is the **Robert H. Goddard Planetarium**. Roswell pioneer, father of rocketry, Robert Goddard, is honored here with science exhibits and hands-on exhibits as well as a recreation of his lab.

From Roswell, take US 285 North to a stretch of road that seems to go on forever, with a switch to NM 20 for the last 47 miles. But it is actually only 85 miles to Fort Sumner; the road is arrow-straight, punctuated by irrigation, silos, sheep, cattle, water tanks, and occasional ranch signs on fences. Named after former New Mexico Territory military governor Edwin Vose Sumner, this military fort was charged with the internment of nearby Navajo and Mescalero Apache populations from 1863 to 1868. Fort Sumner is the site not only of Billy the Kid's grave, where he is buried with his two "pals," but of Fort Sumner State Monument, where Navajo and Apache people were confined during the 1860s following the Long March, 450 miles in which many died, leaving their homeland, devastated by the US military, led by Colonel Kit Carson. The **Bosque Redondo Memorial** here is the only site to tell that story, and the story of the Mescalero Apache imprisoned here, from their point of view. By late 1864, the military held 498 Mescalero and 8,567 Navajo as prisoners of war at the Bosque Redondo Indian Reservation. Engineered by General James H. Carleton and executed by Kit Carson, the destruction of the Indians' homeland and the relocation to Bosque Redondo that resulted in the death of hundreds was an attempt to turn them into farmers and was declared a failure after three years. At that point, they were again relocated to the current Navajo Reservation in the Four Corners.

LEARN THE STORY OF THE LONG MARCH OF THE NAVAJO AT BOSQUE REDONDO MEMORIAL

Billy the Kid's Grave is located in the military cemetery at **Fort Sumner Historic Site**, directly behind the closed building marked Chamber of Commerce. Land baron Lucien B. Maxwell is buried there also. The Kid's grave is encased in iron security bars, as the tombstone was stolen twice. In remembrance of that event, Fort Sumner celebrates **Old Fort Days** in early June, with the World's Richest Billy the Kid Tombstone Race and Weiner Dog Dash. On July 14, 1881, Sherriff Pat Garrett ambushed Billy while he was hiding out at the Maxwell home in Fort Sumner.

From here, travel to **Santa Rosa** 41 miles northeast on US 84 and west to Albuquerque on I-40 or east to Tucumcari on I-40—or re-trace your path to Las Cruces.

IN THE AREA

Accommodations

INN OF THE MOUNTAIN GODS, Carrizo Canyon Road, Mescalero. Call 800-446-2963. $$–$$$.

SMOKEY BEAR CAFÉ & MOTEL, 316 Smokey Bear Boulevard, Capitan. Call 575-354-2253. $–$$.

WORTLEY HOTEL, a historic bed and breakfast at 585 Calle la Placita, Lincoln. Call 575-653-4300. $$.

Attractions and Recreation

BILLY THE KID MUSEUM, 1435 East Sumner Avenue, Fort Sumner. Call 575-355-2380.

BILLY THE KID NATIONAL SCENIC BYWAY, 26305 US 70, Ruidoso Downs. Call 575-378-5318. Website: www.billybyway.com.

BITTER LAKE NATIONAL WILDLIFE REFUGE, 4200 East Pine Lodge Road, Roswell. Call 575-623-5695. Website: www.fws.gov/refuge/bitter_lake.

BOTTOMLESS LAKES STATE PARK, Bottomless Lakes Rd, Roswell. Call 575-624-6058. Website: www.emnrd.state.nm.us/SPD/bottomlesslakesstate park.html.

FORT STANTON, Call 575-354-0341. Website: www.fortstanton.org.

HUBBARD MUSEUM OF THE AMERICAN WEST, 26301 US 70, Ruidoso Downs. Call 575-378-4142. Website: www.hubbardmuseum.org.

HURD-LA RINCONADA GALLERY, GUEST HOMES, AND WINERY, 105 La Rinconada Lane, San Patricio, US 70, at MM 284 between Roswell and Ruidoso. Call 575-653-4331.

HONDO IRIS FARM & GALLERY, MM 284, US 70, Hondo. Call 575-973-0006. Website: www.hondoirisfarm.com.

LINCOLN NATIONAL FOREST, 3463 Las Paloma, Alamogordo. Call 575-434-7200. Smokey Bear District 901, Mechem Drive, Ruidoso. Call 575-257-4095.

LINCOLN STATE MONUMENT, Lincoln. Call 575-653-4025.

MESCALERO APACHE CULTURAL CENTER & MUSEUM, Call 575-671-4494. Website: www.mescaleroapachetribe.com/mescalero-apache-cultural -center-museum.

ORGAN MOUNTAINS DESERT PEAKS NATIONAL MONUMENT. Website: www.blm.gov/nm.

ROBERT H. GODDARD PLANETARIUM, 912 North Main Street, Roswell. Call 575-624-6744.

ROSWELL MUSEUM AND ART CENTER, 100 West 11th Street, Roswell. Call 575-624-6744.

SPENCER THEATER FOR THE PERFORMING ARTS, 108 Spencer Drive, Alto. Call 575-336-4800.

SPRING RIVER PARK AND RECREATION TRAIL, 1101 West 4th Street, Roswell. Call 575-624-6700.

UFO MUSEUM AND RESEARCH CENTER, 114 North Main Street, Roswell. Call 575-625-9495.

WHITE SANDS NATIONAL MONUMENT, 19955 US 70. Call 575-479-6124. Website: www.nps.gov/whsa.

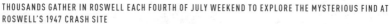
THOUSANDS GATHER IN ROSWELL EACH FOURTH OF JULY WEEKEND TO EXPLORE THE MYSTERIOUS FIND AT ROSWELL'S 1947 CRASH SITE

Dining and Drinks

ANNIE'S LITTLE SURE SHOT COFFEE SHOP, 1068 Calle La Placita, Lincoln. Call 575-937-3755. $.

BONITO VALLEY BREWING COMPANY, 692 Calle La Placita, Lincoln. Call 575-653-4810. $.

CERRITOS MEXICAN CUISINE, 2013 North Main Street, Roswell. Call 575-622-4919. $–$$.

GLENCOE DISTILLERY AND TASTING ROOMS, 27495 US 70, Glencoe. $.

MARTIN'S CAPITOL CAFÉ, 110 West 4th Street, Roswell. Call 575-208-5161. $–$$.

OLD ROAD RESTAURANT, 692 Old Road, Mescalero. Call 575-464-4674. $–$$.

OSO GRILL, 100 Lincoln Avenue, Capitan. Call 575-354-2427. $–$$.

SIPPY AND OPAL'S ICE CREAM AND SWEET TREATS, 327 N Main Street, Roswell. Call 734-536-8727. $.

TASTE OF THAI CUISINE, 1303 West 2nd Street, Roswell. Call 575-622-2412. $–$$.

TINNIE SILVER DOLLAR STEAKHOUSE & SALOON, 28842 US 70, Hondo. Call 575-653-4425. $$–$$$.

YUM YUM'S DONUT SHOP, 460 Central Avenue, Tularosa. Call 575-585-2529. $.

Events

OLD FORT DAYS, early June, with the World's Richest Billy the Kid Tombstone Race and Weiner Dog Dash. Call 575-355-7705. Website: www.fortsumnerchamber.com.

OLD LINCOLN DAYS, and the Last Escape of Billy the Kid, first weekend in August, Lincoln. Call 575-653-4372.

SWEEPING VISTAS ALONG ROUTE 99

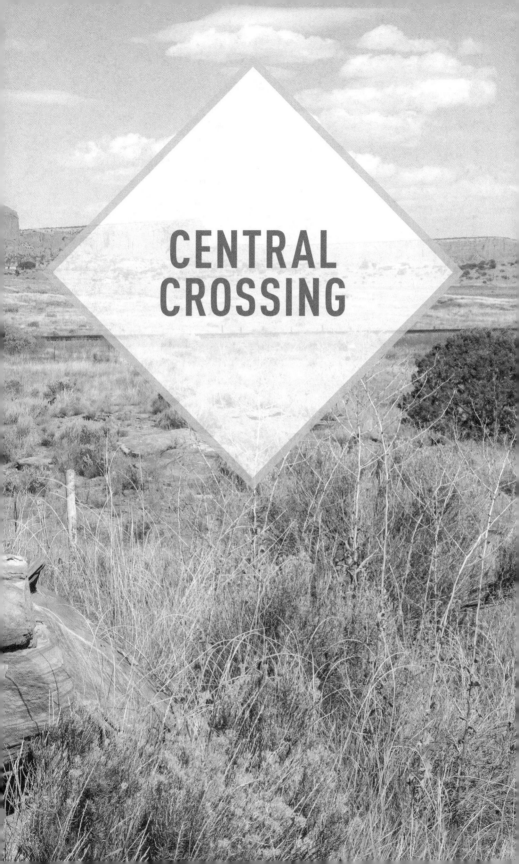

CENTRAL
CROSSING

7

OLD US 66

MOTHER ROAD MYSTIQUE ENDURES

ESTIMATED LENGTH: 400 miles

ESTIMATED TIME: One day driving straight through; at least a weekend to stop and see the sights. It takes about two-and-a-half hours to drive from Albuquerque to Gallup; taking two-lane Old Route 66 parallel to I-40, now NM 124, will take between one and two hours longer, depending on your personal pace.

GETTING THERE: This trip may be taken east–west, from Glenrio to Gallup; or, you can start at Gallup and travel west to east, reversing driving instructions.

HIGHLIGHTS: Blue Swallow Motel, Russell's Truck Stop Vintage Auto Museum, Sky City (Acoma), San Esteban del Rey Mission, Inscription Rock, Richardson's Trading Post

---

Route 66, the Mother Road, unfurling through eight states and 2,400 miles from Chicago to the Santa Monica Pier, California, has given birth to a worldwide nostalgia for the way we once were in America. It's about possibilities, dreams, migration, transformation, hope, memory, and an endless America. Each decade has had its own story of America's Main Street, Route 66. It was celebrated as a path of hope out of the poverty of the Great Depression and the Dustbowl in John Steinbeck's *Grapes of Wrath* and immortalized in the film starring Henry Fonda; as a road to freedom and adventure in a Corvette in a 1960s television series; and as a song you can't get out of your head, written by Bobby Troupe and first sung by Nat King Cole in the postwar 1940s. The road today is a paradox of fantasy and haunted highway. Judging by the thousands of fans it has garnered worldwide, and its ever-expanding mystique, the road exerts its own quintessential magic on anyone who encounters it.

LEFT: A VIEW OF EL MORRO (INSCRIPTION ROCK) FROM BACKROAD NM 53

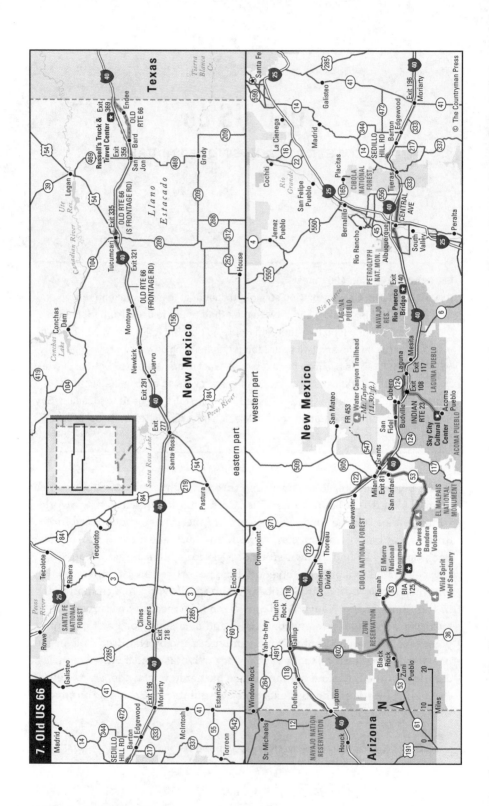

7. Old US 66

The road evokes the yearning for what everyone loves: endless horizons of possibility and discovery punctuated with mom-and-pop cafés, carny roadside attractions, and cozy motels. As time bleaches and fades these images, they grow more vivid in our imagination. Meanwhile, we repair neon signs, preserve bridges, and repurpose motor courts such as the El Vado on Central Avenue in Albuquerque, now remodeled into a network of spiffy themed condos, cafés, studios, and shops. Every culture needs its legends. It's safe to say Route 66 is enshrined in the American psyche; the road embodies just as much quintessential Americanness as America's Highway and the Will Rogers Highway, and it's not going away any time soon.

FOLLOW THE ROUTE 66 SIGNS ALONG THE MAIN DRAG OF GRANTS FOR SIGHTS OF VINTAGE MOTELS AND CAFÉS

In 1921, the US Congress, through the Federal Highway Act, initiated an interstate highway system to link the United States. Route 66, born of a merging of the National Old Trails Road and the Ozark Trails, and it meandered through New Mexico more or less north to south from Pecos to Santa Fe to Los Lunas. In 1926, it was realigned following Governor Hannet's 1926 term to run straight through New Mexico for 399 miles. This realignment became official in 1937 when the road was paved. It ran through several New Mexico cities as a main street: **Tucumcari, Santa Rosa, Moriarty, Albuquerque,** and **Gallup**. While the realignment cut 107 miles from the journey, and shooting through the central corridor of the state saved four hours and avoided the perilous switchbacks of La Bajada Pass, the reason for the realignment was political revenge, not practicality. Governor Arthur Thomas Hannett, looking to get back at the unscrupulous group of Republican politicians and businessmen known as the Santa Fe Ring who had (he believed) thwarted his re-election, diverted the road away from Santa Fe. The new straight road became known as Hannett's Joke.

And it is possible to drive many miles on this original, post-1937 two-lane Route 66, renamed NM 124 when the road was de-commissioned in 1985, parallel to I-40, functioning as a state-maintained frontage road in many places, say, from Albuquerque west toward Gallup. In places, I-40 overrides the original route. In addition, sections of the pre-1937 alignment still exist and are drivable in New Mexico. This chapter speaks to the post-1937 alignment only.

While space prevents detailing every existing road segment, in general, Historic 66 is marked with brown and tan signs. I strongly suggest you consult detailed, recent maps for specifics before heading out, because certain jogs along the way can be confusing, especially when you're navigating traffic. To have the best trip, it is necessary for the driver to do a bit of homework and be prepared for changes in speed limits, road construction, and weather. An excellent website to check daily for road conditions is NMroads.com. In the big picture, accessible east-west road segments include: Glenrio to San Jon; San Jon to Tucumcari; Palomas to Montoya; Montoya to Cuervo; Cuervo to NM 156; Albuquerque to Rio Puerco; Laguna to McCartys; McCartys to Grants; Milan to Continental Divide; Iyanbito to Rehobeth; and Manuelito to the Arizona border. Many guidebooks and maps are available to assist in navigation, in particular the *EZ66 Route 66 Guide for Travelers*, by Jerry McClanahan.

Route 66 Westbound: Enter New Mexico from the Texas border heading west at Exit 0, Texas on I-40 and pass under the Welcome to New Mexico arch entering the state. About 2 miles in, at Exit 369, you'll find **Endee**. Exit right to **Russell's Travel Center.** You'll find a retro café, souvenirs and snacks galore, gas, of course—and most outstanding, the multi-car museum, the passion of the senior Russell, a mind-blowing collection of shiny vintage automobiles plus toys and collectibles of all sorts. Elvis was definitely here (and still may be). And it is free. From Endee, which got its name from the ND Ranch, the main goal is to return to old Route 66 ASAP.

While I do not believe in backtracking, here is the exception that proves the rule. While this direction may seem counter-intuitive, a quick return here is probably the simplest way to both experience the **Russell's Truck Stop** and get back on westbound Route 66. Exit Russell's and return to I-40 eastbound. Stay in the right lane. See a sign to Historic Route 66 before you cross the state line. Turn right.

Carry on. A bit of rough road, a bit of washboard road, and voila! Some of the most photogenic and memorable ruins on the road can be found, slowly melting into the earth as they are buffeted by the winds of the plains, on this 18-mile stretch of good dirt and gravel roadway, through Endee, such as the "modern rest rooms" outhouse still standing, **Bard**, **Montoya** and **San Jon** (pronounced "san hone"). Caution: best to avoid this route in bad weather. It is 43 miles to Tucumcari, at Exit 335, and most of the drive can be made on Old 66. If you choose to avoid this "dirt" road, the alternative is to turn right at 369 for Endee, visit the truck stop, then left on the north frontage road for 13 miles to **San Jon**, Exit 356. Cross I-40, then turn right and proceed 25 miles to Tucumcari. This trip leads to traveling across the **Llano Estacado**, the Staked Plains, of eastern New Mexico.

THERE IS NOTHING LIKE RUSSELL'S TRAVEL STOP MUSEUM NEAR GLENRIO—ABSOLUTELY NOTHING

Tucumcari is visually the purest remaining Route 66 town in New Mexico, and there is an abundance of neon there, lighting up the night sky. For the Route 66 fan, it is Mecca, a required pilgrimage; the town seems suspended in time. Some of the authentic picturesque highlights are the Blue Swallow Motel, Del's, Tee Pee Curios, La Cita, Buckaroo Motel, Whiting Brothers gas station, and so much more. Some of the most decrepit and abandoned motels and gas stations are the most gorgeously photogenic. Cruise Tucumcari Boulevard, actually Old Route 66, and take your time taking it all in.

On the west end of town, in the Tucumcari Convention Center, is the **New Mexico Route 66 Museum**, which boasts the world's largest Route 66 photo exhibit and a recreated vintage diner. Out front is an iconic Route 66 sculpture. Tucumcari also has the **Mesalands Dinosaur Museum** and the **Tucumcari Historical Museum**. The restored railroad station downtown also makes a worthwhile stop.

Leaving Tucumcari—the name has various explanations, one meaning "lookout"—indeed, Tucumcari Mountain on the eastern edge of town makes a fine lookout on those approaching from the plains—and the other from a tragic Romeo-and-Juliet-style love story. But the original name was Six Shooter Siding. Take I-40 on the west end of Tucumcari, go 8 miles, take Exit 321 turn right on the frontage road and proceed with caution 4 miles to a one-lane tunnel, requiring a sharp turn under the interstate. On the north side of I-40, go left and continue to mostly deserted **Montoya,** 21 miles west of Tucumcari, a 20th-century ranch and railroad center that catered to Route 66 travelers once upon a time. There are plenty of photo ops to be found here.

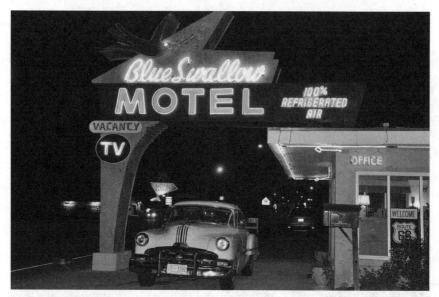

THE BLUE SWALLOW MOTEL REMAINS AS ICONIC AS EVER, THE LOVINGLY PRESERVED PLACE TO STAY THAT SAYS "ROUTE 66" LOUD AND CLEAR

Cross to the south frontage road and continue west until the road passes over I-40, then continue to **Newkirk** and then to **Cuervo**. I have taken some of my best Route 66 photos on this stretch, with gloriously deserted, rusty, and broken-down structures, with deliciously faded signs painted on the buildings. At Cuervo take I-40 Exit 291, going 17 miles to Santa Rosa Exit 277. On the main street, Santa Rosa's most iconic Route 66 sign, the smiling Fat Man from the Club Café, has been preserved at Joseph's Bar & Grill. Part of the film *The Grapes of Wrath* was shot here, on the bridge over the Pecos River. Be careful getting out here to photograph—there are many photo seekers probing about, just like you! The railroad-era Fourth Street Business District with the Ilfield Warehouse and old storefronts has been known as a Route 66 stop since 1926. Located on the Pecos River, Santa Rosa is blessed with plenty of water, including **Blue Hole**, an 82-foot-deep sinkhole that makes the town the Scuba Diving Capital of New Mexico, as well as the water slide and pedal boats on **Park Lake**. The central corridor is old Route 66, known as Will Rogers Drive. The **Route 66 Auto Museum** is the place for lovers of vintage automobiles, and this place is dedicated to the preservation of Route 66 memorabilia and custom cars.

From Santa Rosa heading west, return to I-40 for highway driving; the interstate has subsumed the old road. The first place to hop out is at the mega-truck stop at **Clines Corners**, a stretch from Santa Rosa of 57 miles. More Route 66 immersion awaits in **Moriarty**, 24 miles from Clines Corners, which was not named for Holmes' nemesis, but rather, for health seeker Michael Moriarty, founded in 1902. Several period motels remain, like the

Sunset, and the restored Whiting Brothers sign is the pride and joy of the community. Find out more at the **Moriarty Historical Society & Museum.** The **US Southwest Soaring Museum**, documenting the history of gliding, is another worthwhile local attraction.

There's a rich stretch of Route 66 to navigate past Moriarty, though the road numbers may not coincide. Simply avoid getting back on I-40 at Exit 194 and hop on backroad **NM 333** instead. This approximately 14-mile portion leads through the communities of **Edgewood** and **Barton** as you approach Albuquerque through Tijeras Canyon, cutting through the Manzano Mountains to the south and the Sandias to the north. At Exit 181, cross I-40 and curve left onto Sedillo Hill Road. Warning: this road is notoriously icy during bad weather and the site of numerous wrecks. Back when NM 333 was Route 66, Herman Ardans opened a curio shop around 1956. He

JOHN STEINBECK SET A SCENE FROM *GRAPES OF WRATH* AT THE LANDMARK SANTA ROSA BRIDGE

fabricated the name **Zuzax**; however, he told customers it had had to do with the Zuzax Indians. Today the name endures as an exit off I-40.

Following the realignment of the original 1926 roadway, Albuquerque's population tripled as motels opened and businesses serving tourists thrived. Central Avenue has many architectural remnants of the Route 66 era. Cruising it from Tramway Boulevard on the eastern end in search of these vintage, mostly run-down and largely deserted buildings is possible, but be warned: there is a good deal of both construction and confusion along Central Avenue. A dysfunctional transit program begun during a previous city administration excavated the middle of the street. The problems it created are massive and continue to spawn other problems, putting local enterprises out of business and irritating the citizenry. Consequently, street signs are extremely confusing, even to local residents. We will do our best to highlight intact Route 66 sites of note along Central Avenue in Albuquerque; undoubtedly, you will spot a few of your own.

Outstanding Albuquerque sites along the 17 miles of Route 66 in this city include the Streamline Moderne Nob Hill Shopping Center (113 Carlisle Boulevard SE), built in 1947 and called Waggoman's Folly because it was considered too far out of town to be successful; Jones Motor Company, a garage repurposed as a brewpub; downtown at 5th and Central and worth a stop is the 1927 KiMo Theater, a 1927 Pueblo Deco style movie theater whose name means "the king of his kind" and is now an arts venue; and Maisel's Indian Jewelry, built by Maurice Maisel in 1937 and the largest post along the road at the time, with murals painted by well-known Indian artists when they were students. You can't miss the Dog House, scene of *Breaking Bad* incidents. If you want to stay in Old Town, the **Monterey Motel** at 2402 Central is an excellent choice. **El Vado**, across from the Biopark, once considered the purest Route 66 motel architecture on the road, has been redeveloped as motel rooms, condos, shops, cafés, and outdoor dining; then, cross the Rio Grande and cruise up West Central, noting the Grandview and Americana Motels, Mac's Steak in the Rough, and the Western View Café (a personal favorite) at West Central and Coors Boulevard on the way out of town.

However, you can also set out from **Western View Diner & Steakhouse**, an original Route 66 diner still open and serving biscuits, gravy, and homemade pie at the corner of West Central Avenue and Coors Boulevard. From there, cross the intersection of Central and Coors, look to the left, and follow the signs to Route 66. Continue up Nine Mile Hill and notice original Route 66 motels and cafés like the Westward Ho. In 15 miles, come to the **Rio Puerco Bridge**. The Rio Puerco was notorious for flooding and washing out bridges, so the Parker through truss bridge built in 1933 solved many travel difficulties. The strong steel bridge may be found on the frontage road at Exit 140 off I-40. It is possible to get out of the car and take photos of this landmark survivor of the road. On the opposite side of the highway is the

LANDMARK PARKER THROUGH TRUSS BRIDGE ACROSS THE RIO PUERCO

Route 66 Casino operated by Laguna Pueblo, offering some campy and cool artistic interpretations of the road that are Disney-fied and just fun.

Take I-40 to Exit 117 at **Mesita**. Take a right after leaving I-40, then first left to Old Route 66, which parallels the interstate for almost 5 miles to Exit 114, where NM 124 begins. This stretch of Route 66, from Mesita onward, goes through **Laguna Pueblo**, home of the NM State Fair first-prize-winning burger at the 66 Pit Stop, (505-552-1022, call for directions) and leads to some of my favorite vintage sites: **Budville, Cubero,** and **San Fidel**, offering some of the very best photo opportunities on the entire route. The incredible fact is that from here you can now pretty much stay on old 66, which parallels the interstate all the way to **Grants, Continental Divide,** and ultimately, Gallup, so long as you are willing to stay alert, have patience, follow the signs, and go under a few narrow old tunnels with sharp turns along the two-lane. As you approach Gallup, 66 is again subsumed by I-40, and that

---

SIDE TRIP

Acoma Pueblo: Sky City

Since you are so close, it would be a shame to pass up the opportunity to visit **Acoma Pueblo**, one of the nineteen Indian Pueblos, or villages, each a sovereign nation, in New Mexico. Exit I-40 at Exit 108, 65 miles west of Albuquerque. Follow Indian Route 22 south to **Sky City Cultural Center**, 12.5 miles. A village of 300 adobe structures on a sandstone mesa 357 feet high above the desert, this place has been occupied for at least a thousand years, making it the oldest inhabited place in North America. The Acoma people are known for fine pottery, and village potters sell their wares directly to visitors atop the 357-foot mesa. Here it is best to be aware that some pottery is made from hand-dug clay, while other, known as "green ware" pot designs are painted onto pre-molded completely regular pots. This is a big distinction from handmade, and it naturally affects price. The best, and only, way to see Acoma is to take the van up to the mesa top and receive a tour from one of the excellent native guides. Purchase a ticket inside the Cultural Center, which has a video, exhibits, and a gift shop, and is free. For tour information, please call 800-747-0181. Tours impart information on history, architecture, religion, culture, food, water gathering, customs, where you may and may not walk. People do live up here, but not all year round; they mainly live here at ceremonial times. There is no electricity or running water and people still live in the old way. Photographs for personal use are allowed if you purchase a photo permit, which must be displayed on your camera. One of the highlights is the **San Esteban del Rey Mission**, a massive adobe and wood structure built from 1629 to 1640. While Pueblo languages are traditionally unwritten, the Acoma people, the only Keresan-speaking tribe, are gradually compiling a dictionary and writing their language for the first time.

El Morro/Inscription Rock

This side trip requires half to a full day. Take Exit 81 off I-40 west of Grants and turn left on NM 53. Known as the **Ancient Way** (byways.org/explore/states/NM), this drive parallels the ancient trade route between **Acoma** and **Zuni Pueblos**, the route originally taken by Coronado. It's a 73-mile scenic trip to Zuni Pueblo. This is an intriguing backroad, full of surprises and a variety of natural beauty. The biggest surprise I ever had out here was when a mountain lion leapt in front of my car and bounded across the two-lane road with one spring while I was driving along on a Sunday afternoon. Three miles southwest of the interstate, come to the quiet Hispanic community of **San Rafael**, a stop for the Navajo on the Long March to Fort Sumner. Immediately pass the villages of **San Mateo** and **Cebolleta**.

Exit 81, west of Grants, will take you along NM 53 where you can travel to the northern boundary of the El Malpais National Monument (505-876-2783). This monument holds 200 miles of lava flow. There are several hiking opportunities here, including the El Calderon Trail and Zuni-Acoma Trail, the remaining rugged 8-mile path marked by cairns of an ancient 73-mile trail between the two pueblos across the lava flow. The final stop is the vast **El Malpais National Monument**. Pronounced *el-mahl-pie-ees*, meaning 'bad land' in Spanish, it consists of almost 200 square miles of lava flows bounded by NM 53 to the north and NM 117 to the east. Five major flows have been identified, the most recent pegged at only 2000 to 3000 years old. Paleo Indians may have witnessed the final eruptions: local legends refer to "rivers of fire." Stop by the Information Center on NM 53 to pick up permits to explore nearby lava tubes (some of which are ice caves) or get the lowdown on possible hikes. Alternatively, pick up the same info at the Northwest New Mexico Visitors Center in Grants.

An experience like no other is the **Ice Caves and Bandera Volcano**, 25 miles southwest of Grants. Inside the temperature never gets above 31 degrees Fahrenheit due to the 20-foot thick ice on the cave floor. Bandera is the largest of the 29 quiet volcanos in this region. This cave was known to Pueblo Indians as the Winter Lake, and the ancients mined the ice. The cave is located in part of Bandera's collapsed lava tube. Bandera Volcano erupted 10,000 years ago, and its lava flow is 23 miles long. There is a trail around the side of the volcano. Called the Land of Fire and Ice, the walk to the trail is a 0.25-mile long and takes 40 minutes to make the round trip. Viewing the ice cave requires climbing up and down a lengthy flight of steps and takes about 20 minutes. The old-time Trading Post displays ancient artifacts found in the lava, plus local Indian art.

One mile further on, cross the **Continental Divide**. Approximately 170 miles west of Albuquerque on I-40 is the pinnacle of a geological ridge that separates the nation's waterways. East of the Divide all waters flow east to the Atlantic Ocean, while those west of the divide flow toward the Pacific.

Cimarron Rose Zuni Mountain Bed & Breakfast, 30 miles southwest of Grants on NM 53, is a green retreat on the Continental Divide. Breakfast is delivered to your room, and there are three suites, two with cooking facilities. A splendid perennial garden attracts dozens of bird species.

Ancient Way Café (4018 NM 53, Ramah, 505-783-4612) 4018 NM 53, Ramah offers a café, cabins, tents, and RV spots in this unexpectedly lively scene of art, good food, wellness, and New Age spirituality. The vegetarian-friendly natural foods café, where home-baked cakes and pies fill the display case and the house-cured pastrami rueben is to die for, is **Inscription Rock Trading Post & Coffee.** The food is healthy, delicious, and somewhat gourmet! You can also visit the **Old School Gallery** and a sculpture trail behind the Ancient Way Café.

El Morro National Monument (505-783-4226) is 42 miles southeast on NM 53 from Grants. "Paso por aqui" (I passed by here) wrote conquistador Francisco Coronado in the sandstone cliff above the water pool in 1640. His signature is among over 2,000 on this bluff, or cuesta, including petroglyphs made by ancestral Puebloans, Spanish explorers, the military, and Anglo settlers, beneath which travelers throughout history have found a permanent water source. The paved 0.5-mile trail from the visitor center leads here. In addition, a two-hour moderate hike to the mesa top reveals the 13th- and 14th-century ancestral pueblo of Atsinna. Zuni Pueblo is 30 miles west.

Eleven miles further lies Ramah, primarily a Mormon and Navajo town, with one small museum, the **Ramah Museum**, open Friday 1 to 4 p.m. Through displays, the museum exhibits tell the story of the town. Ramah Lake is 2.5 miles northeast of town.

In 20 miles, arrive at Zuni Pueblo, the westernmost of New Mexico's 19 Indian Pueblos, and the largest. The people specialize in fine distinctive inlay and "needlepoint" and "pettipoint" jewelry, and jewelry shops and trading posts line the main street. **Zuni,** also known as *Haiikawa*, was the first Native American village encountered by Coronado on his search for the Seven Cities of Gold. The restored mission church, Nuestra Senora de Guadalupe de la Candelaria de Halona, established in 1630–66, has life-sized restored murals. The A:shiwi A:wan Museum and Heritage Center (02E Ojo Caliente Road, Zuni, 505-782-4403, www.ashiwii-museum.org) displays artifacts retrieved when Haiikawa, or Zuni Pueblo, was excavated in 1920. Please note photos are not allowed here. At the junction of NM 53 and NM 602, go left for 25 miles on NM 602, which will bring you into Gallup.

will be your entrance to the city. It's about 20 miles from Gallup to cross the state line into Fort Lupton, Arizona, following I-40.

Grants, formerly the Uranium Capital of the World at the base of **Mount Taylor**, is a favorite place to rest. A cruise through Grants along Santa Fe Avenue shows the remains of much vintage Route 66 architecture, including the **Sands Motel**, a place Elvis Presley enjoyed staying. The **New Mexico Mining Museum** has the world's only underground uranium mining museum where you can ride "the cage" down an actual mineshaft. Cibola ("buffalo") County has a long history of mining, including copper, gold, silver, uranium, and coal. At Riverside Park across the street from the museum, find the **Route 66 Arch,** designed for a drive-through selfie. At night, it is a beacon of colorful neon.

During the 1880s, the Atlantic & Pacific Railroad laid tracks; the contractors heading up the project were three Grant brothers from Canada, giving their name to the coal loading area and depot. So, the settlement originally named Los Alamitos (small willows) became Grants.

For visitors interested in more of the intertwined history of Route 66 and Grants, Double Six Galleries (1001 West Santa Fe Avenue) features a permanent exhibit called The Route 66 Vintage Museum. Vintage postcards from trading posts and other stops are on display, as well as automobiles, including a 1923 Model T Ford.

At one time, during the 1920s and 30s, Grants was known as the Carrot Capitol of the United States. Continue on Santa Fe Avenue into the adjacent community of **Milan**, where the road again becomes Route 66. It leads west toward Gallup.

Mount Taylor, at 11,301 feet, is a dormant stratovolcano which erupted last between 1.8 and 3.2 million years ago. It was named for President Zachary Taylor. It is considered one of the four sacred mountains of the Navajo and is also known as Turquoise Mountain. To access Mount Taylor, take NM 547 from Grants, a roadway also known as Lobo Canyon Road. Follow until the pavement ends. Continue on the dirt road for 5 miles, then take a right on Forest Road 453 to Water Canyon Trailhead.

Note: If you choose to get off at **Thoreau** ("threw"), midway between Grants and Gallup, you can get on NM 371, 27 miles to **Crownpoint**, where the monthly Crownpoint rug auction is held in the high school, and then you can ultimately find the backroad to Chaco Culture National Historical Park.

The **Continental Divide** is 33 miles west of Grants. It is the highest point on Route 66, at 7,295 feet, along the hydrological divide that runs through the Americas, where water divides and flows east or west. Here the curio shop is built exactly on the divide.

Called the Indian Capital of the World, Gallup's population swells by thousands each weekend when people come in from the Navajo Reservation to shop and visit. It is the trading, shopping, medical, and educational center

DETOUR

Wild Spirit Wolf Sanctuary

If you have the time, you should check out the Wild Spirit Wolf Sanctuary (378 Candy Kitchen Road, Ramah, 505-775-3032, wildspiritwolfsanctuary.org). Continue past El Morro for 2 miles. Go left on BIA 125 for 8 miles. Go right on BIA 120 for 4 miles; the sanctuary is on the left. Meet wolf-dogs and captive wolves in natural enclosures. Open Tuesday to Sunday. Closed Monday. Guided tours daily. $4 children, $7 adults, $6 seniors, under age 7 free.

for the Navajo and Zuni. Over 100 trading posts sell all manner of Indian jewelry and wares, and Gallup is the site of the annual **Intertribal Ceremonial**, a gathering of tribes from throughout the hemisphere for parades, powwows, rodeos, market, and dances, in late July or early August. Lacking a formal banking system, many of the early trading posts functioned as pawnshops offering ready cash, and now old pawn or dead pawn jewelry, guns, saddles, and more are sought-after items. Gallup started out as a railroad and coal mining town, and it got its name because the paymaster was named David Gallup, and workers would announce they were "going up to Gallup's" to collect their wages. Prior to the 1880s, it consisted of a station, saloon, and store.

IN THE AREA

Accommodations

BLUE SWALLOW MOTEL, 815 Route 66, Tucumcari. Call 575-461-9849. $$. Owned and operated by former Harvey Girl Lillian Redman for over 40 years, the current owners cherish the 1939 stucco motel character of the place where the neon blue swallow flies proudly as a symbol of the Mother Road.

CIMARRON ROSE ZUNI MOUNTAIN BED & BREAKFAST, Route 9407, 689 Oso Ridge Road, Grants. Call 800-856-5776. Website: www.cimarronrose .com. $$$.

EL RANCHO HOTEL, 1000 East Route 66, Gallup. Call 505-863-9311. $$. Where Western stars stayed while filming in the area. With 24 rooms, each named for a movie star, this 1937 motel is the epitome of Hollywood-gone-Western nostalgia. It has a pool, a lounge, and a decent restaurant, as well as a bar. The floor-to-ceiling stone fireplace and rustic

ROOMS ARE NAMED FOR STARS WHO STAYED IN GALLUP'S EL RANCHO MOTEL

wooden lobby furnishings are always welcoming to visit.

MONTEREY MOTEL, 2402 Central Avenue SW, Albuquerque. Call 505-243-3554. $. Modest, inexpensive, clean, circa 1936.

Attractions and Recreation

BANDERA VOLCANO & ICE CAVE, The Land of Fire and Ice. Call 888-ICECAVE. Website: www.icecaves.com.

DOUBLE SIX GALLERIES, 1001 West Santa Fe Avenue, Grants.

GALLUP CONVENTION & VISITOR BUREAU, 103 West Route 66, Gallup. Call 505-863-3841.

GRANTS/CIBOLA COUNTY CHAMBER OF COMMERCE, 100 North Iron Avenue, Grants. Call 505-287-4802.

LAGUNA PUEBLO, 22 Capitol Road, Laguna Pueblo. Call 505-552-6654.

MESALANDS DINOSAUR MUSEUM, 222 East Laughlin Avenue, Tucumcari. Call 575-461-3466.

MORIARTY HISTORICAL SOCIETY & MUSEUM, 202 South Broadway, Moriarty. Call 505-832-0839.

NEW MEXICO MINING MUSEUM, 100 North Iron Avenue, Grants. Call 505-287-4802.

NEW MEXICO ROUTE 66 ASSOCIATION, Website: www.rt66nm.org.

NORTHWEST NEW MEXICO VISITOR CENTER, 1900 East Santa Fe Avenue, off I-40 at Exit 85, Grants. Call 505-876-2783.

OLD SCHOOL GALLERY, 46 NM 53, Ramah. Call 505-369-4047.

RICHARDSON'S TRADING CO., 222 West Route 66, Gallup. Call 505-722-4762. Nearly overwhelming selection of turquoise, silver, coral, Navajo, and Zuni jewelry; Navajo rugs; sand paintings; pottery; and old pawn fill the walls and cases of this creaky 1913 post. Reliable.

ROUTE 66 AUTO MUSEUM, 2436 Will Rogers Drive, Santa Rosa. Call 575-472-1966. Website: cibolaartscouncil.com/museum.html.

THE ROUTE 66 VINTAGE MUSEUM, Website: cibolaartscouncil.com /museum.html. Vintage postcards from trading posts.

RUSSELL'S ENDEE TRUCK AND TRAVEL CENTER, 1583 Frontage Road 4132, Glenrio. Call 575-576-8700.

SANTA ROSA LAKE STATE PARK, NM-91, Santa Rosa. Call 575-472-3110.

SANTA ROSA PARK LAKE HISTORIC DISTRICT, 913 Blue Hole Road, Santa Rosa. Call 575-472-3763.

SANTA ROSA VISITOR INFORMATION CENTER, 1085 Blue Hole Road, Santa Rosa. Call 575-472-3763.

SKY CITY CULTURAL CENTER, Haaku Road, Acoma Pueblo. Call 505-552-7861.

TEE PEE CURIOS, 924 East Route 66, Tucumcari. Call 575-461-3773.

TUCUMCARI HISTORICAL MUSEUM, 416 South Adams Street, Tucumcari. Call 575-461-4201.

TUCUMCARI/QUAY COUNTY CHAMBER OF COMMERCE, 404 Route 66, Tucumcari. Call 575-461-1694.

US SOUTHWEST SOARING MUSEUM, 918 Route 66, Moriarty. Call 505-832-9222.

WILD SPIRIT WOLF SANCTUARY, 378 Candy Kitchen Road, Ramah. Call 505-775-3032. Website: wildspiritwolfsanctuary.org.

ZUNI VISITOR CENTER, 1231-1245 NM-53, Zuni. Call 505-782-7238.

Dining and Drinks

ANCIENT WAY CAFÉ/EL MORRO RV PARK AND CABINS, 4018 NM 53, Ramah. Call 505-783-4612. Website: elmorro-nm.com. $$.

DEL'S RESTAURANT & GIFT SHOP, 1202 East Route 66, Tucumcari. Call 575-461-1740. $$. Home cooking with a salad bar, juicy burgers, and great chicken-fried steak, all served up in original 1956 style. Look for the big bull sign.

EARL'S FAMILY RESTAURANT, 1400 East Route 66, Gallup. Call 505-863-4201. $-$$.

EL CAFECITO, 820 East Santa Fe Avenue, Grants. Call 505-285-6229. $.

EL VADO, 2500 Central Avenue SW, Albuquerque. Call 505-361-1667. Restored and repurposed 1937 motel, $$.

MAC'S LA SIERRA RESTAURANT, 6217 Central Avenue NW, Albuquerque. Call 505-836-1212. $.

MR. POWDRELL'S BBQ HOUSE, 11301 Central Avenue NE, Albuquerque, Call 505-298-6766. $$.

SILVER MOON CAFÉ, 3501 Will Rogers Drive, Santa Rosa. Call 575-472-3162. $$.

66 DINER, 1405 Central Avenue NE, Albuquerque. Call 505-247-1421. $$.

VIRGIE'S RESTAURANT & LOUNGE, 2720 West Route 66, Gallup. Call 505-863-4845. $.

WATSON'S BAR-B-QUE, Tucumcari Ranch Supply, 502 South Lake Street, Tucumcari. Call 575-461-9620. $.

WESTERN VIEW DINER & STEAKHOUSE, 6411 Central Avenue NW, Albuquerque. Call 505-836-2200. $.

LEFT: A ROUTE 66 ICON

8

US HIGHWAY 60

SAILING THE OCEAN-TO-OCEAN HIGHWAY TO THE PIEWAY

ESTIMATED LENGTH: 140 miles

ESTIMATED TIME: Two hours driving, half-day to explore

GETTING THERE: Drive through Socorro to south end of town. (Socorro is 82 miles south of Albuquerque on I-25.) Go right (west) on US 60.

HIGHLIGHTS: Very Large Array, Pie Town

The first transcontinental highway, from Virginia Beach, Virginia, to Los Angeles, California, was begun in 1912 and not completely paved until 1947. This road began well before Route 66; it followed an old wagon road from Springerville, Arizona, to **Socorro**. Today's US 60 basically follows the same configuration. Unlike Route 66, it was never realigned. It remains the slow road two-lane through New Mexico going east to west, with a 65-mph speed limit, no billboards, no chain restaurants, and no chain motels. This is a journey through several of New Mexico's parallel universes: the Old West, the high-tech scientific world, the world of the arts, and the world that was opened up by the railroad. If instead of heading west, you turned east, taking off from I-25, you would pass through many miles of "big empty," ancient Spanish mission ruins (see Chapter 9), the salt lakes east of Willard, and farming communities devastated by the drought after drought brought by 20th century climate change. Continuing on to Clovis and the eastern border with Texas are little towns and iconic Santa Fe Railway mission-designed stations. The stations were spaced 17 miles apart, for that was how long steam engines could travel before needing to take on more water.

But much of the trip west feels like a trip on a roadway to the sky, without landmarks or bearings along the roadside. There's so little traffic the driver

LEFT: FIND LOTS OF BIG SKY AND OPEN SPACE ALONG OLD US 60

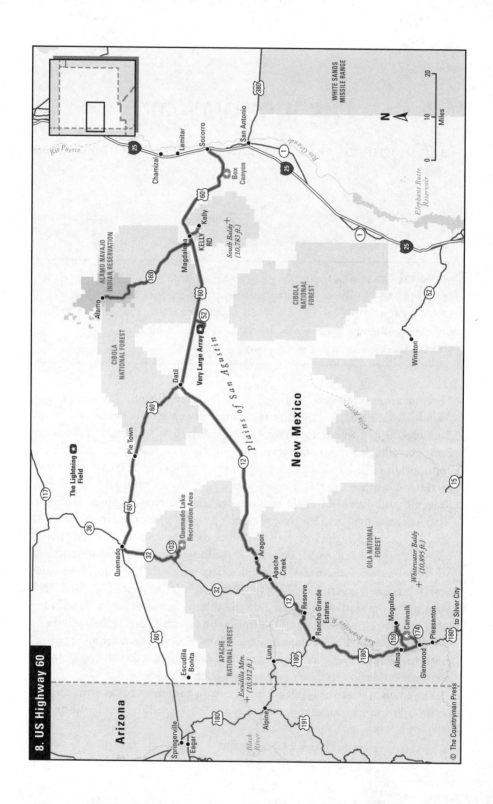

8. US Highway 60

© The Countryman Press

feels like they own the road, traveling at a speed that allows for taking in both the vastness and the emptiness. Along the way, pass through the villages of **Magdalena, Datil**, the **Very Large Array, Pie Town**, and **Quemado**. Travel through the **Plains of San Agustin**, a stretch of desert about 50 miles west of Socorro that spans Socorro and Catron Counties and extends south of US 60. Coinciding with the 1947 Roswell Incident that inspires UFO curiosity (see Chapter 7) was a report of another incident out here, according to Grady L. "Barney" Barnett, involving the reported crash of an intact craft and the recovery of several alien bodies on the Plains of San Agustin. He supposedly passed a lie detector test, but otherwise, little is actually known about this "other Roswell incident." For the past decade, the area has been generating controversy because of plans afoot to drill the aquifer and pipe water to metropolitan areas like Rio Rancho. The floor of the valley held a lake during the Pleistocene, from about 2.8 million years ago to the last Ice Age, 11,700 years ago. It is possible to travel on US 60 all the way through New Mexico from the Texas to the Arizona borders.

Socorro is a hub of history and modern technology. The town was named by Juan de Onate in 1598 because he and his party, crossing what became the Camino Real, were aided by native Piros. It remains a fascinating place with historic architecture and is the home of the New Mexico Institute of Mining and Technology, founded when Socorro was a center of mining activity. It remains a pleasant small town with a pretty plaza for special events and farmers markets, and it makes a good jumping off place for points east, south, and west.

The **Socorro Heritage and Visitor Center,** a block west of the Plaza, exhibits vintage photos that tell the story of old Socorro. Here is the place to pick up the brochure for the City of Socorro Historic Walking tour and get oriented. The tour is organized into three historic districts: the San Miguel Church District; the Church-McCutcheon District, and the Kittrel Park-Manzanares District.

A highlight is the **Garcia Opera House.** Built in 1884–87 by the widow of, and dedicated to the memory of, Juan Garcia, the adobe walls are almost 3 feet thick and the raked stage makes for a fine presentation; it is a preferred venue for community arts events.

San Miguel Church is one of the oldest Catholic churches in the United States, believed to be built between 1615 and 1626. The massive walls are almost 5 feet thick and the church's hand-carved *vigas* (beams) were hauled many miles. Following the Pueblo Revolt of 1680, area Piro Indians fled south with the Spanish to El Paso. The church was rebuilt in 1816. It is estimated that 100 to 200 people are buried beneath the church, including General Manuel Armijo, the last governor of New Mexico Territory.

Local legend tells that an Apache Indian raid in the early 1880s was thwarted when attackers saw a man with wings and a shining sword hovering

Box Canyon

From Socorro, go west on US 60 for 6.8 miles. Immediately after the bridge, go left (south). The second left is a gravel road leading to a parking area. This is a favorite red rock climbing and rappelling area west of Socorro.

over the church door. Consequently, the church's name was changed to San Miguel. San Miguel Fiestas are celebrated here September 27–29.

The Capitol Bar, on the east side of the Plaza, started out as the Bianaschi Saloon in 1896 for the sale of local wine. It remains one of the oldest ongoing bars in the United States.

Continue 27 miles west of Socorro on US 60. The face of Mary Magdalena, also known as the Lady of the Mountain, is supposedly visible on the mountainside on the eastern edge of town, but it takes a keen imagination to see it. Magdalena had its glory days as the shipping railhead of the Hoof Highway or Beefsteak Trail, the destination of cattle drives from ranches 125 miles west to Arizona and through the Plains of San Agustin. This little town is undergoing something of a revival and has sprouted a dozen galleries, several coffee shops, and a busy annual schedule of events, notably Old Timers Day during the second weekend in July, when a Queen who must be over age 70 is selected.

The **Magdalena Public Library**, located in the repurposed 1915 AT&SF station, keeps things lively with biweekly lectures and cultural events. The library has an excellent permanent exhibit of posters, magazine advertisements, photos, and art reproductions once displayed in railroad depots and Fred Harvey hotels throughout the Southwest.

The **Box Car Museum** is a restored AT&SF boxcar alongside the library stocked with local memorabilia about local history, mining, and cattle drives circa 1885–1930. The Box Car Museum displays old photographs and objects from yesteryear's frontier life. The park bench area on the old train station loading dock is a great place to rest under the shade of the cottonwood trees and imagine what life might have been like in this Old West town.

The **Magdalena Café and Steakhouse** serves only fresh, never frozen, fruit and vegetables. During summer weekends, diners are treated to a mock, old-fashioned gunfight during lunch. The clientele is an interesting mix of movie crews, ranchers, longtime locals, artists, and more recent arrivals.

The **Magdalena Hall Hotel** is an original cowboy hotel built in 1917, with **Kelly's Café,** which serves health-conscious food and coffees.

The **Route 60 Trading Post and Gallery** sells authentic jewelry made by Navajo living in nearby Alamo along with cowboy art. There's quite a collection of "junque" alongside the post that proprietor James Chavez refers

THE MAGDALENA PUBLIC LIBRARY IS A REPURPOSED AT&SF TICKET OFFICE

to as his "Museum of Rust," featuring many "antiques on wheels." He knows the area well and gives tours booked in advance.

Magdalena has several interesting coffee shops, including **Ex-presso** and **Evett's Gallery and Coffee**. You can usually find at least one of them open, though here, as in most small towns, hours are uncertain and vary by season.

Datil, 35 miles west of Magdalena on US 60, was named for the nearby Datil Mountains. The name translates as "date" and may refer to a wild fruit that once grew here.

DETOUR

Alamo Navajo Reservation

The Alamo Navajo Reservation (575-854-2686), 30 miles north of Magdalena on NM 169, is 63,000 acres in the northwest corner of Socorro County. It is bordered on the south by the Gallinas Mountains. There are 2,200 residents of this place, called T'iisTsoh—a cottonwood near a spring settled en route home from Fort Sumner. A celebration of culture takes place each October. Alamo Indian Days are held the weekend before Columbus Day, with singing, drumming, dancing, and the Miss Alamo Indian Pageant. It is actually 220 miles southeast of the Navajo Nation. The maintained scenic dirt road cuts across to I-40, with plenty of mountain views, rolling hills, and mesas, bordered on the south by the Gallinas Mountains. Petroglyphs are visible, painted on rocks bordering the Rio Salada, and sheep graze here.

Kelly

Considered one of New Mexico's top ghost towns for exploration, Kelly is located only 3.5 miles from Magdalena. Turn south on Kelly Road at the US Forest Service Office. Drive south 2 miles to a fork in the road. At the fork are the ruins of the Graphic Mill. Take fork on the left. Kelly is 1.5 miles ahead. Its remnants are accessible on foot, and photo opportunities are plentiful. Mines, head frames, remains of mills and smelters are all visible. Note: do not attempt this journey in winter.

John Hutchinson found minerals here in 1866, and the town of Pueblo Springs, now Magdalena, developed in the 1870s. The main mining camp above the town was named for Hutchinson's friend, Andy Kelley, but the name was misspelled when the camp was registered at the courthouse in 1879. During the 1880s, silver and lead and zinc mining brought a boom to the area. The population grew from 1,500 to 2,000. The AT&SF arrived in Magdalena in 1885, with a daily stage to Kelly. Sherwin Williams Paint Company purchased the Kelly mine and Graphic Mill in 1904. A gradual descent came about, and the Great Depression continued its toll-taking. The post office closed in 1945, and by 1947 the remaining residents moved to Magdalena and Socorro.

The mine head frame was erected in 1906 by Gustav Billing, the owner. It was purchased from the Traylor Engineering Company of New York. They acquired this head frame in kit form from the Carnegie Steel Works of Passaic, New Jersey, after it was designed by Alexander G. Eiffel to be the state-of-the-art technology of that era. Local tales that it was built by Eiffel himself are false, but there is indeed a connection. This area is a rockhound's delight.

The landmark **Eagle Guest Ranch** is located at the intersection of US 60 and NM 12, in Datil. This roadhouse began as a gas station and grocery shop in the early 20th century to serve automobiles that began coming through. Steaks and burgers are the usual fare, and the Mexican food on Friday will heat your soul. It's a favorite of dusty cowboys and well-armed hunters.

Datil Well Campground, US 60 to Datil, south 1 mile on NM 12, has a 1-mile moderate hiking trail through pinon-juniper and ponderosa pine. This site is one of 15 wells that supplied water along the 1880s cattle driveway between Magdalena and Springerville. Firewood is provided at 22 campsites.

Driving into **Glenwood**, 104.4 miles south of Datil via US 180 and NM 12, is like discovering a little piece of countrified Shangri-lá. This is a pleasant stop for gas and a bite to eat at any café that happens to be open.

To find the **Catwalk** (575-539-2481), come to Glenwood and go left on NM 174 for 5 miles. Originally constructed by miners in 1889, this high walkway and suspension bridge leads to a waterfall through narrow Whitewater Canyon. Flooded out a few years ago and then rebuilt, it is especially beautiful

The Kelly Church is still an active mission church for San Miguel parish and is still used for weddings, Masses, funerals, and the annual fiesta.

A pretty green stone found here called Smithsonite is named for the founder of the Smithsonian Institution. The rock is zinc carbonate, mined from tailings piles of the Sherwin Williams Paint Company.

IF YOU THRILL TO THE SIGHT OF RUSTY OLD MACHINERY, YOU'LL BE IN YOUR ELEMENT IN MAGDALENA

in the fall, hiking among the sycamore and rock walls. The trail is easy and maintained for the first 0.5-mile. Please check status and carry water.

Mogollon is one hour south from Datil on NM 180, left on NM 159 between Glenwood and Alma. Considered one of the state's more remote and well-preserved ghost towns, this gold and silver mining village deep in the Gila Wilderness is accessible only by a 9-mile road, NM 159, that climbs 2,080 feet with many sharp switchbacks and without guardrails. The last 5 miles become a one-lane road. Founded in 1895, this gold rush boomtown was the state's leading mining district by 1915. For accommodations, check the restored 1885 **Silver Creek Inn**, open on weekends during summer, and check road conditions carefully before taking this trip.

Returning to US 60, many will recognize the **Very Large Array** from the movie *Contact*, starring Jodie Foster. The Karl G. Jansky Very Large Array is 50 miles west of Socorro on US 60. Twenty-seven dish antennae, movable on tracks across the roadway around 100 square miles of desert. Each dish is 82 feet across and weighs 230 tons. You can learn more about radio

DETOUR

Backroad to Silver City

Reserve is 67.2 miles south of Datil via NM 12 and US 189. This is the land of cowboys, real ones, yes ma'am. There are a couple of bars, a gas station, and, if otherwise stranded, a motel. Best keep your political opinions to yourself, podner. A chief attraction is a commemorative monument to New Mexico character Elfego Baca, a lawyer and lawman who performed amazing feats in a gunfight, fending off a large group of attackers, and who was viewed as a champion of the people.

astronomy at the visitor center. Scientists are not looking for life beyond planet Earth here—they are measuring radio waves. The visitor center and gift shop offer displays and videos and are open all year from 8:30 a.m. to sunset. You may find information on star birth, galaxy growth, and black holes here. There is a self-guided tour for viewing the antennas up close.

As you travel across the **Plains of San Agustin**, the vegetation changes as the elevation increases, transforming from a grassy plain to a cooler pine forest within the **Cibola National Forest.**

Pie Town, located right on the Continental Divide, is 21 miles northwest of Datil on US 60, a 20th-century homesteader community immortalized by photos made by photographer Russell Lee for the Farm Security Administration. Although they were lured here by desperation, the land was too dry to farm, so these tough pioneers baked their way through the Depression by selling homemade pies to cowboys who came through on the Hoof Highway. The tradition of homemade pie-making is carried on to this day, and people come from all over the world for the experience. In the early 1920s, WWI-veteran Clyde Norman began making and dried apple pies on the Ocean-to-Ocean Highway, staying in the spot where his car broke down.

While other cattle drives such as the Chisum and Goodnight-Loving trails faded away with the coming of the railroad, the Magdalena Trail remained vital in use until the 1970s. The trail for livestock began in January 1885, when the AT&SF completed its branch line from Socorro to Magdalena. Ranchers from western New Mexico and eastern Arizona drove their cattle as far as 120 miles to ship them. Because the area was protected from homesteading claims, the trail was designated the Stock Driveway. In places it was 5 to 10 miles wide, to provide grass for stock. To improve the driveway, the Civilian Conservation Corps was established. The CCC built wells at 10-mile intervals along the Driveway, considered one day's journey.

A highlight of Pie Town is **Pie-O-Neer Café**, US "Pieway" 60, with a reputation for the best pie in New Mexico, served on the Continental Divide by proprietor Kathy Knapp, the Pie Lady of Pie Town. Savory green chile apple, sky-high coconut cream, and so many other varieties—so much pie, so little time—make it difficult to choose.

Quemado is 43 miles west of Pie Town on US 60 and 33 miles from the Arizona border. The name means "burnt" in Spanish. This is the place to meet with transportation for Walter de la Maria's Lightning Field, an installation of 400 polished steel poles that catches changing light and New Mexico's high desert lightning. The location is 45 miles away. Reservations must be made several months in advance.

Quemado Lake Recreation Area (575-773-4678). From Quemado, west on US 60 0.5 mile, south on NM 32 for 16 miles to NM 103. Eight hundred quiet, unspoiled acres of ponderosa pine border a 131-acre trout lake. There is camping, along with 7 miles of hiking trails with good birding.

KATHY KNAPP IS THE PIE LADY OF PIE TOWN—MAKING THE WORLD A BETTER PLACE ONE HOMEMADE PIE AT A TIME

IN THE AREA

Accommodations

HIGH COUNTRY LODGE, 303 First Street, Magdalena. Call 575-854-2062. $–$$.

SILVER CREEK INN, NM 159, Mogollon. Call 866-276-4882. $$–$$$.

WESTERN MOTEL & RV PARK, 404 First Street, Magdalena. Call 575-854-2417. $–$$.

Attractions and Recreation

ALAMO NAVAJO RESERVATION. Call 575-854-2686.

BOX CAR MUSEUM, 108 North Main Street, Magdalena. Call 575-854-2361.

CAPITOL BAR, 110 Plaza, Socorro. Call 575-835-1193.

DATIL WELL CAMPGROUND, US 60 to Datil, south 1 mile on NM 12. Call 575-835-0412.

ELVIRES' ROCK SHOP AND SAW SHOP, East US 60, Magdalena. Call 575-854-2324.

KARL G. JANSKY VERY LARGE ARRAY, 50 miles west of Socorro on US 60. Call 575-835-7000.

MINERAL MUSEUM, 801 Leroy Place, southeast corner of Canyon Road and Olive Lane on New Mexico Tech campus, Socorro. Call 575-835-5420.

QUEMADO LAKE RECREATION AREA, Quemado. Call 575-773-4678.

ROUTE 60 TRADING POST & GALLERY, 400 1st Street, Magdalena. Call 575-854-3560.

SOCORRO FARMERS' MARKET, 101 Socorro Plaza, Socorro. Call 575-312-1730.

SOCORRO HERITAGE AND VISITOR CENTER, 217 Fisher Avenue, Socorro. Call 575-835-8927.

WALTER DE LA MARIA'S LIGHTNING FIELD, Quemado. Call 505-898-3335.

Dining and Drinks

EAGLE GUEST RANCH, US 60 and NM 12, Datil. Call 575-772-5612. $$.

FRANK & LUPE'S EL SOMBRERO, 210 Mesquite, Socorro. Call 575-835-3945. $–$$.

M MOUNTAIN COFFEEHOUSE, 110 Manzanares Avenue, Socorro. Call 575-838-0809. $.

MAGDALENA CAFÉ AND STEAKHOUSE, 109 South Main Street, Magdalena. Call 575-838-0809. $$.

PIE-O-NEER CAFÉ, US "Pieway" 60, Pie Town. Call 575-772-2711. $.

SOCORRO SPRINGS RESTAURANT, 1012 North California Street, Socorro. Call 575-838-0650. $$.

9

SALT MISSIONS TRAIL

HOLY RUINS AND HOMESTEADERS

ESTIMATED LENGTH: 140 miles

ESTIMATED TIME: One day

GETTING THERE: Following the natural curve of the road as it nudges the Manzano Mountains, take NM 333 east from Albuquerque, NM 337 south from Tijeras, and a few well-marked quick jogs along the way south. On your return, take US 60 West from Mountainair to I-25 North, exit Belen, and continue on NM 47 to Los Lunas. Continue on NM 47 through Isleta Pueblo, then either take I-25 back to Albuquerque or continue on 47 North back to Albuquerque.

HIGHLIGHTS: Ruins of Spanish Mission churches built atop Indian kivas and dwellings at Quarai, Abo, and Gran Quivira form the Salinas Pueblos Mission National Monument—all three sites are within a 50-mile radius from Mountainair; also, the Belen Harvey House, Cerro Tome, Through the Flower Art Space

In 1598, conquistador Juan de Onate pronounced salt one of the "four treasures of New Spain," as New Mexico was then known. Salt, in addition to being an essential foodstuff, was used to cure meat, and the Spanish used Indian labor to mine and haul it to silver mines in Chihuahua. Salt was also essential to the process of silver mining. Evaporation within the Estancia Basin, a landlocked region created by glaciation from ice ages, resulted in abundant salt lakes. In their quest for "gold and souls," the Spanish church and crown found societies of as many as 10,000 indigenous dwellers, who had inhabited this land for at least 7,000 years, living in at least 10 villages the Spanish named the Salines. The Spanish forced the native dwellers to construct their grand mission churches. These Native Americans the Span-

LEFT: ASTONISHING MISSION RUINS AT QUARAI RISE OUT OF THE PLAINS WITH NO WARNING

ish enslaved and attempted to convert traced their origins to the Mogollon pit-dwelling hunter-gatherer culture from the southwest and the Ancient Puebloan (formerly Anasazi) people of the north. They were traders and farmers who fended off attacks from Apache tribes in the east. Their villages were largely abandoned by the 1670s, due to devastations of drought, disease, and exhaustion. Those that remained accompanied the Spanish to El Paso when they were driven out by the Pueblo Revolt of 1680.

The **Salt Missions Trail** leads to the village of **Mountainair**, founded in

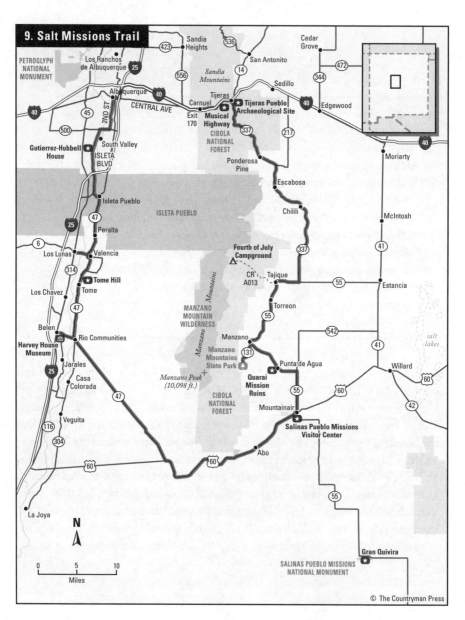

1908, which, from the 1920s through the drought of the 1950s, had a reputation as the Pinto Bean Capital of the World. The effects of what we now know as climate change during the 20th century devastated this area. This region contains visible overlays and admixtures of New Mexico's cultural vitality: Indian, Spanish, and homesteader. Be prepared with a full tank of gas, food, and water. There is little in the way of supplies available on the route, and the occasional far-flung grocery store or gas station offer at best irregular hours of operation.

While indigenous people walked this winding route that seems to flow alongside gentle undulations for millennia in sacred pilgrimage, seeking salt from salt lakes east of **Willard,** today's traveler will encounter hiking, biking, and camping opportunities; centuries-old Spanish villages, each with its own church that continues to draw the faithful; and, ultimately, the haunting, photogenic ruins of 350 to 400 year-old multistoried Spanish mission churches built of local sandstone atop ancient Indian sites.

MASSIVE SCULPTURE, *LA PUERTA DEL SOL,* COMMEMORATES THE CULTURES OF CENTRAL NEW MEXICO, MARKING TOME HILL

Watch for the MUSICAL HIGHWAY sign, about 5 miles before **Tijeras.** On this segment of Old Route 66 driving at 45 mph, the road itself plays "America the Beautiful," one of only two such roads in the United States that does this, designed to slow traffic. To the left is **Tijeras Canyon,** separating the **Manzano Mountains** from the **Sandia Mountains** to the north. Vegetation ranges from desert yucca to pinon-juniper to Ponderosa pine forest. Continue 6.5 miles (from Albuquerque) to the village of Tijeras (which means "scissors," referring to the meeting point of two scissor-like canyons) and exit south (right) on NM 337. On the corner see **Roots Farm Café,** a farm-to-table restaurant specializing in salads. Directly beyond the café about a 0.5-mile, just behind the Sandia Ranger Station, is the **Tijeras Pueblo Archaeological Site**, a district of the **Cibola National Forest.** An Indian village was constructed and occupied here between CE 1313 and CE 1425. Members of the contemporary pueblo of Isleta consider this an ancestral site. There is a 0.33-mile self-guided trail, along with a museum (open weekends May through October) that demonstrates archaeological techniques and gives an intimate view of the lives of Ancestral Puebloan people, as well as a native plant garden.

Numerous hiking and biking trails run throughout this Manzano Mountain canyon, with its views of the Manzano Mountains, and you are likely to encounter bicyclists along the way, as this is a popular getaway for Albuquerque cyclists. Several campgrounds are found here, some of which are by reservation only. At 14.5 miles from Tijeras, see the tiny settlement of **Escobosa;** continue another 4.4 miles to the **Chilili Land Grant.** A sign declares this place is inhabited by descendants from the original Spanish land grant dating to 1841, La Merced del Pueblo del Chilili. It is a sovereign, self-governing entity, known for land disputes that may be generalized as a bitter battle between preservation of traditional ways of life and development. Photography is forbidden. The cemetery is colorful and highly adorned with plastic flowers and personal memorials; the resting place, or *camposanto*, is to be observed respectfully from the roadside only.

Each tiny roadside settlement is built upon land grants given to petitioning families to occupy and protect this frontier from Apache raiding, likely positioned on pueblo sites. Many were abandoned and then reoccupied in the 1800s.

NM 337 dead ends at a stop sign. Go right at junction 55 to **Tajique,** 13.3 miles from **Chilili,** the oldest village along this route, then see the sign to the **Fourth of July Campground** (about 7 miles of gravel off the main road), famous for blazing red oaks and the state's largest stand of big tooth maple fall foliage. One hike into the **Manzano Mountain Wilderness** starts at the Fourth of July Campground and leads 1.5 miles to the crest of the area. From there, a trail runs along the crest for 22 miles to **Manzano Peak.**

At **Punta de Agua,** the site of an ancient spring, go right on NM 55 about 2 miles and arrive at the first of the Salinas Pueblo sites, **Quarai.** As noted New Mexico author Charles Lummis wrote in his classic, *Land of Poco Tiempe,* "An edifice in ruins but so tall, so solemn, so dominant of that strange lonely landscape. . . . On the Rhine it would be a superlative; in the wilderness of the Manzano it is a miracle."

DETOUR

Manzano Mountain Retreat and Apple Farm

Tucked away at 2.7 miles beyond Torreon ("watch tower"), be on the lookout for a sign on the right for the Manzano Mountain Retreat and Apple Farm, selling a dozen varieties of apples, cider, and offering a hot dog stand during peak fall weekends. This is the perfect family weekend destination, and many local families make this trip a fall ritual. The gravel road is tricky but well-marked. Have faith. Follow signs patiently and you will arrive.

Manzano Mountains State Park

Continue heading into **Manzano Mountains State Park** and arrive at the village (in truth, a ghost town) of **Manzano**, no doubt named for the apple trees planted by early missionaries, though the precise age of apples here is still debated, given that some claim they were planted by later settlers in the 1830s. Some believe they are the oldest apples in the United States. Here you can access several lovely hiking trails, including one of my favorites, **Red Canyon Trail**, which has excellent birding, given that this is a raptor flyway. You will see many alligator junipers growing along the trail. Or, you can camp on sites forested with Ponderosa pine. Manzano Peak, at 10,098 feet, is the highest point in the mountain range. **Capilla Peak**, meaning "chapel," at 9,368 feet, also resembles a hood when viewed from the east.

Manzano Mountain Wilderness

Spread out across the western slope of the Manzano Mountain Range, the Manzano Mountain Wilderness varies in elevation from about 6,000 feet to 10,098 feet atop Manzano Peak. This is steep and rugged terrain for the most part, cut with canyons and marked with outcroppings of rock. More than 64 miles of a well-developed trail system provide access to the Wilderness, but access to water and campsites is limited.

Prepare to be thunderstruck by the three-story monumental red sandstone edifice before you. The mind floods with questions: Who built this? How did they build it? Who lived here? What happened to them? Dozens of unexcavated Indian mounds surround the ruin. The sophistication of the architecture and construction is dazzling. The 5-mile trail around the ruins, mostly accessible, leads through an unexcavated Tiwa Indian village. It's best to walk the straight path toward the 17th-century Franciscan mission, **Nuestra Senora de La Purisma Concepcion de Cuarac**, and allow your imagination to wander as it will.

The convent within was used during the Spanish Inquisition, and at least three of Quarai's priests served as heads of the Inquisition in New Mexico. By 1677, it was abandoned and the population retreated to Isleta Pueblo. However, following the Pueblo Revolt of 1680, many natives and Spanish people from this area fled south to El Paso and Ysleta del Sur.

Do stay on the trail and be alert for rattlesnakes.

Beside the ruin is a meadow along with picnic tables in the shade of giant cottonwoods, making this one of the most sublime picnic spots ever. It is a good place to pause and begin to comprehend the enormous cultural collision that occurred here when the Spanish Franciscan missionaries subjugated and attempted to convert the indigenous population. You can also begin to understand ways in which this process links New Mexico to the cultural developments that occurred throughout the hemisphere.

Return to Punta de Agua and proceed 13 miles south on NM 55 to Mountainair, once a center for homesteading, ranching and farming, and now largely boarded up. A New Mexico folk art treasure is the gate beside the 1920s Shaffer Hotel, embellished with fanciful animal forms of local stone by Pop Shaffer, an early 20th-century entrepreneur, mechanic, and jack-of-all-trades. The hotel he built is located at 103 Main Street West. This hotel has reopened with a café and art gallery, La Galeria. Mountainair has a trading post, as well as a café or two. You can try **Alpine Alley** for decent coffee, or go to a grocery store, the B Market, for grab and go, but there is little else besides endless photo ops of abandoned buildings, some with Art Deco touches. By all means, visit the co-op gallery, **Cibola Arts**, to see a sampling of work by local artists and find out what's going on.

Founded in 1903 to headquarter the construction of the Belen Cutoff, Mountainair was a destination for 20th-century homesteaders offered free land on the condition that they could farm it and "prove up" on it for a designated period of time. Health-seekers, or "lungers," as people suffering from tuberculosis were known, also arrived here, seeking relief in the pure, high mountain air. While the offer of free land was appealing, many

JACK-OF-ALL-TRADES POP SHAFFER NEVER CALLED HIMSELF A FOLK ARTIST, BUT THE STONEWORK GATE NEXT TO HIS SHAFFER HOTEL IS A NEW MEXICO FOLK ART TREASURE

people worked heartbreakingly hard, lived in poverty in dugouts, attempted dry farming, and ultimately gave up their claim in exchange for "a team of horses or anything that would get them out of town." Others toughed it out, and many surrounding ranches are conglomerations of abandoned claims, now held by descendants of homesteaders. The **Salinas Pueblo Missions National Monument** visitor center is in the center of town.

Salt lakes are located east of Willard, about 11 miles east in the dry deserted landscape of US 60. Another option is to drive 26 miles on NM 55 to **Gran Quivira**. The most far-flung of the Salinas Pueblos and substantially different from the other two, it was an important trading center for Plains Indians. As many as 3,000 Pueblo and Plains Indians would gather here for religious events and trade fairs. The occupants staged an ambush of Spanish colonists, and in retaliation the Spanish killed as many as 900 Indians and took an additional 400 as prisoners to make into slaves. The **Church of San Buenaventura** was never completed and was abandoned in 1670. Gran Quivira reveals the most extensive pueblo ruins of the three sites, built largely from limestone quarried nearby and mortar. The University of New Mexico has made extensive excavations here.

Alternatively, from Mountainair, head 9 miles west on US 60 to Abo, another abandoned Spanish mission church ruin that is particularly glorious at the golden hour before sunset. This 0.75-mile trail is fully accessible. The mission of **San Gregorio de Abo** is built on a site occupied for at least 500 years, starting in the 12th century CE, by Tompiro Indians, and became important as a pottery and trade center after 1400. **Abo** was occupied by

Spanish missionaries from 1622 to 1673. The existence of an Indian kiva, or ceremonial chamber, within the mission, remains a mystery.

Paralleling this drive is freight train traffic traveling the **Belen Cutoff** as it crosses **Abo Pass.** This Atchison, Topeka & Santa Fe Railway track connected Belen to Amarillo, Texas, eliminating the need to haul freight across steep Raton Pass to the north, and opening the flow of commerce from east to west.

After touring Abo, you have a few options for a return route. Heading straight west on US 60 to I-25 for 62.7 miles, then traveling 48 miles back to Albuquerque, may be the fastest route. Alternatively, it is 36 miles on US 60 then bearing right at NM 47 through **Rio Communities** to Belen. This is a remote rural road with little traffic. From Belen, continue 21 miles on NM 47 to **Los Lunas** through a rural farming region toward **Tome.** Remaining on NM 47, go through Isleta Pueblo and on to the South Valley of Albuquerque on Isleta Boulevard.

This journey will occasionally coincide with the Camino Real, the road north forged by conquistador Juan de Onate, who made the first permanent settlement in New Mexico in 1598 north of Santa Fe at **Okeh Owingee Pueblo.** For centuries, the 1,590-mile Camino Real d'Adentro, the Royal Road of the Interior from Mexico City to Okeh Owingee Pueblo, was the only route in and out of New Mexico, the northern reach of the Spanish empire known as New Spain.

Most notable in Belen is the trackside **Belen Harvey House Museum,** a fine example of the Fred Harvey chain of lunchrooms and hotels along the AT&SF Railway. This 1910 Harvey House is special; it once served as a Harvey Girl dormitory as well as a restaurant and celebrates Harvey history with many unique artifacts. To get to the museum, Exit 195 off I-25. Turn left into Belen. Follow Main Street south to Becker Avenue. Turn left on Becker and drive east to the end. Turn left on First Street, and the museum will be on the right. Artifacts are interwoven to create a delightful visit to early 1900s Belen. See the uniforms and dormitories of the Harvey Girls, view the interior of an old beauty shop, and revisit the bygone days of railroad travel.

Return to Becker Street and walk one block east to reach Judy Chicago's new **Through the Flower Art Space.** Chicago has lived and worked in Belen for nearly two decades, and she and her husband, photographer Donald Woodman, have, with the help and support of the city, opened an exhibit space/gallery.

In Belen you may get a bite to eat at **Pete's Café,** serving railroaders and locals local cuisine based on green and red chile over 70 years. About 110 freight trains pass through Belen daily as they travel the Belen Cutoff. The word *Belen* means "Bethlehem." Each year the city holds what they call "the world's largest matanza," a traditional pig roast and feast, in late January.

Tome Hill, on the south end of **Los Lunas,** is known as a Good Friday pilgrimage site, but throughout history many of various faiths have been called to make the steep trek to the top, from ancient Aztecs all the way to Mennonites. World War II native son veteran Edwin Berry built three crosses at the top and established the contemporary Catholic ritual on his return home from the war, as part of his own healing from illness and the brutality he witnessed and endured. The hill itself is considered a shrine, and many signs of faith embellish its sides. From the top of this volcanic hill, there is a good view of the Rio Grande Valley. A sculpture, *La Puerta del Sol,* by Armando Alvarez, honors those who journeyed on the Camino Real. To reach El Cerro, take paved NM 263 east, then south around the mountain. You also can take Tomé Hill Road east from NM 47. There are signs directing visitors, but you have to keep your eyes focused to see them.

El Cerro's two main trails are the Via Cruces ("Crosses Way") from the west and the South Path, from the parking area near the junction of Tomé Hill Road and La Entrada Road. The South Path is the quickest—and steepest—route to the top, though spur and side trails allow for breaks. While El Cerro's trails are short, they are often steep, and the volcanic rocks make for tricky footing. Bring a hat, dark glasses, sunscreen, solid shoes, and a walking stick, and beware of rattlesnakes.

Continue on NM 47 through **Tome,** an agricultural valley of pleasant farms and ranchitos, where horses and cattle graze in green fields while time stands still.

Travel at a leisurely pace on this two-lane until Los Lunas, once a traditional agricultural village and now a fast-growing suburb of Albuquerque

NOTED ARTIST JUDY CHICAGO OPENED HER ART SPACE, THROUGH THE FLOWER, IN BELEN WHERE SHE LIVES AND WORKS.

Fred Harvey

The man, whose imagination and unrelenting work turned his vision of gracious fine dining on the railroad into reality, arrived in New York from England in 1850 at age 15, with $10 in his pocket. Starting out as a dishwasher, by 1873 Fred Harvey operated three eating houses along the Kansas Pacific (later a branch of the Union Pacific) Railroad. He was convinced that railroad passengers deserved better than bitter coffee, hard biscuits, tough-as-nails antelope steak, and ancient beans likely left over from the plate of a diner on an earlier train.

But it was his initiative with the AT&SF that resulted in the opening of his first lunchroom in 1876 in Topeka, Kansas, the railroad's headquarters city. Its popularity with travelers and locals launched his success: an 1889 partnership with the railroad led to the creation of eateries and hotels across the West, serving delicious fresh food in generous portions, served with high standards of customer service. His motto was "It is our business to please cranks, for anyone can please a gentleman." And to prove his point, he hired the chef of the renowned Palmer House in Chicago at the then-unheard-of salary of $5,000 a year.

The result was America's first chain restaurant, with trackside restaurants and hotel dining rooms from Kansas to California.

And it was Harvey's drive toward innovation as well as his ability to recognize a good idea when he heard it that gave life to the iconic female wait staff.

Not merely "waitresses," they belonged to a special sorority—the Harvey Girls—as popularized by Judy Garland in a nostalgic 1946 movie of the same name. Drawn from a pool of middle-class young women from New England and the Midwest, screened through recruiting offices in Chicago and Kansas City, applicants had to be both attractive and intelligent and between the ages of 18 and 30. In exchange for a weekly salary of $17.50, plus tips, room and board, they lived tightly supervised lives in Harvey dormitories and obeyed a 10 p.m. curfew rule. (Friday night dances were the only exception to the rule.) In addition, they had to promise they would not get married for a year.

thrust into prominence as the site of Facebook's off-the-grid new location. This is where you'll find the highly-haunted Victorian **Luna Mansion** at 110 West Main Street. This architectural anomaly of a three-story adobe and terron (mud brick) structure resembles a grand Georgian mansion. The building was a gift to Solomon Luna from the AT&SF Railway in exchange for the right of way through the Luna-Otero Land Grant; locals come here to celebrate birthdays and anniversaries with steak and prime rib, but the menu includes burgers and chicken-fried steak specials as well. The politically powerful Luna-Otero family, who built a fortune in land and sheep in the days of patriarch Solomon Luna, dates to 1530 in this area. The upstairs bar features vintage photos of family members, and reports of supernatural activity are frequent enough to attract dedicated ghost hunters.

NM 47 leads to Isleta Pueblo, 10 miles from Los Lunas and only 15 miles south of Albuquerque. It is possible to drive through the Pueblo on NM 47 and visit one of the oldest mission churches in the country, San Agustin de la Isleta, dating to 1710. It is also possible to purchase oven bread, horno (oven) roasted blue corn meal, and artwork here.

Continuing north on NM 47, you will find Isleta Boulevard leading through Albuquerque's South Valley. At 6029 Isleta Boulevard SW is the Guttierez-Hubbell House, a nearly 6,000-square-foot adobe structure restored as a community education center that teaches about life at a respite on the Camino Real. During New Mexico's Territorial Period from 1848 to 1912,

MANZANO MOUNTAIN RETREAT AND APPLE RANCH RAISES DOZENS OF APPLE VARIETIES, INCLUDING HEIRLOOM VARIETIES DATING TO THE CIVIL WAR

this was a way station along the highway, a trading post, a farm, and much more. Today, agriculture-based festivals are celebrated, traditional crafts are demonstrated, and lectures and exhibits celebrating local culture may be found here. Eight miles farther, and you will come to Albuquerque, completing the loop.

IN THE AREA

Attractions and Recreation

BELEN HARVEY HOUSE MUSEUM, 104 North 1st Street, Belen. Call 505-861-0581.

CIBOLA ARTS, 217 Broadway, Mountainair. Call 505-847-0324.

BUILT AS A HARVEY GIRL DORMITORY AS WELL AS A RESTAURANT, THIS OLD HARVEY HOUSE IS TODAY A FASCINATING MUSEUM

GUITIERREZ-HUBBELL HOUSE, 6029 Isleta Boulevard SW, Albuquerque. Call 505-244-0507.

MANZANO MOUNTAINS STATE PARK, County Road B062, Mountainair. Call 505-469-7608.

MANZANO MOUNTAIN RETREAT AND APPLE RANCH, Call 505-384-4467. Website: retreatinfo@manzanoretreat.com.

SALINAS PUEBLOS MISSION NATIONAL MONUMENT, US 60, Mountainair. Call 505-384-2418.

SHAFFER HOTEL, 103 West Main Street, Mountainair. Call 505-847-2888.

THROUGH THE FLOWER ART SPACE, 107 Becker Avenue, Belen. Call 505-864-4080.

TIJERAS PUEBLO ARCHAEOLOGICAL SITE, 11776 NM-337, Tijeras, behind Sandia Ranger Station, a district of the Cibola National Forest. Call 505-281-3304.

Dining and Drinks

ALPINE ALLEY, 210 N Summit Ave, Mountainair. Call 505-847-2478. $.

LUNA MANSION, 110 Main Street SW, Los Lunas. Call 505-865-7333. $$$.

PETE'S CAFÉ, 105 North South 1st Street, Belen. Call 505-864-4811. $$.

TEOFILO'S RESTAURANTE, 144 Vallejos Lane, Los Lunas. Call 505-865-5511. $$.

10

TURQUOISE TRAIL

BACK DOOR TO SANTA FE: MINING TOWNS AND ARTIST
HAVENS FROM TINKERTOWN TO MADRID TO CERRILLOS

ESTIMATED LENGTH: 65 miles along NM 14

ESTIMATED TIME: Half-day

GETTING THERE: From Albuquerque take I-40 for 6 miles east to Tijeras Exit
175 and go left (north). Alternatively, from the intersection of Tramway and
Central, take NM 333 (Old Route 66) to Tijeras. Just before Tijeras, see a
sign with a bar of music. Slow down to 45 mph and as you do, roll down the
windows and listen to the road, yes the road, play "America the Beautiful."
This is one of only two such "musical highways" in the nation, designed to
slow traffic.

HIGHLIGHTS: Tinkertown Museum, Madrid

The **Turquoise Trail National Scenic Byway** coincides with NM 14 north
from the village of Tijeras 65 miles to **Santa Fe**. Known locally as either the
Turquoise Trail or North 14, it is actually the scenic backroad to Santa Fe,
first passing the east side of the Sandia Mountains, then traversing gentle
hills as it follows the contours of the land. The Ortiz Mountains stand to
the east, with views of the Jemez Mountains to the west. It's a pretty alternative to I-25 if you have the extra hour or so it takes to drive from **Albuquerque,** and this loop can be completed expeditiously by returning on the
freeway. This two-lane road is a popular, accessible weekend getaway, with
sightseeing, shopping, entertainment, ghost towns, and food galore. It is
also a favorite route for motorcyclists out on a Sunday jaunt. The elevation
rises to 5,275 feet.

As you head north to **Cedar Crest**, a well-populated East Mountain bedroom community, with cafés and grocery stores along the way, take note that

LEFT: CERRILLOS STATION, WHERE OLD WEST MEETS TRENDY

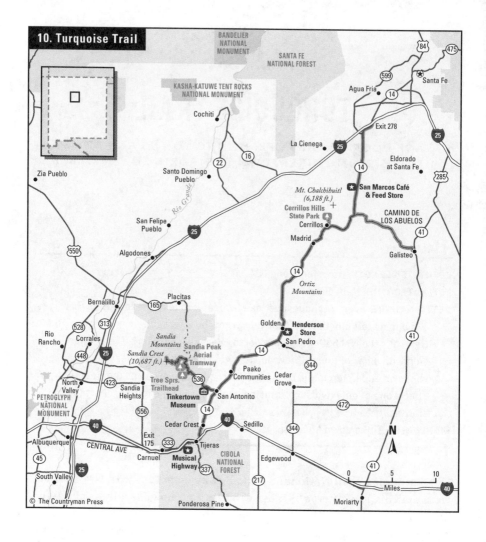

the east side of the Sandia Mountains has a completely different ecosystem than the high desert side facing Albuquerque. Here is it green, with deciduous trees and wildflowers. When Spanish explorers marched through here more than four centuries ago, they found indigenous pueblos with settled dwellers along this route. The people of Tijeras (see Chapter 9), **Pa'ako,** and **San Marcos** lived, hunted, farmed, and mined this area from as long as 1,000 years ago.

On the way to Albuquerque, at 1.5 miles on your left, find the **Tinkertown Museum,** the lifetime creation that is the unique vision of outsider folk artist Russ Ward. It is part Disney, part upcycled machinery and throwaway materials, part medicine show, part Wild West, oodles of nostalgia, and pure imagination. This giant environmental art piece is a series of 22 rooms (along narrow hallways) of diorama miniatures in motion. A week would not

Sandia Ski Area

Travel through Cedar Crest and continue 5.6 miles until you see the sign for Tinkertown, 6 miles north of Tijeras. Make a left turn on NM 536, also known as the Crest Road, which leads to the Sandia Ski Area. Along the way are marvelous hikes. Some are part of a trail system where it is possible to hike all the way to the Crest. My favorite is Tree Springs Trail, a moderate, blessedly green 3-mile hike that in early summer reveals a brilliant display of wild primrose. At the top is a mind-blowing panorama of Albuquerque.

be enough time to appreciate the ornate, dreamlike world of Tinkertown. Put a quarter in a slot in one display and tiny figures sing and dance. The wall of 5,000 bottles embedded in adobe is also a phenomenon. As self-taught artist Russ Ward said, "I did all this while you were watching television." Tinkertown has its roots in handmade displays Ward first brought to fairs and carnivals starting in 1962.

This is a place for the old and the young to marvel together and become ageless. It is a perfect spot for a family outing or picnic. There simply is no other place like it, and the crammed gift shop, the place to stock up on joke gifts, alone is worth the visit. However, to be perfectly honest, the conglomeration of signs, buttons, dolls, and miniature toys might make you a little crazy. If you are at all claustrophobic, do yourself a favor and take a pass.

Although a diversion, if you have the urge, continue on NM 536 for 13.6 miles to the top of 10,687-foot rugged **Sandia Crest**, Albuquerque's landmark east of the city. The **Sandia Crest Scenic Byway** is a refreshing green route in warm weather and a ski destination in winter. In addition to hiking, mountain biking and cross-country skiing are also popular sports here. At the crest is a 100-mile view. This is the destination of the **Sandia Peak Aerial Tramway** as well, which approaches the crest from the Albuquerque side of the mountain. There are also a gift shop, café, and a new restaurant. Note: Beware of the increased altitude up here. Both alcohol and caffeine can more easily affect you and upset your trip if consumed before you are acclimated. The Tram, one of the world's longest, travels through five of the earth's six biozones.

Meanwhile, it's 12.6 miles from Tinkertown, counting the return to NM 14, to the ghost town of **Golden** along the pinon-juniper studded roadway. The big blue sky, decorated with white fluffy clouds breezing by, is as much a part of the visual experience as the roadside. True to its name, this semi-deserted village owes its existence to gold, and more accurately the search for gold. In 1828, 21 years before the California gold rush, gold was discovered in the Ortiz Mountains. Then, in 1839, placer gold was discovered on Tuerto Creek, on the Real de San Francisco. Golden grew up as a result. There mostly local folks with burros panned for gold. The name was changed in 1879 or 1880 when outside mining companies attempted to expand operations, but lack of water hindered that expansion. Some silver and lead ores were mined and sent to England for smelting. But big ambitions flopped, and Golden was pretty much deserted by 1884. Today the **Bottle House** is the town's main attraction, with recycled bottles decorating the structure and trees, to be found across the road from the **Henderson Store**. This store, at 1710 NM 14, Golden, is a highlight of the **Turquoise Trail**. A general store before 1918, it was purchased by the family of the current owners and stands as an emporium of collectible Indian wares.

Near Golden are the ruins of the inaccessible Ancestral Pueblo archaeological site **Pa'ako Pueblo**. However, the name **Pa'ako** has been given to the upscale golf community located along the west side of NM 14, with its unobstructed views of the Ortiz Mountains and Santa Fe–style custom-built residences.

The **Ortiz Mountains** are composed of Tertiary-era intrusions up to 65 million years old, pushed up along the east side of the Rio Grande Rift, with remnants of even earlier rock as well as volcanic matter. Land formations known as the Ortiz Surface existed before the Rio Grande became a continuous river flowing through its current channel.

Mining has been important here since prehistoric times. The indigenous people mined turquoise, which they traded throughout the hemisphere, and lead, for pottery glaze, from **Mount Chalchihuitl**, near **Cerrillos** to the north. Cerrillos turquoise, sometimes in distinctive sea foam green, is especially prized. Lewis Tiffany had mine claims here, declared it the finest turquoise, and popularized the semiprecious stone in jewelry he designed and sold in his Manhattan shop, setting a trend. The Spanish mined silver here in the late 1600's, making Cerrillos the oldest mining community in the country. They had no interest in turquoise; ironically, the Indians had interest neither in silver nor gold.

Up the road 11.4 miles is **Madrid** (MAH-drid)—emphasis on first syllable—unlike the city in Spain. On that drive the volcanic plug, sacred to indigenous people, known as **Cabezon** (the head) is visible on the western horizon. From 1880 onward, Madrid was a coal-mining town, producing both bituminous and anthracite coal, once entirely for sale by the mine superintendent, Oscar Huber. His asking price was $250,000, as advertised in the *Wall Street Journal*. Yet even that price brought no buyers. Huber designed Madrid to be the ideal mining town, with higher living standards for miners and their families, with good housing, medical care, team sports, and holiday celebrations. Abandoned since 1954, artists began rediscovering it in the 1970s, moving in, building galleries, and renovating the miners' houses.

Today Madrid's reinvention seems somewhat over-the-top, with crowds each summer weekend, ginormous RVs lumbering through streets designed for horse-drawn wagons, and pricey real estate. Dozens of art galleries, in diminutive houses that once held humble working miners' families, line the streets, opening their doors to visitors from all over the world, selling everything from garden sculpture to hand-carved flutes, and a mind-boggling variety of locally made jewelry and wares. Two of my favorite shops are **Cowgirl Red**, which has not-unreasonably priced vintage silver and turquoise jewelry, secondhand cowboy boots, and other well-curated items for the urban cowgirl, and **Heaven**, a well-stocked boho boutique featuring lacy, flowing garments you can be sure no one else will be wearing at the next concert, be it the Rolling Stones or the Santa Fe Symphony. Madrid has long been known for its charming Christmas light display. In fact, one legend is that Walt Disney, on a coast-to-coast TWA flight, was inspired by its twinkling lights to create Disneyland. It was known that commercial flights would alter their routes to give passengers a view of the 150,000-light Christmas display. The Oscar Huber Memorial Ball Park was the first lighted ballpark in the state and possibly the nation, built in 1920 for the Madrid Miners, an AA minor league team that was the farm team for the Brooklyn Dodgers. Today it's amusing to watch the crowds amble by from the deck of the ice cream parlor or the patio of the **Mine Shaft Tavern**, a favorite stop of bikers (there is usually a crowd of hogs parked out front). This is one of the oldest ongoing bars in New Mexico, and it was specifically built so miners could stand up straight after working hunched over in the mines all day. The 40-foot-long lodge-pole pine bar is the longest in New Mexico. There has been a tavern on this spot since 1895; the original burned in 1944 and was reopened as the Mine Shaft Tavern in 1947. This is a classic rowdy roadhouse, with live music most weekends, stupendous burgers, and ever-flowing beer. The menu contains locally raised Wagyu burgers that are sourced from Lone Mountain Ranch in Golden. The annual Crawdaddy Blues Fest is held here mid-May and is a great draw for those who love blues and enjoy the fresh crawfish brought in from Texas. It will be obvious from your first look that this town can be so overcrowded on weekends you can safely assume that if you intend to eat here, you are in for a wait. If what you are looking for is coffee and a snack, **Java Junction**, a coffee shop with a bed-and-breakfast upstairs, may fit you to a tee.

The **Old Coal Mine** houses Engine 767, the most complete non-operating steam locomotive in the United States. The coal mineshaft and original mining headquarters are on display.

Only 2 miles beyond Madrid is Cerrillos (Spanish for "little hills"), a sleepy town slowly coming to life. The crammed, dusty old What Not Shop, with shelves stuffed with treasures from abandoned houses and arroyos (previously the site of the Tiffany Bar), has been replaced by the spiffy arcade of **Cerrillos Station**, selling jewelry, local crafts, upscale bath care and housewares, a gallery with monthly opening events, and a spa. The **Black Bird Saloon**, which began life as Tomas De Lallo's saloon, then morphed into a mercantile, serves a fantastic burger, salads, and spirits in a lively atmosphere that evokes saloons of yore. From the pet-friendly patio it is possible to hear the chug of the Southwest Chief as it whistles through town, a reminder of the Cerrillos Coal Railroad Company, constructed in 1892, then sold under foreclosure to the Santa Fe a few years later.

Still, with its adobe architecture and dusty streets essentially intact, the village of Cerrillos has an unmistakable and delicious ghost-town feel, which equates to its irresistible magnetism for artists, photographers, hideaways, wanderers, and souls who don't feel they belong in the 21st century. At **Mary's Bar**, just about as funky and creaky a place as you can find anywhere, you can sip a cold one with a story-telling old-timer or an AWOL Hollywood star without makeup. Cerrillos has long served as a set for movies, like *Young Guns*. Walt Disney discovered it when he filmed the *Nine Lives of Elfego Baca* in 1958. The **Eaves Movie Ranch**, the set of so many Hollywood westerns, is nearby. The town still has its **Casa Grande Trading Post, Petting Zoo & Turquoise Mining Museum**, a good place to bring children to visit and feed the goats or llamas. Admission is free, and animal feed is available for purchase inside the shop. Proprietor Todd Brown mines Cerrillos turquoise from his own claim, and it is available for purchase here, along with handmade jewelry. The 28-room adobe is stocked with rocks and bottles and rusty items that might be from out of *The Pickers*. The scenic overlook outside the operation is worth the trip. Nearby, **Broken Saddle Riding Company** is open year-round and offers rides through **Cerrillos Hills State Park** on Tennessee Walkers and Missouri Foxtrotters.

Yet another famous visitor who spent time in Cerrillos was Thomas A. Edison. He was hired by a mining company to develop a method of extracting placer gold from ore using static electricity, thus conserving scarce water. However, Edison was stumped, and even the great inventor could not

DETOUR

Cerrillos Hills State Park

With 5 miles of hiking trails, Cerrillos Hills State Park is a year-round, day-use park that offers the perfect blend of hiking, history, and awesome views. The 1,000-year documented history of mining in the area is explained, and from a park elevation of 5,900–6,100 feet, the Sandia, Ortiz, Jemez, and Sangre de Cristo Mountain Ranges are all in view. Trails range from easy to moderate.

Galisteo

A backroad cuts across from the Turquoise Trail to **Galisteo** called the **Camino de los Abuelos** (Road of the Grandfathers). This road connects the Turquoise Trail to the village of Galisteo, a very old, very quaint hamlet with art studios, historic church, and a classic Old West cemetery, in the Galisteo Basin. The 25-mile round-trip route, rough in spots, climbs through 1,500 vertical feet of rolling hills with gorgeous views of mountains and mesas on all sides. It also crosses the Southwest Chief rail line that still connects Los Angeles to Chicago along much the same path as the old Route 66 once did. You are unlikely to encounter much, if any, traffic. From Galisteo, it is 22.7 miles back to Santa Fe, and then you would make a loop back to Albuquerque south on I-25, or continue 39.2 miles to I-40, traveling east and west.

figure out how to complete this task. In 1898, He produced the first movie shot in New Mexico: *Indian Day School.*

From Cerrillos, exit and turn left to drive 9 miles north on NM 14 through stunning wind-sculpted red hills to the cozy local spot of the **San Marcos Café & Feed Store,** where peacocks strut the front yard and greet customers with fanfare. Breakfast with fried potatoes and red chile is so good that people from Santa Fe drive here to eat. Further up the road 6 miles is the popular **Santa Fe Brewing Company**, one of the oldest microbreweries in the state, offering weekend tours of its facility. One mile farther and you will arrive at the I-25 interchange.

IN THE AREA

Accommodations

ELAINE'S: A BED AND BREAKFAST, 72 Snowline Road, Cedar Crest. Call 505-281-2467. Website: www.elainesbnb.com. $$.

Attractions and Recreation

BROKEN SADDLE RIDING COMPANY, 26 Vicksville Road, Cerrillos. Call 505-424-7774.

CASA GRANDE TRADING POST, CERRILLOS TURQUOISE MINING MUSEUM & PETTING ZOO, 17 Waldo Street West, Cerrillos. Call 505-438-3008.

CERRILLOS HILLS STATE PARK, County Road 59, Cerrillos. Call 505-474-0196.

CERRILLOS STATION, 15B First Street, Cerrillos. Call 505-474-9326.

COWGIRL RED, 2865 NM 14, Madrid. Call 505-474-0344.

EAST MOUNTAIN CHAMBER OF COMMERCE, 12129 NM 14, North Suite B, Cedar Crest. Call 505-281-1999. Website: www.eastmountainchamber.com.

HEAVEN BOUTIQUE, 2853 NM 14, Madrid. Call 505-474-8359.

J. W. EAVES MOVIE RANCH, NM 14, then west on NM 45, 75 Rancho Alegre Road, Santa Fe. Call 505-474-3045. Website: www.eavesmovieranch.com.

OLD COAL MINE MUSEUM, 2846 NM 14, Madrid. Call 505-473-0743.

SANDIA PEAK SKI AREA. Call 505-242-9052.

SANDIA RANGER DISTRICT VISITOR CENTER, 11776 NM 337, Tijeras. Call 505-281-3304.

VINTAGE RESTORATION CERRILLOS-STYLE

THE BLACK BIRD SALOON IS THE PLACE TO BE ON TURQUOISE TRAIL SUNDAY AFTERNOONS

TINKERTOWN MUSEUM, 121 Sandia Crest Road, Sandia Park. Call 505-281-5233. Website: www.tinkertown.com.

TURQUOISE TRAIL ASSOCIATION, Website: turquoisetrail.org.

Dining and Drinks

BLACK BIRD SALOON, 28 Main Street, Cerrillos. Call 505-438-1821. $$$.

MARY'S BAR, 15A 1st Street, Cerrillos. $.

MINE SHAFT TAVERN, 2846 NM 14, Madrid. Call 505-473-0743. $$–$$$.

SAN MARCOS CAFÉ & FEED STORE, 3877 NM-14, Santa Fe. Call 505-471-9298. $$.

SANTA FE BREWERY & TASTING ROOM, 35 Fire Place, Santa Fe. Call 505-424-3333. $$.

11

THE HIGH ROAD

FORGOTTEN VILLAGES FROM SANTA FE TO TAOS: STORIES
OF SANTEROS, SURVIVAL, AND FAITH

ESTIMATED LENGTH: 56 miles

ESTIMATED TIME: One day

GETTING THERE: From Santa Fe, take US 84/285 north to Espanola 27.3 miles.
Along the way, see the National Cemetery on the left just north of DeVargas
Shopping Center at the intersection of Paseo de Peralta and US 84. The Santa
Fe Opera, with its annual summer repertory festival, is on the right at approximately 6.9 miles. At the Pueblo of Pojoaque, one of the pueblos that nearly
disappeared and, through great effort, was revived during the 20th century, see the Poeh Cultural Center at 16 miles, with the tower that holds the
expressive sculptures of beloved Pueblo artist Roxanne Swentzell. The Poeh
Cultural Center's primary exhibit is a well-crafted journey through time that
tells the story of the indigenous people of the area. Numerous casinos, the
newest being the Tesuque Pueblo casino directly to the south of the Opera,
line the roadway, and beyond that lies the splendid Buffalo Thunder Resort,
with four restaurants and Las Vegas–style gaming, and also with the intriguing bazaar that is the Santa Fe Flea Market directly across the highway during
the warmer months. To the left are the 14-million-year-old Jemez Mountains,
home of Los Alamos, the Secret City, and Bandelier National Monument, as
well as the **Valle Caldera National Monument**, the collapsed volcano caldera
that spewed as far as Kansas when it erupted a million years ago.

HIGHLIGHTS: Santuario de Chimayo

Traveling the 56-mile two-lane **High Road** between **Santa Fe** and **Taos** is
a necessary journey into northern New Mexico's deep and complex past.
Although—and perhaps because—it is slow, inconvenient, and remote, it

LEFT: NOWHERE IS AUTUMN MORE GLORIOUS THAN ALONG THE HIGH ROAD

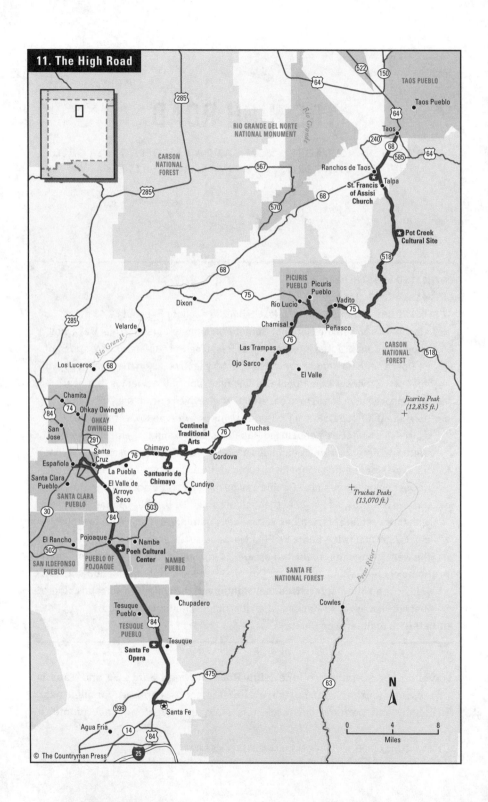

522
150
TAOS PUEBLO
64
Taos Pueblo
285
RIO GRANDE DEL NORTE
NATIONAL MONUMENT
64
CARSON
NATIONAL
FOREST
567
Taos
240
68
585
64
Ranchos de Taos
St. Francis
of Assisi
Church
Talpa
285
68
570
★ Pot Creek
Cultural Site
518
68
PICURIS
PUEBLO
Picuris
Pueblo
75
Dixon
Rio Lucio
Vadito
75
285
Chamisal
Peñasco
Velarde
76
Las Trampas
CARSON
NATIONAL
FOREST
518
Los Luceros
68
Ojo Sarco
El Valle
Jicarita Peak
(12,835 ft.)
Chamita
74
Ohkay Owingeh
OHKAY
OWINGEH
Centinela
Traditional
Arts
76
Truchas
San
Jose
291
Chimayo
76
Santa
Cruz
Cordova
Truchas Peaks
(13,070 ft.)
Española
La Puebla
Santuario de
Chimayo
Santa Clara
Pueblo
El Valle de
Arroyo
Seco
Cundiyo
SANTA CLARA
PUEBLO
503
30
84
Pecos River
El Rancho
Pojoaque
502
Nambe
SAN ILDEFONSO
PUEBLO
PUEBLO OF
POJOAQUE
Poeh Cultural
Center
NAMBE
PUEBLO
SANTA FE
NATIONAL FOREST
Tesuque
Pueblo
Chupadero
Cowles
TESUQUE
PUEBLO
84
Tesuque
Santa Fe
Opera
475
63
N
599
Santa Fe
0   4   8
Agua Fria
14
Miles
84
25

© The Countryman Press

remains authentic. There is no pretense here, and locals are quick to spot it should it appear. There is no push toward change or economic development or anything the outside world might term "progress." The road follows the same path taken by burros for centuries carrying wood down from the mountains. Most of New Mexico is more receptive to visitors than this area. There are few services, and if you should need assistance with your vehicle, it's best to go to the local bar and see who might help you out. Keep in mind people here are savvy. They have to be to survive. They will, of course, peg you for an outsider, but they might take pity on you and fix your flat tire.

But remove satellite dishes, doublewides, and asphalt, and life goes on very much as it in has in these isolated mountain villages since the 18th century. If you want a true gut understanding of New Mexico—its faith, its art, its history, its people and its diverse culture, its beauty and its dark side, a drive here will go a long way toward opening the door to just that. Many inhabitants are descendants of original settlers and Native Americans who traveled and hunted this region for centuries, and who continue to live sustainably on small plots of land. Many of these holdings are remnants of land grants made by the Spanish Crown to encourage habitation on the frontier and combat the Indian invaders. They plant chile—the landrace plant, grown from nonhybridized seeds and traded over the back fence—and beans; water their crops from the *acequias*, the ancient gravity-fed ditch system; raise chickens and sheep; hunt wild game; and fish. They shop at Walmart, and they make their own tortillas; they hunt wild game and forage foods like pinon nuts and chokecherries. Rather than go to the doctor, they rely on the art of *curanderismo*, or herbal cures based on a combination of Native American and ancient Old World knowledge. Barter remains a significant part of the economy, as do traditional crafts of weaving, wood carving, straw inlay, and *colcha* embroidery. Food is preserved by sun drying, and they butcher their own meat. They practice building and auto repair. They are handy and know how to get by.

And most of all, these people of what is termed *manito* culture continue practicing their faith, worshipping in the Spanish mission churches and meeting in the Penitente *moradas*, or chapter houses. They live side by side with contemporary commercial culture, plugging in when they need to, but never giving away their hearts—or their secrets—to the outside world they do not completely trust.

One of those secrets is Crypto-Judaism, a phenomenon that has come to public awareness during the last generation: the belief—and through academic and DNA research, now the knowledge—that many of the families in these villages are descendants of Jews who fled the Spanish Inquisition and came to New Mexico with Juan de Onate and other conquistadors. Over time, they lost most, if not all, their Jewish practice and became devout Catholics, but they kept their Jewish identity alive in fragments of customs.

Today, many of these people consider themselves both Jewish and Catholic. And out of the deep fear instilled by the Inquisition, they maintained—and still maintain—secrecy around this piece of their identity. Their "hiddenness," physically, geographically, and psychologically, is part of their coolness to outsiders.

The Penitente Brotherhood, referred to as the Brothers of Light, or the *Hermanos*, have in New Mexico a history of ascetic practices such as self-flagellation and the actual reenactment of Christ's crucifixion on Good Friday. They continue to function actively today as a lay society responsible for the community's welfare. Their mournful hymns, called *alabados*, are sung from their windowless *morada* meeting houses. While some association continues to be made with the Crypto-Jews, scholar Dr. Stanley Hordes says that in communities where Crypto-Jews lived, there was more likely to be an overlap between cultures.

Espanola is the low rider capital, full of the colorful painted and altered automobiles that are considered a high art in New Mexico; to get there, turn right on NM 76 at Santa Cruz Road to begin the journey up the **High Road**. Pass **El Parasol**, the local place for tacos, where you are just as likely to run into a Hollywood star without makeup as a Sikh in full headgear—**Yogi Bhajan's Sikh Center** is nearby, and next to the drive-in is parent restaurant **El Paragua**. Just beyond is **Santa Cruz**. Go left at McCurdy Street to find the 1733 adobe **La Iglesia de Santa Cruz de la Canada**, one of the oldest churches in the state, which contains some of the earliest and finest regional religious, or *santero*, art. This village was the second permanent settlement in New Mexico, founded in 1695. The village of **Chimayo** is 10 miles further east on NM 76. Galleries, studios, and weaving shops beckon along the narrow road lined with adobe homes, charming gardens, and cottonwood trees. A good bet is **Theresa's Art Gallery** (NM 76 between Espanola and Chimayo), operated out of the home of Theresa and Richard Montoya, artists who paint Spanish colonial-style folk art, displaying a colorful assortment of folk art, Santa Clara Pueblo pottery, and work by local artists.

At 10 miles further, find **Galeria Ortega and Ortega's Weaving Shop** (55 Plaza de Cerro, Chimayo), now in its eighth generation. Loom demonstrations are offered. While 100-percent pure wool jackets and vests may seem pricy, garments are all handmade here and durable enough to last a lifetime, in addition to providing a living for local residents. The name *Chimayo* is derived from the Tewa Indian word meaning "good flaking stone." Founded after the Spanish reconquest of New Mexico in 1692 following the Pueblo Revolt of 1680, Chimayo is home to the 1816 **Santuario de Nuestro Senor de Atocha Chimayo**, the Lourdes of America. It is said that many of those who built the Santuario were Guatamalans who brought their worship of *Escuipalas*; perhaps the tradition of "holy dirt" as their connection to Jesus is connected to their legacy, because they practice the custom of eating clay.

NO VISIT TO THE HIGH ROAD IS COMPLETE WITHOUT A STOP AT THE SANTUARIO DE CHIMAYO

Although this antique building appears rustic and a bit tumble-down, it is precisely built on sacred numerical and geometric principles. If you would like to light a candle in the chapel, you must purchase a regulation candle for $3.50 from the **Santuario Gift Shop** to the right. If you would like to shop for local art, chile, or find a cold drink, the **Vigil Trading Post**, also known as **El Portrero Trading Post**, to the left of the **Santuario** makes for interesting browsing, with its *milagros, retablos*, books, and folk art.

The Santuario is a pilgrimage site that draws 300,000 visitors a year. People come to this place to be healed by the "holy dirt" from the *posito,* or little well, in a back room of the village church. The Good Friday pilgrimage here draws over 30,000 souls, many of whom have traveled great distances, perhaps hundreds of miles. Don Bernardo Abeyta, as the story goes, was making his evening prayers on Good Friday when a shaft of light appeared, leading him to find a crucifix. He returned it to the **Santa Cruz Church** in the town below. After the same thing happened two more times, he understood that he was to build a chapel on this site. Another version of the story tells that he was praying for healing here and found it. Actually, the heavy-beamed adobe Santuario is built on an ancient site where Native American warriors came to bathe in the healing waters.

The art within, including *El Senor de Esquipalas* on the altar, is typical of Spanish mission art, created by *santeros*, often anonymous, with natural materials, such as yucca brushes, earth pigments and plant dyes, on carved cottonwood.

A few blocks to the left of the Santuario, the nearby shrine dedicated to **Santo Nino de Atocha,** built in 1856, is also considered holy. Hundreds of baby shoes represent replacements for those of the Christ child, who is said to wear his out by going around the village performing good deeds at night.

Santo Nino is associated with aid to prisoners, law officials, and the military, and the pilgrimage to the Santuario became popular during World War II, when the young men of these villages serving in the military were captured and forced to go on the Bataan Death March in the Philippines. Only half returned. Hundreds of photos of family members in the police and military line the walls in a tiny room crowded with discarded crutches arrayed around the glass encased figure of Santo Nino. Surrounding the *santo*, or saint figure, are dozens of crutches, supposedly discarded by pilgrims who visited here and received healing. No photos of the church interior, please. It is okay to take photos of the exterior.

Rancho de Chimayo Restaurante, in a thick-walled century-old adobe, is the quintessential New Mexican restaurant and not to be missed. The recipient of a James Beard Culinary Heritage Award, its margaritas are legendary, as are the green and red chile, sopaipillas, and enchiladas. The owner, Florence Jaramillo, known as Mrs. J., presides beside the dining room as the grande dame she is, ensuring all is well with her customers and staff.

Five miles further east up the mountain on NM 76, go 1 mile south to the tiny village of **Cordova**, famous for its unpainted aspen and cedar carved *santos*, a skill passed on through the generations. Carvers open their home studios to visitors. Of note is the **Castillo Gallery**. Another option for purchase is at the Spanish Market, held annually the last weekend in July, on Santa Fe Plaza.

DETOUR

Centenela Traditional Arts

A hand-built traditional family weaving gallery, Centinela Traditional Arts is home to artists Lisa and Irvin Trujillo and their daughter Emily. The humble gallery also carries weavings of a dozen other locals. Much of their work is made of natural dyed wool sheared from churro sheep raised by Irvin's sister. Hand-woven original pieces such as hats, placemats, and coasters are available in all price ranges.

This inconspicuous gallery, located behind an apple orchard and beside an *acequia*, or ditch, actually holds the work of two master weavers who often win first place at the Spanish Market, held the last weekend in July in Santa Fe Plaza, and whose dazzling, complex weavings grace the Smithsonian.

Best of all, Lisa and Irvin are kind, patient people who gladly explain the art of Rio Grande weaving, how they do what they do having come out of a multi-generational family tradition, as well as the place of weaving in their part of northern New Mexico. Lisa is often at work at her loom, and she is happy to demonstrate and explain her creative process.

Driving along, you will see handmade crosses, some stark, some colorful and highly ornamented, along the roadside and affixed to fences. Known as *descansos*, these roadside memorials mark the place where someone lost their life, usually in a car wreck, and are a vital part of the living folk culture of New Mexico. Each *descanso* tells a story, marks a life, and informs us that a departed loved one is still missed and remembered. The term *descanso* originally referred to a stopping place for the pallbearers between the rural church where a funeral was held and the cemetery. In New Mexico, *descansos* are protected by law and it is a crime to deface them in any way.

Continue climbing NM 76 into the **Sangre de Cristo Mountains** toward the staggering **Truchas Peaks**, 13,070 feet. **Jicarita Peak** (12,835 feet) is sacred to the Picuris Indians. While the name means "little cup," there is a creation story that the mountain was originally a basket the Great Spirit turned upside down, and from it came all the things of this world. Take time at turnouts to enjoy dramatic overlooks. Reach the town of **Truchas** (trout) at 4 miles beyond Cordova. At the junction of NM 76 and CR 75, find the High Road Marketplace, Artists Co-op, & Gallery, (1642 NM 76) a nonprofit community store representing 70 local traditional and contemporary artists in every imaginable medium, from clay to weaving to woodcarving to punched tin in every price range. The last two weekends of September offer a self-guided Artists' Studio Tour. Along the way, see the Cardona-Hine Fine Art Gallery at 82 NM 76, which features the transcendental work of Los Angeles artists Alvaro Cardona-Hine and Barbara McCauley, contemporary fine artists who located themselves here almost four decades ago, and the old Mercantile building, now serving coffee and baked goods. Robert Redford set the film *Milagro Beanfield War*, based on New Mexico author John Nichols' classic novel and directed by Redford, in this village. Continue on NM 76 14.5 miles to **Penasco**, the largest High Road village, which has gas, an ATM, and the fine **Sugar Nymphs Bistro**, known for its dishes made from scratch with local ingredients, such as soups, stews, desserts, and burgers. The chocolate maple pecan pie is the signature dish, but the towering three-layer chocolate cake is irresistible. This brainchild of two female chefs who learned and practiced their craft in the Bay area has garnered four-star reviews from prestigious food magazines, whose foodie critics somehow found their way up here. Continue driving through the **Carson National Forest**, with its stands of pine, pinon, and juniper, along with thick evergreen at higher elevations. Altogether, the Carson is a million and a half acres of four-season recreation that includes **Wheeler Peak**, the state's highest mountain at 13,171 feet.

Along the way, see the villages of **Las Trampas**, **El Valle**, **Chamisal**, **Ojo Sarco**, and **Vadito**. These are quiet, private places where families reside, and they are, frankly, not particularly welcoming to "outsiders."

From Penasco, take NM 75 3.3 miles north to **Picuris Pueblo**. Here, locate the historic restored **San Lorenzo de Picurís** church and the **Picuris Pueblo**

Museum and gift shop. The Pueblo is known for its gold-flecked mica pottery. Haunting Matachine Dances, a traditional masked dance-drama pageant representing conquest, is performed annually throughout New Mexico, largely around the holidays, and in Picuris on December 24–25.

Following the swings and curves of the road through the Carson National Forest, come to **Pot Creek Cultural Site,** only 9 miles From Taos on NM 518. Open late June through early September, Wednesday to Sunday, an easy 1-mile trail leads to a reconstructed pueblo. This site was inhabited by Ancestral Pueblo people between BCE 1100 and CE 1300. Many pots were found here when the Spanish arrived, hence the name.

From here back to Taos is a short drive, only about 24 miles. The road continues following the curvatures of the earth, along the path of least resistance, was clearly designed more for burro-drawn carts and buggies.

At 18 miles from **Picuris Pueblo** is **Fort Burgwin**, the summer home of Southern Methodist University, which presents lectures and music during warm months. It is also the remains of an actual fort. In approximately 6 miles, keep an eye open for a gate post marked with numerous taillights at Espinoza Road. Go right. The adobe building is a Penitente *morada*, and behind it is the Jesus Nazarene Cemetery. Should you choose to venture out there, you will find the grave of actor Dennis Hopper, a Taos resident who inhabited the **Mabel Dodge Luhan House** and remains venerated as a folk hero for the emblematic road film celebrating the spirit of the 1960s, *Easy Rider*, which he directed, co-wrote, and co-starred in with Peter Fonda, both actors playing archetypal rebel dropouts.

Continue on NM 518 for 1 mile to the junction with NM 68 and go right to **Ranchos de Taos.** In a mile or so, to the right, find **Ranchos Plaza** and the highly recognizable bulk of the adobe **St. Francis de Assis Church**, a.k.a. **Ranchos Church**. This is the most painted and photographed church in America, made famous by Georgia O'Keeffe and Ansel Adams. Its curvilinear adobe buttresses are maintained by the community, which each June 4 performs an annual "mudding" to maintain it. A few other galleries and cafés occupy the Plaza. Ranchos de Taos is actually one of three entities that came together to form what we call Taos today, including **Taos Pueblo** and **Don Fernando Plaza** (Central Taos). Continue north 4 miles on Paseo del Pueblo Norte to arrive at Taos.

IN THE AREA

Accommodations

CASA ESCONDIDA, CR-100, Chimayo. Call 505-351-4805. Website: www .casaescondida.com. $$$.

RANCHO MANZANA, 26 Camino de Mision, Chimayo. Call 505-351-2227. Website: www.ranchomanzana.com. $$.

Attractions and Recreation

CARSON NATIONAL FOREST, 208 Cruz Alta Road, Taos. Call 575-758-6200.

EL SANTUARIO DE CHIMAYO (OR THE SANTUARIO), 15 Santuario Drive, Chimayo; northeast of Santa Fe 25 miles on US 84/285 to Espanola; turn east on NM 76, follow signs. Call 505-351-4889. Website: www .elsantuariodechimayo.us.

GALERIA ORTEGA AND ORTEGA'S WEAVING SHOP, 55 Plaza de Cerro, Chimayo.

HIGH ROAD MARKET PLACE ARTISTS' CO-OP AND GALLERY, 1642 NM 76.

HOLY CROSS CHURCH, 26 South McCurdy Road, Santa Cruz.

SAN JOSE DE GRACIA DE LAS TRAMPAS, Las Trampas. NM 76, 46 miles northeast of Santa Fe.

SIPAPU SKI AND SUMMER RESORT, 5224 NM 518, Vadito, 25 miles southeast of Taos via NM 68 and NM 518. Call 800-587-2240. Website: sipapunm .com.

Dining and Drinks

EL PARAGUA, 603 Santa Cruz Road, Espanola. Call 505-753-3211. $$–$$$.

RANCHO DE CHIMAYO, 300 Juan Medina Road, Chimayo. Call 505-351-4444. $$–$$$.

SUGAR NYMPHS BISTRO, 15046 NM 75, Penasco. Call 575-587-0311. $$–$$$$.

Events

ANNUAL GOOD FRIDAY PILGRIMAGE, Chimayo.

A MORNING STROLL TO THE HILLSBORO POST OFFICE PROVIDES
MEDITATIVE FITNESS TIME TAKEN AT YOUR OWN PACE

SOUTHWEST

12

BLACK RANGE

SEEKING SILVER CITY: GHOST TOWNS AND FORGOTTEN
GLORY IN THE GILA

ESTIMATED LENGTH: From Truth or Consequences to Silver City across the Black
Range on NM 152 is 88 miles; from I-25 Silver City is 75 miles. The Silver City
I-25 exit is 13 miles south of Truth or Consequences.

ESTIMATED TIME: Half-day

GETTING THERE: Starting from Truth or Consequences, visit the Geronimo Trail
headquarters at Foch Street for information.

HIGHLIGHTS: The ghost towns of Hillsboro and Kingston are loaded with gold
mining history and crumbling wood and adobe buildings alluring to photographers; thrilling panoramic views from the 55-mile-long Black Range (also
known as the Devil's Range or Sierra Diablo) within the Aldo Leopold Wilderness of the Gila National Forest

---

This land was once inhabited by the Mimbres (willow) people, related to the
Mogollon, considered early Puebloan people, who dwelled in these mountains and along the Mimbres river, known for their classic black-and-white
pottery. It was also the territory of warrior-shaman Geronimo, descendent
of the Mescalero and Chiracaua Apache tribe, during the 19th century; his
determination led his people in remaining the last holdouts against American expansion.

Cross 8,000-foot **Emory Pass** in low gear to navigate the steep, steady
climb of 8 miles from Kingston to Emory Pass. Then come the sweeping
turns downhill to NM 61 at San Lorenzo. From there see the rolling hills
leading into **Silver City.** The descent through the ponderosa forest is wonderful. Continue the descent west through Gallinas Canyon, which has dramatic rock formations. *Bicycling Magazine* has written up the ride as one

of the great climbs in the country. Find views of the Hurley open-pit mine and Kneeling Nun rock formation along the way. William Emory, a topographical engineer, with Kit Carson as a guide, charted this remote area proximate to the Continental Divide with the Army of the West in 1846. You will be traveling along the southern portion of the **Geronimo Trail National Scenic Byway.** A century ago, this was the summer land of the Chiracauhua Warm Springs Apaches. Magnificent scenery highlights this curvy drive through the Black Range and over the 8,200-foot Emory Pass. The Vista Point at Emory Pass is a handicap-accessible place to take a break and enjoy the eye-popping views. Restroom, tables, and grill are available at the Vista, also a trailhead.

Starting in the town of **Caballo** just south of **Truth or Consequences**, the

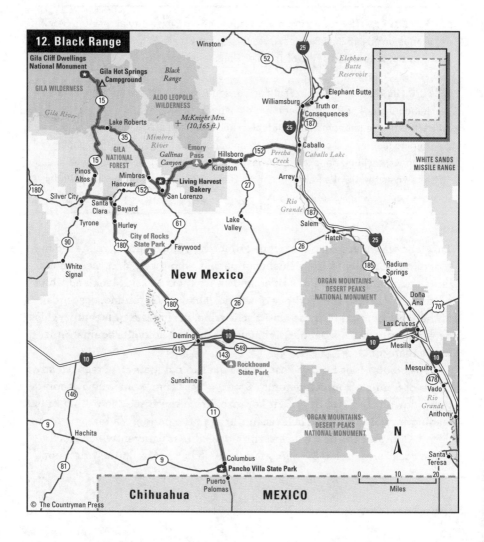

road snakes along, dips and climbs from 4,100 to 5,140 feet as it heads west to Silver City. From I-25 to Silver City is 75 miles.

From **T or C**, travel 13 miles on I-25 south to the NM 152 exit. Go right. Be prepared to travel slowly with extreme caution over the shoulderless switchbacks of **Emory Pass**. Allow time to browse the ghost towns of **Hillsboro** and **Kingston** and to take photos from the summit of McKnight Mountain at 10,165 feet. There is no cell phone coverage between Hillsboro and Silver City.

From the I-25 exit, go 17 miles on NM 152 to Hillsboro (once the center of gold and silver mining activity and the gateway to the Black Range. Or take the backroad, NM 187, from T or C down to **Caballo Lake State Park**.

It doesn't take long, once you leave the main highway, to know you are headed for somewhere long ago and faraway. In fact, the Old West is only a whisper away here. It only happened yesterday, it seems. Over $6 million in precious metal was extracted here back in the day, when as many as 10,000 prospectors lived here. Cowboys drew from a hat for the honor of naming it. Hillsboro was well on its way to becoming a true ghost town when it was discovered by a few urbanites who moved in and fixed up the old houses, built between 1877 and 1940, or built new ones indistinguishable from vintage properties. Turning first from mining, then to ranching, it became celebrated as a center for apple growing, before settling into its current station as home to artists, old-timers, and visitor's intent on exploring every corner of the state. The **Hillsboro Café**, in addition to serving homemade food and coffee, with daily specials, is an excellent place to meet those old-timers, who may stroll in with spurs on, and who, with a little patient prodding, may part with their tales. Biscuits and gravy, steak specials, and healthy portions of healthy food may make this your dream come true of a roadside café. The Black Range Museum was once home to British-born madam Sadie Orchard, local lady of the night with a heart of gold. She served the town during epidemics, donated to good causes, and ran a stagecoach line. The museum tells the story of Sierra County's early days with an emphasis on mining. Hillsboro was the county seat for 30 years and the site of one of the state's most famous, or infamous, trials: that of Oliver Lee for the murder of Judge Albert Fountain and his son Henry, which brought Sheriff Pat Garret to town and remains unsolved to this day. **Percha Creek Traders** is a co-op gallery featuring a few dozen local artists who do clay, photography, weaving, and quilting. It is a stop on the New Mexico Fiber Arts Trail. **Black Range Vineyards** specializes in New Mexico vintages, gourmet snacks and occasional live music. The road to **Lake Valley**, a deserted silver mining town, winds out of Hillsboro.

It's only 9 miles west down NM 152 through the Box Canyon of Percha Creek and dramatic rock formations to a for-real ghost town, Kingston, where a sign proclaims THE SPIT AND WHITTLE CLUB DWELLS HERE. Hard as

NO MATTER HOW YOU GET THERE, THE HILLSBORO CAFÉ IS WELL WORTH THE TRIP

it is to believe, this spot in 1890 was a rip-snortin' mining town of 7,000 with 22 saloons, plus brothels and banks and the distinction of being New Mexico's largest city. Even the most famous singer of her day, Lillian Russell, performed here with her troupe. The **Percha Bank Museum and Gallery** is the only intact building remaining from those days, and it offers an education on what it was like to live here back then.

When **Las Cruces** native Catherine Wanek drove here from **Los Angeles** on her honeymoon, she spotted the old mining hotel called the **Black Range Lodge** and fell in love with it. She and her new husband decided to buy it on the spot. She turned this rather dark, out-of-the-English-countryside lodge into a merry B&B. Massive stone walls and log-beamed ceilings date to 1940, but the original building dates to the 1880s, when it was built to house miners and cavalry. Cyclists and tourists from all over the world are drawn here to enjoy Wanek's informal hospitality, her breakfast buffet featuring preserves made from apples and plums from her orchard on home-baked bread, and her claw-foot tubs. Catherine has become a well-known authority on straw bale construction and has built several straw bale buildings on her premises, including an all-natural meeting room that hosts live music, talks, films, and special events.

If you are planning on driving the entire **Geronimo Trail Scenic Byway**, which begins in **T or C** and loops back at **San Lorenzo** on NM 152, plan for an all-day trip at 220 miles, and you may want to overnight in Kingston. At the intersection of NM 152 and NM 356 is the small, easy-to-miss Santa Rita Shrine, fronted by a memorial to Vietnam veterans killed in action. Be on the lookout for the rock formation landmark known as the Kneeling Nun looming over the massive strip mine.

The journey across Emory Pass to Silver City begins in 8 miles as you leave Kingston and gain altitude. Travel 48.5 miles to Silver City, a drive of one hour and 20 minutes, an excellent base for exploring the Gila Cliff Dwellings; attending the many annual arts, music and food festivals; and enjoying birds and other wildlife. In 1821, this area changed from Spanish

BLACK RANGE LODGE IN THE GHOST TOWN OF KINGSTON PROVIDES RUSTIC COMFORT WITH HOMEGROWN PRESERVES AND CLAW-FOOT TUBS

to Mexican control; then, in 1853, it became an American territory with the signing of the Gadsden Purchase.

Silver City, population 10,000 and elevation 6,000 feet, originally the site of an Apache encampment, has two museums; Western New Mexico State University; an abundance of artist studios, galleries, and cafés; and an historic downtown to explore. Founded in 1870 and named for rich silver deposits west of town, its period architecture is well preserved, with dozens of Queen Anne and Victorian homes to admire. It is one of the most pet-friendly places you will ever visit. Billy the Kid, known then as Henry Antrim, roamed these streets when he was growing up, as did Butch Cassidy and the Wild Bunch. Billy's mother, Catherine Antrim, is buried in Silver City in the Memory Lane Cemetery. The Visitor Center parking lot holds a log cabin from a movie set for *The Missing* that replicates the sort of place Billy would have lived in. Two historic downtown hotels, the Palace, a Victorian brick, and the art deco Murray Hotel, are of interest. A popular walking and birding area is Big Ditch Riverwalk Park, with the feel of a small forest hidden away in town. A series of devastating floods between 1895 and 1910 washed away the original Main Street and created a Big Ditch. Businesses started using their back door entrances on Bullard Street, and eventually Bullard became the new Main Street.

Silver City has something of a dual nature; the town seems divided between newcomers like tourists and amenity migrants and old-time copper miners. If you just stay in the downtown, you may not be aware this town continues to struggle with issues of poverty, unemployment, addiction, and

San Lorenzo

Cross the Mimbres River at San Lorenzo, pass the intersection with NM 61 to Deming on the left, and begin climbing again.

Notice: Regarding San Lorenzo, serious ghost town hunters only need apply to visit here. You won't need a 4WD vehicle on this narrow road, but a high clearance vehicle is a must. With a population under 100, the post office founded in 1876–77 is closed. If you are a true New Mexico aficionado addicted to the beauty of deserted places, you'll want to be able to say, "been there, done that." And the visit to Living Harvest Bakery, located on the east bank of the Mimbres River, makes the trip so worthwhile. The devoutly Christian congregation who live and bake here (using only the freshest of grains) operate a bakery that serves breakfast and lunch Tues.–Sat. 7 a.m.–noon. They also sell their flour and baked goods at the Las Cruces Growers market on Saturday. There is a ranching community on NM 180, 10 miles east of Santa Rita, founded in 1714 by Governor Juan Ignacio Flores Mogollon. Deming served as a military outpost during American occupation.

health problems specific to miners. The downtown, loaded as it is with galleries, cafés, microbreweries, and one of the state's oldest food co-ops, may seem at first like the place where old hippies never die, they just retire and write poetry and play the guitar. The Chino Mine, also known as the Santa Rita Mine, an immense strip mine, is located 15 miles east of town on NM 152. The 1950s film *Salt of the Earth,* about miners organizing, was made here.

The Silver City Museum, a brick Mansard-Italianate style home built by prospector Harry Ailman in 1880, showcases local history exhibits. Western New Mexico University is a hidden treasure housing the largest collection of prehistoric Mimbres black on white pottery in the nation. Casas Grande pottery, mining artifacts, prehistoric tools and jewelry are also on display.

Gila Cliff Dwellings National Monument is 44 miles north of Silver City along the Trail of the Mountain Spirits Scenic Byway. Take N 15 north from Silver City into the Gila National Monument for 115 miles through **Pinos Altos**, Lake Roberts, Mimbres River and the Santa Rita open pit copper mine. Allow at least two hours.

The **Gila Hot Springs Campground** is a private business owned by Allen and Carla Campbell. It offers camping and natural hot spring pools beside the Gila River in southwest New Mexico. The springs vary in temperature from 147° to 154°F and are considered sweet springs (no sulphur odor). It is located 40 miles north of Silver City and about 4 miles from the Gila Cliff Dwellings National Monument, declared a national monument in 1907 by President Theodore Roosevelt. The area is surrounded by the **Gila Wilderness** and the larger **Gila National Forest.**

Festivals of Silver City

Silver City loves to celebrate itself and does so almost monthly with a cornucopia of joyous festivals.

February brings Chocolate Fantasia, when the town paints itself chocolate. Downtown businesses give the stuff away, and chocolate artists from near and far show off their finest, most fanciful creations. There are tastings, contests and more. It's an absolute must-do for the chocoholic, and a warm-up for Valentine's Day. The theme of 2019 was Children's Storybook Fantasia.

May is time for Tour of the Gila, a major bike race of 10,000 feet of climbs and a thrilling in-town high-speed contest that draws Olympians. Silver City has almost as many cyclists as artists. It is a stop on the USA Cycling Pro Road Tour.

May is also Blues Fest, a perfect way to celebrate spring; this celebrated weekend of blues and jazz is free.

July is Clay Fest, when the town celebrates its abundance of potters and clay artists who may trace their artistic lineage all the way back to the indigenous Mogollon makers. Get your hands dirty and throw a pot and shop among the most diverse work in clay imaginable.

September is time for Gila River Fest, with river events and education about the life force that nourishes wildlife and civilization in this part of the world. In October is the juicy Festival of the Written Word, a multicultural, diverse showcase of journalism, theater, poetry, and fiction with readings, roundtables and performance.

December brings a Victorian Christmas to the Silver City Museum, in time for the holiday spirit in this most Victorian of towns.

A short drive from the visitor center along the West Fork of the Gila River, a 1-mile loop leads through the dwellings, natural caves fashioned into 40 rooms with stone quarried by the indigenous farmers who lived here starting in CE 100 to 400. These Mogollon people raised squash, corn, and beans on the mesa tops and along the river, also making exquisite black and white pottery between the 1280s and the 1300s.

The trail actually passes through rooms used by the ancient Puebloans as it rises 180 feet above the Gila River, gleaming on the canyon floor. A drought in the 13th century probably drove them out. The trail is steep in places, with a 180-foot elevation gain above the river, making for a lovely, shady walk during which to contemplate the spirits of the ancients.

Back at NM 35 junction, follow the road east along Sapello (Spanish for "little toad") Creek toward Lake Roberts for 63 miles until you reach the lake. Continue down NM 35 along the Mimbres River into the valley.

Leave Silver City for **Las Cruces** via US 180, and then go 56 miles to Deming, a town named for a woman. Deming is named after Mary Ann Deming Crocker, wife of railroad industrialist Charles Crocker, known for her good works in the area. A silver spike was driven here in 1881 to

Gila National Forest

Measuring over 3.3 million acres—the nation's sixth largest national forest—the vast Gila National Forest is beyond compare in its diversity and recreational opportunities. Terrain ranges from high desert at 4,200 feet to rugged mountain and canyon lands at 10,900 feet. Four of planet Earth's six life zones may be found here. "Gila" is a Spanish corruption for a Yuma Indian word meaning "running water that is salty." Birding, hiking, camping—in mostly primitive settings, but also with RV hookups—is all here, at all levels, especially birding. Nearly 400 species make this their habitat. The forest includes the Gila Wilderness and the **Aldo Leopold Wilderness**, the nation's first wilderness, founded in 1924 and named in honor of the great environmentalist. This area is considered a significant bird habitat and contains a New Mexico Birding Trail. Vegetation switches from pinon-juniper to mixed conifer; wildlife includes black bear, wild turkey, mule deer, and javelina, a hairy native mammal also known as a peccary or skunk pig; many switchbacks make travel in winter chancy and not a good idea to attempt after dark (always check conditions before you go). A section of the Continental Divide Trail lies within the forest. In recent years, fire has devastated much of the Gila.

SIDE TRIP

Pinos Altos

Located 6 miles north of Silver City on NM 15, **Pinos Altos** (tall pines) sits directly on the Continental Divide. Walking into this town is like walking into an unchanged corner of the Old West. Splendidly decaying weathered wooden buildings mean it doesn't take much imagination to imagine a duel—or a hanging—on Main Street. Here the Hearst Mine found and supplied the gold for the Hearst Castle. Stroll about and find an occasional ice cream parlor or rock shop that may be open. A good reason to make the trip is to dine at the **Buckhorn Saloon**. This 1860s establishment is saturated with Old West flavor, embedded in the foot-and-a-half thick adobe walls. Dine in Victorian elegance or be like the locals and belly up to the Old West bar. Steaks are served with fresh sourdough bread, and there are live entertainment shows on weekends. **Bear Creek Motel and Cabins** is the place to stay.

SIDE TRIP

Bayard Historical District

Located 9 miles east of Silver City via US 180 and owned by Phelps Dodge Mining Company, you'll find the Bayard Historical District, where the six underground shafts of this once bustling mining district produced more gold, silver, copper, lead, zinc, iron manganese, and molybdenum than all other NM mining districts combined. The area may be toured by automobile. It is popular with mountain bikers, horseback riders, and birders. Buffalo Soldiers, the African American troops of the 9th Cavalry, were stationed here from 1866 to 1899. Tour information available at Bayard City Hall.

commemorate the meeting of the Southern Pacific with the AT&SF railroad and the second transcontinental railroad line. Today Deming is a quiet place of 14,000, peopled largely by retirees and snowbirds, that bills itself as Rockhound's Paradise, although it remains a center of ranching and farming activity. The town's big event used to be the Deming Duck Race, but now it is the annual Rockhound Roundup, held in March, generally coordinated with Pancho Villa Day, in honor of the Mexican revolutionary who "invaded" the United States by crossing the border at **Columbus**, 32 miles on NM 11 to the south.

A worthwhile attraction is the **Deming Luna Mimbres Museum**, with a quilt room, a doll room with over 600 antique dolls, the military room with mementos of the Pancho Villa Raid, and the Indian kiva, with outstanding Mimbres pottery and native basketry. The museum is housed in a 1916 armory with a motorized chairlift. It also holds the "silver spike" mentioned above. Another worthwhile stop is the mothership of St. Clair Vineyards. Tours are offered Saturday and Sunday, and tastings are generous with a

DETOUR

Pancho Villa State Park

Columbus is now where many US citizens cross over to Mexico in quest of cheaper dental services and prescription drugs than they can find at home. However, its main attraction is Pancho Villa State Park, with a visitor center doubling as a museum about Mexican revolutionary Villa's March 9, 1916, invasion in which 17 Americans perished in the Battle of Columbus. General John J. Pershing pursued Villa with a force of 10,000 as well as an early version of a tank (on display at the center), on top of automobiles and airplanes that provided a trial run for US involvement in WWI, but Villa eluded the force and was never captured.

free glass of the wine of the month plus tastes of two additional wines. Cabernet, Chardonnay, Zinfandel, and sparkling wines are made here. Nearby **Adobe Deli Steakhouse** has been featured on food TV and is known for the décor of wall-to-wall mounted heads and more importantly, for sublime sandwiches on freshly baked bread and signature onion soup.

To visit **Rockhound State Park,** go south 5 miles on NM 11, then east on NM 141 for 9 miles. Each visitor is permitted a haul of 25 pounds of rocks and can select among jasper, perlite and geodes. Return to the main road and continue to **City of Rocks State Park** on US 180 (24 miles from Deming, should you skip Rockhound), then 4 miles northeast on NM 61 leads to City of Rocks State Park With the feel of a natural Stonehenge, monumental rock formations—pillars of 34.9-million-year-old, wind-sculpted volcanic ash as high as 40 feet—are separated by paths to give the feeling of a city. A premier dark skies location, there is an astronomy observatory that offers frequent starry-night programs. Truly surreal. Right next to City of Rocks is **Faywood Hot Springs Resort** at 165 NM 61, with over a dozen shaded outdoor, natural geothermal mineral water soaking pools, both public and private. Overnight guests may use public pools all night. "Limp in, leap out" is the motto here. Faywood offers cabins, RV hookups, and tent sites.

From here it's 86.4 miles further along NM 80 and I-10, the high lonesome road that shoots straight as a bowling lane through dry empty stretches of creosote, ocotillo, yucca, and tumbleweed along the road to **Las Cruces,** home of New Mexico State University's Aggies and the attractions of the Mesilla Valley: New Mexico Farm and Ranch Heritage Museum, Mesilla Plaza, the state's best Mexican food, and high desert hiking at **Organ Mountains Desert Peaks National Monument**, whose 496,000 acres surround Las Cruces. Our nation's newest protected area features recreational opportunities like strolling through desert nature trails and the chance to encounter petroglyph and archeological sites, with Picacho Peak Recreation Area within it, as well as the remarkable Farmer's and Craft Market downtown on Saturday mornings.

IN THE AREA

Accommodations

BEAR MOUNTAIN LODGE, 80 Bear Mountain Road, Silver City. Call 575-538-2538. $$$$.

BLACK RANGE LODGE, 119 Main Street, Kingston. Call 575-895-5652. Website: www.blackrangelodge.com. $$.

Attractions and Recreation

BAYARD HISTORICAL DISTRICT, 9 miles east of Silver City via US 180. Call 575-537-3327.

GERONIMO TRAIL VISITOR CENTER, 301 South Foch Street., Truth or Consequences. Call 575-894-1968. Website: geronimotrail.com.

GILA NATIONAL FOREST RANGER DISTRICT, HC 68 Box 50, Mimbres. Call 575-536-2250. Website: www.fs.usda.gov/detail/gila/about-forest /districts/?cid=fse_006126.

GILA NATIONAL FOREST SUPERVISOR'S OFFICE, 13005 East Camino del Bosque, Silver City. Call 575-388-8201.

PERCHA BANK MUSEUM AND GALLERY, 119b Main Street, Kingston.

SILVER CITY VISITOR CENTER, 201 North Hudson, Silver City. Call 575-538-5555. Website: silvercitytourism.org.

WESTERN NEW MEXICO UNIVERSITY MUSEUM, Light Hall Theater, 1000 West College Avenue, Silver City. Call 575-538-6386.

Dining and Drinks

ADOBE DELI STEAKHOUSE, 3970 Lewis Flats Road, Deming. $$.

DIANE'S RESTAURANT, 510 North Bullard, Silver City. Call 575-538-8722, Website: dianesrestaurant.com. $$$. Across the street at 601 North Bullard is Diane's Bakery and Deli, with takeout sandwiches, 20 kinds of artisan breads, and more.

HILLSBORO GENERAL STORE CAFÉ, 0697 Highway 152, Hillsboro. Call 575-895-5306. $$.

JALISCO CAFÉ, 103 South Bullard, Silver City. Call 575-388-2060. $$.

LITTLE TOAD CREEK BREWERY & DISTILLERY, 200 North Bullard, Silver City. Call 575-956-6144. $$.

ST. CLAIR VINEYARDS, 1325 De Baca Road, Deming. $$.

THE RIO GRANDE
IN LOS ALAMOS

NORTHWEST

13

THE OLD SPANISH TRAIL

A WOVEN ROAD FROM ABIQUIU TO CHAMA

ESTIMATED LENGTH: 58.6 miles

ESTIMATED TIME: Half-day

GETTING THERE: Climbing past the National Cemetery, Opera Hill, Camel Rock, Buffalo Thunder Resort and the Poeh Cultural Center out of Santa Fe, drive north on US 84/ US 285 to Espanola. In Espanola, go left at Junction US 84/ US 285 north to Abiquiu. Cross Rio del Oso (river of the bear). Pass Northern New Mexico Community College on the right, see Ohkay Owingeh Pueblo on right in 3 miles. Along the shoulder of this road is the location where photographer Ansel Adams in 1941 shot his revolutionary black and white photograph, "Moonrise, Hernandez, New Mexico" in 1941. Also notice outdoor beehive adobe ovens known as *hornos* and decorated roadside memorials known as *descansos* (meaning "resting place") along the way, characteristic markers of northern New Mexico backroads. In 8 miles, reach the Rio Chama, a tributary of the Rio Grande. Dry washes intersect sand hills as the striking scenery for which this high desert country is renowned comes into view. Huge fluffy white clouds scud across brilliant blue skies contrasting with pink, gold, and rose layered cliffs and basalt-capped mesas. This road follows the Chama River through the valley. In early spring, if the rains have come and snow has watered the land, a bouquet of brilliant wildflowers adorn emerald meadows. Just past the village of Medanales (a family name or the name for sand dunes), enter the Santa Fe National Forest. Medanales is 8 miles before Abiquiu. In 2 miles after this village, to the right notice the crumbling adobe mission church of Santa Rosa de Lima, the first New World saint canonized, situated overlooking the Rio Chama and dating to 1744. Sublimely peaceful or eerily haunted, depending on your perspective, this venerable site emanates both the faith and the handmade labor that created

LEFT: ALL ABOARD THE CUMBRES & TOLTEC!

it, invoking the hard lives of the farmers who struggled in this outpost for survival and attempted to defend their land from continual Indian attacks. The church was in use until the 1930s. Built in the 1730s by early settlers along the Old Spanish Trail, this site marks the beginning of cohesive Abiquiu Genizaro Pueblo history.

HIGHLIGHTS: Ghost Ranch, Georgia O'Keeffe Home, Cumbres & Toltec Railroad, Purple Adobe Lavender Farm, Tierra Wools

---

In 1828, Santa Fe merchant Antonio Armijo assembled 60 men and 100 mules for the journey to San Gabriel Mission in California. His route became the road known as the Old Spanish Trail, and it created a landline between Spanish provinces. Mountain men Kit Carson and Lucien B. Maxwell traveled this route. It originally ran 2,700 miles from Santa Fe to Los Angeles to move woolen goods and sheep to California to trade for horses. In 1848, it ended when the Treaty of Guadalupe Hidalgo and the California Gold Rush opened wagon trail routes. Called "the longest, crookedest, most arduous pack mule route in the history of America," it has three branches, one based on ancient Native American foot paths. Armijo camped along the Animas River near what is today the Aztec Ruins in Aztec, New Mexico, on the southern branch of the trail (see Chapter 15).

The original trailhead is on the site of what is today **Bode's General Store** in **Abiquiu.** It was also a slave trafficking route. *Genizaros*, or detribalized Indians in California, were sold or traded as slaves in the New Mexico market. There they were assimilated into households and ranchos of Spanish settlers and converted to Catholicism.

But the history of this place is utterly ancient. Dinosaur and fossil remains found in these cliffs, denoting ancient ocean beds, date back 300 million years and more. Paleo people roamed here 12,000 years ago. Ancestral Tewa people and bands of Ute, Navajo, Jicarilla, Apache, and Comanche nomads hunted, farmed, and traded here.

About 3 miles further, find the **Abiquiu Inn.** This gracious Southwest-style lodge has 25 rooms, including private casitas, and offers classes, workshops, lectures, and tours.

Abiquiu is perhaps best known for the **Georgia O'Keeffe Home and Studio.** O'Keeffe's residence is walled and cannot be seen from the road; however, you can book a tour at the **O'Keeffe Welcome Center**, which runs eight tours daily, maximum twelve participants. Tours run Tuesday through Saturday from first week of March through the third week of November. Tours are best reserved at least two weeks in advance. However, you could get lucky if you just drop in.

Just beyond the Abiquiu Inn and O'Keeffe Welcome Center is Bode's General Store (21196 US 84). A gas station for more than a century, Bode's is

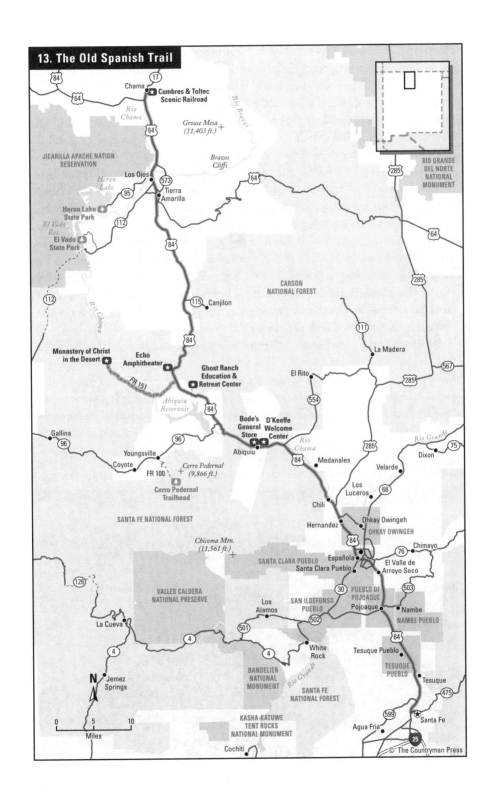

13. The Old Spanish Trail

84

17

Chama

Cumbres & Toltec
Scenic Railroad

64

Rio Chama

Grouse Mesa
(11,403 ft.)

64

Rio Brazos

Brazos
Cliffs

285

RIO GRANDE
DEL NORTE
NATIONAL
MONUMENT

JICARILLA APACHE NATION
RESERVATION

Los Ojos

573

64

Heron
Lake

95

Tierra
Amarilla

Heron Lake
State Park

112

El Vado
Res.

El Vado
State Park

84

CARSON
NATIONAL FOREST

285

64

112

Rio Chama

115

Canjilon

84

111

La Madera

567

Monastery of Christ
in the Desert

Echo
Amphitheater

FR 151

Ghost Ranch
Education &
Retreat Center

El Rito

285

Abiquiu
Reservoir

84

554

Bode's
General
Store

O'Keeffe
Welcome
Center

Gallina

96

96

Youngsville

Abiquiu

Rio
Chama

285

Rio Grande

75

Medanales

Dixon

Coyote

FR 100

Cerro Pedernal
(9,866 ft.)

84

Velarde

Cerro Pedernal
Trailhead

Los
Luceros

68

SANTA FE NATIONAL FOREST

Chili

Hernandez

Ohkay Owingeh

OHKAY OWINGEH

Chicoma Mtn.
(11,561 ft.)

84

Chimayo

76

126

SANTA CLARA PUEBLO

Española

Santa Clara Pueblo

El Valle de
Arroyo Seco

VALLES CALDERA
NATIONAL PRESERVE

Los
Alamos

30

SAN ILDEFONSO
PUEBLO

PUEBLO OF
POJOAQUE

503

Pojoaque

Nambe

La Cueva

501

502

NAMBE PUEBLO

84

4

4

White
Rock

Tesuque Pueblo

TESUQUE
PUEBLO

N

Jemez
Springs

BANDELIER
NATIONAL
MONUMENT

Rio Grande

SANTA FE
NATIONAL FOREST

Tesuque

475

0   5   10

Miles

KASHA-KATUWE
TENT ROCKS
NATIONAL MONUMENT

599

Santa Fe

Agua Fria

25

Cochiti

© The Countryman Press

now a café, hardware store, grocery, take-out food establishment, wine shop, camping store, and souvenir shop famous for cinnamon rolls, breakfast burritos, Frito pies, and green chile cheeseburgers. It is still in the family of founder Martin Bode, who opened it as a trading post.

Fifty-three miles from Santa Fe, Abiquiu was built on an abandoned pueblo above the Rio Chama. The name comes from the 13th-century Indian pueblo known as *Ave shu*. It remains a stronghold of Penitente culture. It is a center home for descendants of Genizaros; in 1754, 34 Genizaro families received a 16,000-acre land grant for grazing and lumber. These residents are of mixed tribal and Spanish heritage. In recent years, they have celebrated this heritage, as more is becoming known and made public. To reach Abiquiu, drive across US 84 from Bode's toward the post office. Make a left on the road that runs in front of the post office and go up the hill. Bear around and eventually come to the plaza, with the church of San Tomas, the library, and assorted galleries. The **Galeria de Don Cocohuate**, on the west end of the plaza, is the home-studio of folk artist Leopoldo E. Garcia, the genuine article, who carved *santos* (saint figures), walking sticks, and various authentic, painted folk art pieces.

Abiquiu Reservoir fronts Triassic red rocks aged 300 million years as well as Jurassic-age sandstone. It is here that many coelophysis skeletons have been unearthed near **Ghost Ranch**. The state fossil, it is one of the earliest dinosaurs and stood about as tall as a man, at 6 to 10 feet. Known as "the little dinosaur," it's on display at the **Ruth Hall Museum of Paleontology** at Ghost Ranch. An omnipresent natural feature of Abiquiu and Ghost

GEORGIA O'KEEFFE LOVED IT AND SO WILL YOU—GHOST RANCH GETS INTO YOUR HEART AND WRAPS UP YOUR SOUL

Ranch is **Pedernal**, meaning "flint mountain." It is the flat-topped dark mesa that Georgia O'Keeffe loved and painted, saying famously, "God told me if I painted it often enough, He would give it to me." It was a site where ancient people gathered stone to make hunting points. To reach: off US 84, go west (left) on NM 96 for 11.5 miles. At a small sign for Forest Road 100, go left 5.7 miles. There is a 3-mile hike to the base.

The "jewel in the crown" of this tour, Ghost Ranch Education & Retreat Center is located 40 miles northwest of **Espanola** on US 84, or 13 miles past Bode's and the village of Abiquiu on the same road. The ranch, which acquired its name because locals believed it was haunted—a story spread by cattle rustlers and horse thieves who hid their livestock away from view there—stands on a portion of the **Piedre Lumbre** (shining stone) Land Grant, originally given by King Charles III of Spain in 1776 to a local settler. Over 300 classes and seminars in photography, writing, pottery, silversmithing, tin punching, history, health, and spirituality are offered year-round at this 21,000-acre ecumenical retreat center in the heart of O'Keeffe's red rock country. Specialized historic, movie, archaeology, horseback, and landscape tours are available, but in general must be booked in advance. Owned and operated by the Presbyterian Church, rustic Ghost Ranch is a center of diversity. It is possible to stay at Ghost Ranch even if you are not enrolled for a class, space permitting. Upgraded accommodations are available, as are simple dorm spaces and camping. Breakfast in the dining hall is included with overnight stays. The ranch has five beloved hiking trails, including intermediate hiking trails Kitchen Mesa and Chimney Rock, which traverse the expansive desert landscape with panoramic views. A $5 conservation fee payable at the visitor center grants access to labyrinth, hiking trails, and museums. While Georgia O'Keeffe did live and paint here, her home is closed to visitors.

At the **Ruth Hall Museum of Paelontology**, exhibits include recent discoveries of Tawa, a new species of small carnivorous dinosaur, and Effigia, the fossil reptile species named for Georgia O'Keeffe and Ghost Ranch. Coelophysis, the Little Dinosaur of Ghost Ranch, is about 205 million years old and lived here when this part of North America was located near the equator.

The **Florence Hawley Ellis Museum of Anthropology** commemorates the life of one of the first women to receive a PhD in anthropology. In 1934, Dr. Ellis made her mark on her field here at Ghost Ranch. There are displays of finds from Paleo Indian cultures 10,000 years old. The museum houses the world's largest collection of Gallina artifacts, a culture that existed here from CE 1050–1300.

You reach the **Monastery of Christ in the Desert** by going 6 miles beyond Ghost Ranch on US 84, left on Forest Service Road 151, and 13 miles on a winding dirt road that is pure slippery caliche mud when wet. The road is rocky and perhaps one grade above inaccessible. It leads you out of the world of the everyday into a place of pure contemplation. A Japanese monk designed the primitive rock-and-adobe church at this remote Benedictine monastery perched on the banks of the Chama River. The Benedictine tradition of offering hospitality is the community's reason for being. To make a retreat here, contact the guest master. Bring a journal, a camera, and perhaps your knitting, and be prepared to sit beside the Chama River and watch it flow. Time spent in this wild, silent place offers the opportunity to take part in the life of resident monks during prayers centering on the Book of Psalms, as well as silent meals. Should you feel the call to make a retreat and leave the bustling world behind for a bit, this may be your place. A 2-night minimum stay in a basic dormitory room (a "cell") is required. Suggested donation $75–$150 per night. In my opinion, 4WD required.

The **Echo Amphitheater**, 1 mile beyond the turn to the Monastery or 18 miles north of Abiquiu on US 84, is a red sandstone natural amphitheater-shaped formation where echoes resound. There are a few campsites and a short easy hiking trail. It is under the management of the **Carson National Forest**.

Continue through ever-changing scenery that transforms from the dazzling red rock landscapes to forested mountain lands 26 miles past the Echo Amphitheater to **Tierra Amarilla**. The name means "yellow earth," a name common to all native people who lived here and used the yellow pigment for pottery. It is the county seat of Rio Arriba County. The courthouse of Tierra Amarilla is best known as the place where Reyes Lopez Tijerina staged a raid in 1967. His movement for over 20 years was a fight to return Spanish land grant lands to descendants of original grantees. Today Terra Amarilla is a quiet village populated by old-timers. A drive through here yields many photo opportunities for those entranced by abandoned buildings. The town feels like it long ago hung out a DO NOT DISTURB sign.

Keep an eye out for the turnoff to the right to **El Vado Lake State Park,** with camping, boating, waterskiing, and fishing. This area is close to **Heron Lake State Park**. Popular for all water sports—sailing, fishing, canoeing, kayaking, and cross-country skiing, available in uncrowded conditions. Boat rentals from nearby Stone House Lodge.

Just past this turnoff, look to the left for a grand view of the village of **Los Ojos**, on US 84. You will now be about 10 miles south of Chama. This village reinvented itself during the 1960s by returning to its roots as a sustainable sheep grazing and cooperative weaving center and has served as a model for rural economic development. While it is still a weaving center where weavers of all ages may be found working on traditional Spanish treadle looms, it is no longer a cooperative. Rather, both the weaving workshop and lamb business are owned by Shepherd's Lamb, a multi-generational area ranch. The wool, made from the fleece of the heritage breed four-horned Churro sheep originally brought by the Spanish, is hand-spun and hand-dyed, and

NOTHING CHANGES MUCH IN THE PASTORAL VILLAGE OF LOS OJOS

available in a rainbow of brilliant colors, along with Rio Grande textiles of rugs, blankets, capes, hats and more, in the century-old mercantile building. **Tierra Wools** teaches residents and visitors to dye, spin, and weave.

Visible to the east of US 84 just south of Chama, like watchful sentinels, the **Brazos Cliffs**, a striking 3,000 feet of vertical space, cliffs of sheer Precambrian quartzite, are popular with climbers. And the headwaters of the Brazos River, which flows from these stone mountains over a rocky streambed, are a fisherman's dream.

Only 12 miles past Los Ojos, you'll reach Chama. Surrounded by the **Carson National Forest**, at the base of **Cumbres Pass**, at 7,860 feet, Chama makes for a four-season getaway, known in winter especially for the Chama Chile Classic, a cross-country ski event. The name of the town is a Spanish interpretation of the Tewa name *T'sama*, and indeed, a Tewa pueblo of this name was located near Abiquiu on the Western bank of the Rio Chama. It may mean "here they wrestled." The name is also close to the word for "red," referring to the color of the river. The town was founded in 1880 with the arrival of the railroad.

The main feature of the town is the **Cumbres & Toltec Scenic Railroad**.

CLOUDSCAPES DECORATE THE SKY AND TRANSFORM THE ROADWAY IN GEORGIA O'KEEFFE COUNTRY

The scenic narrow gauge railroad is a national historic landmark historic narrow-gauge coal powered steam locomotive travels across 64 miles, a 10,222-foot pass bordering Colorado in the **Rio Grande National Forest** over **Cumbres Pass** leading to **Antonito**, Colorado. It was originally part of the Denver & Rio Grande Railroad, connecting Denver with Rocky Mountain mining towns designed to carry silver and gold from mining territory. There are special trains, such as the Father's Day geology train, scenic dinner trains, a Fourth of July train with fireworks viewing, and, most beautiful, rides through the golden aspen in fall. Traveling 10,000 feet up, this is the highest narrow gauge in the United States. Open late May to mid-October.

IN THE AREA

Accommodations

ABIQUIU INN, 21120 US 84, Abiquiu. Call 505-685-4378. Website: www .abiquiuinn.com. With Café Abiquiu and Azul Gift Shop, open 7 a.m.–9 p.m. $$$.

BRANDING IRON MOTEL, 151 West Main Street, Chama. Call 575-756-2162. Website: brandingironmotel.com. $.

CHAMA STATION INN, 423 Terrace Avenue, Chama. Call 575-756-2315. Website: www.chamastationinn.com. $$.

CORKINS LODGE, Alamo Road, Chama. Call 575-588-7261. $$$ (some special rates may be available).

LAS PARRAS DE ABIQUIU GUESTHOUSE & VINEYARD, 21341 US 84, Abiquiu. Call 800-817-5955. $$$.

PARLOR CAR BED & BREAKFAST, 311 Terrace Avenue, Chama. Call 505-756-1946. $$.

Attractions and Recreation

ABIQUIU LAKE RECREATION AREA, from Abiquiu, take US 84 to NM 96. Call 505-685-4433. Website: www.emnrd.state.nm.us/PRD/BOATINGWeb /boatingwaterslakeabiquiu.htm.

BODE'S GENERAL STORE, 21196 US 84. Call 575-685-4422. Website: www .bodes.com.

CARSON NATIONAL FOREST, Call 575 758-6200. Website: www.fs.usda .gov/main/carson/home.

CHAMA VALLEY CHAMBER OF COMMERCE, 2372 Highway 17, Chama. Call 575-756-2306. Website: www.chamavalley.com.

CUMBRES & TOLTEC SCENIC RAILWAY, 500 Terrace Avenue, Chama. Call 575-741-3126. Website: cumbrestoltec.com.

EDWARD SARGENT WILDLIFE AREA, Website: www.wildlife.state.nm .us/wp-content/uploads/2014/06/Ed-Sargent-WA-WMA-NMDGF.pdf.

EL VADO LAKE STATE PARK, NM 12, Tierra Amarilla. Call 575-588-7247. Website: www.emnrd.state.nm.us/PRD/elvado.htm.

GALERIA DE DON COCOHUATE, House #8, Abiquiu Plaza, Abiquiu. Call 505-685-0568.

GHOST RANCH EDUCATION & RETREAT CENTER, 1708 US 84, Abiquiu. Call 505-685-1000. Website: www.ghostranch.org.

HERON LAKE STATE PARK, 95 Heron Lake Road, Los Ojos. Call 575-588-7470. Website: www.emnrd.state.nm.us?PRD/heron.htm.

MONASTERY OF CHRIST IN THE DESERT, Call 575-613-4231. Website: www.christdesert.org.

O'KEEFFE WELCOME CENTER, 21120 US-84, Abiquiu. Call 505-685-4016. Website: www.okeeffemuseum.org.

TIERRA WOOLS, 91 Main Street, Los Ojos. Call 575-588-7231. Websites: www.tierrawools.com and www.handweavers.com.

Dining and Drinks

BOXCAR CAFÉ, 425 Terrace Avenue, Chama. Call 575-756-2706. $.

ELKHORN LODGE & CAFÉ, 2663 US 84, Chama. Call 575-756-2105. $$.

FOSTER'S HOTEL BAR RESTAURANT, 393 South Terrace Avenue, Chama. Call 575-756-2296. $–$$.

HAND-SPUN, NATURAL-DYED WOOL FROM LOCALLY RAISED CHURRO SHEEP, AS WELL AS RIO GRANDE WEAVINGS, ARE AVAILABLE AT TIERRA WOOLS IN LOS OJOS

HIGH COUNTRY RESTAURANT & SALOON, 52289 NM 17, Chama. Call 575-756-2384. $$.

Events

CHAMA CHILE SKI CLASSIC, Martin Luther King Jr. weekend. New Mexico's banner cross-country ski event, skichama.com.

14

JEMEZ BYWAY

ANCIENT PUEBLO TO SECRET CITY: HOT SPRINGS AND
SPANISH MISSIONS

ESTIMATED LENGTH: 163 miles

ESTIMATED TIME: Anywhere from a half-day to a weekend

GETTING THERE: US 550, NM 4. 25 miles north of Bernalillo on US 550 to San
Ysidro. Go right on NM 4, which runs through the Canon de San Diego along
the Jemez River. Proceed through Jemez National Recreation Area of the
Santa Fe National Forest.

HIGHLIGHTS: The route includes attractions including hot springs, Jemez Pueblo,
Jemez Springs, Jemez State Historic Site, Battleship Rock, Soda Dam, La
Cueva, the Valle Caldera, and Bandelier National Monument, all the way into
Los Alamos; from there it is possible to loop back to Albuquerque, continue
north to Espanola and on into Taos, or head down the hill to Santa Fe

As a road trip, the **Jemez Mountain Trail National Scenic Byway** has it all—
glorious scenery in all seasons, Native American culture, western history,
Spanish mission ruins, Bandelier National Monument, hot springs, hiking,
fishing, camping, fun cafés, B&Bs and comfortable lodgings. You can style a
getaway anywhere between rustic and posh. In fact, the Jemez Byway is so
accessible from both Albuquerque and Santa Fe that it can become a favorite
getaway. In winter, it is a favorite of cross-country skiers.

If you are setting out from **Albuquerque**, drive north on 4th Street
through the Alameda neighborhood. At the northwest corner of Alameda
and North 4th, see the Glenna Goodacre bronze sculpture, *Olympic Wan-
nabees*. Goodacre is best known for her Vietnam Women's Memorial sculpture in Washington, DC. Across 4th Street, see the **Nativity of the Blessed
Virgin Mary Catholic Church**, with its distinctive double towers, dating

LEFT: SODA DAM IS ONE OF THE NATURAL PHENOMENA ALONG THE JEMEZ SCENIC BYWAY

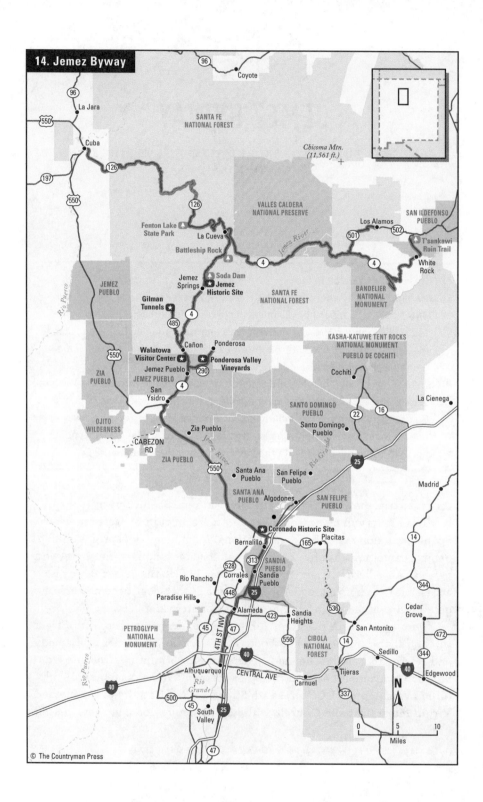

14. Jemez Byway

Coyote

96

La Jara

550

Cuba

197

550

126

126

SANTA FE NATIONAL FOREST

Chicoma Mtn. (11,561 ft.)

VALLES CALDERA NATIONAL PRESERVE

Los Alamos

SAN ILDEFONSO PUEBLO

501

502

T'sankawi Ruin Trail

Fenton Lake State Park

La Cueva

Jemez River

Battleship Rock

4

White Rock

JEMEZ PUEBLO

Rio Puerco

Jemez Springs

Soda Dam

Jemez Historic Site

SANTA FE NATIONAL FOREST

BANDELIER NATIONAL MONUMENT

Gilman Tunnels

485

4

Cañon

Ponderosa

KASHA-KATUWE TENT ROCKS NATIONAL MONUMENT

PUEBLO DE COCHITI

550

Walatowa Visitor Center

Ponderosa Valley Vineyards

Cochiti

La Cienega

ZIA PUEBLO

Jemez Pueblo

JEMEZ PUEBLO

290

4

San Ysidro

OJITO WILDERNESS

Zia Pueblo

CABEZON RD

Jemez River

SANTO DOMINGO PUEBLO

Santo Domingo Pueblo

Rio Grande

22

16

ZIA PUEBLO

Madrid

550

Santa Ana Pueblo

San Felipe Pueblo

25

SANTA ANA PUEBLO

Algodones

SAN FELIPE PUEBLO

14

Coronado Historic Site

Placitas

Bernalillo

165

528

313

SANDIA PUEBLO

Rio Rancho

Corrales

Sandia Pueblo

344

Paradise Hills

448

25

536

Cedar Grove

PETROGLYPH NATIONAL MONUMENT

Alameda

423

Sandia Heights

472

45

4TH ST NW

47

San Antonio

556

CIBOLA NATIONAL FOREST

14

Sedillo

344

Albuquerque

40

CENTRAL AVE

Tijeras

40

Edgewood

Rio Puerco

Rio Grande

Carnuel

337

N

500

45

South Valley

25

0   5   10

Miles

47

© The Countryman Press

to 1734. Other significant neighborhood locations are the **Adobe Theater** and **El Pinto Restaurant**. Continue across the bridge crossing the wetlands, bear left at the roundabout, and head north to **Bernalillo** along NM 313 for 26 miles. This scenic, straight-as-a-string road, a segment of pre-1937 Route 66 as well as a section of the original Camino Real, passes through **Sandia Pueblo** and, in season, is a habitat for sandhill cranes, geese, and even bald eagles. Pass Shady Lakes fishponds and Sandia Lakes, a recreational park operated by Sandia Pueblo, on the left. The road gives a superb view of the 10,000-foot Sandia (watermelon) mountains on the right. They form the eastern edge of the Rio Grande Rift and were uplifted 10 million years ago as part of the formation of the Rio Grande Rift. They are referred to as "turtle mountain" in Indian cosmology. Ahead to the left is the first glimpse of the Jemez (HAY-mez) Mountains, formed of volcanic remnants. Hidden high within these mountains is the "secret city" of **Los Alamos**, home of the Manhattan Project.

West of Bernalillo, a village dating to 1598, on the south side of US 550 is an historical marker noting that the pueblo province of **Tiguez** served as winter headquarters for conquistador Francisco Vasquez de Coronado in 1540–42. Bernalillo was founded after the Spanish reconquest in 1692 by Diego de Vargas. Drive through this traditional Spanish village, now growing but retaining much of its old-time flavor, along Camino Del Pueblo. The original **Range Café and Lizard Lounge**, a colorful explosion of local art, serves fine *huevos rancheros* with green chile as well as American comfort

RED ROCKS HIGHLIGHT THE ROADWAY EN ROUTE TO JEMEZ PUEBLO

food. Their signature dessert is Death by Lemon. The restaurant is located next to Rose's, a shop selling Indian pottery. The building was, at the turn of the 20th century, a general store known as the Seligman Store, where young German and Russian Jewish immigrant men came to be trained in the mercantile business and then were sent out across the state to open supply shops in rural areas.

At the traffic light, go left on US 550, then cross the Rio Grande. Go 2.9 miles west on US 550 to find a sign on the right directing you toward the **Coronado Historic Site**, Bernalillo. Known as Kuaua Pueblo, the northernmost of twelve pueblos of the province of Tiguez, it has been partially excavated and is notable for the restored Indian murals dating to the 1300s as well as the restored painted kiva it is possible to climb into on a ladder. The area has seen human habitation for 10,000 years. The visitor center was designed by architect John Gaw Meem, who popularized Santa Fe Style architecture, and this was the first state historic monument, built over 80 years ago. Panoramic views of the Sandia Mountains and the Rio Grande form a perfect picnic spot at sunset as they turn rosy in the evening light. Admission charged.

Continue on US 550 West through the desert scrub, and pass the pueblos of Santa Ana and Zia, as the red rocks that are the distinctive markers of the Jemez country emerge. Zia Pueblo actually is the origin of the New Mexico symbol that honors the four directions. At 21 miles beyond Bernalillo is the entrance to the **Ojito Wilderness**, a 12,000-acre rugged, austere, and dramatic wilderness area for hiking, primitive camping, and horseback riding. Ruins of previous civilizations, including Spanish, Pueblo and Navajo, as well as shark's tooth and other fossils remain, telling their story to the sky and passersby willing to stop and look. Almost immediately you will see the sign for the **Perea Nature Trail**, a short, gentle walk through the desertscape.

At the junction of NM 4 and US 550, go right toward **San Ysidro** on to NM 4, a narrow, winding two-lane road. Cross Jemez Creek. **Jemez Pueblo**, one of New Mexico's 19 Indian pueblos, each of which is a sovereign state, is about 5 miles from the little village of **San Ysidro**. The 3,400 souls who live here refer to their village as **Walatowa**, from the Towa word meaning "this is the place." While Jemez Pueblo is not accessible to the public other than on declared feast days, much can be learned about their ancient agricultural way of life from the exhibit in the **Walatowa Visitor Center**, across from the Red Rocks at 7413 NM 4. You will find Indian-made goods such as rugs and pottery, beverages, and a small walk-through exhibit that tells the story of the tribe, known for their fine pottery. The pueblo invites the public to attend dances on feast days; please check with Indian Pueblo Cultural Center, www. indianpueblo.org, for dates. This is the sole Towa-speaking pueblo remaining.

DELIGHTFULLY CLUTTERED PONDEROSA WINERY PRODUCES SUPERB VINTAGES

For a short side trip to a rustic winery, go right on NM 290 for 3 miles to the village of **Ponderosa**, so named for the logging industry that was vital there. If you like photographing deserted houses returning to the earth, you will have a field day in this not-quite ghost town. The main attraction is **Ponderosa Winery**, guarded by a lazy Newfoundland and a vocal Chihuahua. Surrounded by half-century-old vineyards, the wooden house holding the winery is like something out of a fairy tale such as Hansel and Gretel, and the tasting room, crowded with knick-knacks resembles the bargain room of your local thrift store. The wine produced here is from New Mexico grapes, either grown on this hill or down south in Deming. This is the antithesis of a slick, shiny winery, trading on its homegrown unpretentiousness and disregard for polish in favor of quality. The pours are generous, and there is an extensive wine list from which to choose, plus a wall loaded with prize ribbons as testament to good quality.

The road is filled with gentle swoops and curves, many leading to river access and picnic areas. Ahead is the best view of **Guadalupe Mesa**, said to be where the Virgin Mary revealed herself in 1947. In her honor, Jemez Pueblo dances the *matachine* dances in both the Spanish and Indian versions on December 12. Guadalupe Mesa served as a defensive stand for the Jemez people against the Spanish; there are ruins atop the mesa and a hike that can be accessed near Gilman Tunnels.

Jemez Springs, a picturesque village dedicated to the care and feeding of tourists, offers B&Bs, cafés, galleries and other pleasant distractions, such

The Gilman Tunnels

Back on NM 4, watch on the left for the NM 485 sign. This road leads 5 miles on NM 485 to the Gilman Tunnels, though access is restricted. NM 485 follows the Guadalupe River Canyon, with its dramatic waterfall. The Gilman Tunnels were blasted out of the rock by the Santa Fe Northwestern Railway through the canyon used to haul lumber from the Jemez Mountains, used in the early 1900s. The tunnels and canyon have been filming locations of several Hollywood hits such as *3:10 to Yuma* and *The Scorch Trials*. They are named for William H. Gilman, former CEO of the SFNW Railway. The road is paved but very narrow. Just past the tunnels, the pavement ends. There is a gate across the road at that point which is often closed well into May because of snow and poor road conditions until the spring and summer heat dries things out.

as the **Jemez Springs Bath House,** whose Victorian-era baths, updated, are fed by a rich mineralized spring, with indoor private soaking tubs, an outdoor riverside tub, and massage and spa treatments; and **Giggling Springs Spa.** The classic western cowboy bar is the landmark **Los Ojos Restaurant & Saloon,** a dark, wood-paneled place with a roaring fire in the massive stone fireplace, billiards, and old-timers hunched over brewskis at the bar. The feature is prime rib specials on the weekend. A patio addition is available in warmer weather to enjoy the Famous Jemez burger and tasty red chile enchiladas. **Highway 4 Coffee** is a good place to pick up a fresh cinnamon roll and latte or stop for a home-cooked meal. The atmosphere refreshingly harkens back to the 1960s or 1970s, a sweet time warp where people are studying the I-Ching. **Casa Blanca** and the **Inn @6300** are two of the beautiful B&B's, and **Jemez Fine Art Gallery** is worth a visit.

Across the highway, find the **Bodhi Manda Zen Center,** at 13 Bodhi Drive, a Zen retreat offering private workshops and open to the general public from December to March with a four-room guest house available by reservation. The public is also invited to attend various Zen ceremonies throughout the year. The center was founded in 1973 by Kyozan Joshu Roshi, a Rinzai lineage Japanese Zen Master.

The **Jemez Historic Site** is located 0.5 mile north of Jemez Springs on NM 4. It was established in 1935 to protect the ancient pueblo and the 17th-century ruins of San Jose de los Jemez Mission Church, with its 7-foot-thick walls and unusual octagonal bell tower, dating to 1621–22. The indigenous name, **Gisewa** (GEE-say-wah), means "by the sulphur" in the Jemez language. This is the ancestral village of the Jemez people, who occupied this site for hundreds of years prior to the Spanish Entrada in 1540, subsisting on farming and hunting. Constructed by Jemez Indians according to plans by Spanish missionaries, using local materials, the mission was abandoned in 1640, well before the Pueblo Revolt in 1680. It is made of the remains of a 14th-century Towa pueblo. Newer archaeological digs are in process to learn more about this mysterious site. An easy 0.5-mile handicapped-accessible, self-guided trail encompasses the site from the visitor center, which also contains an interpretive exhibit. It is possible to climb the ladder down into a kiva, or ceremonial chamber.

CLIMB DOWN INTO THE KIVA AT JEMEZ HISTORIC SITE IF YOU DARE

Soda Dam, 2 miles north on **Jemez Springs** on NM 4, is a 300-foot dam made of natural mineral deposits. From the parking lot, it is only a short hike down to the river and to Spence hot springs.

Battleship Rock, 5 miles north of Jemez Springs on NM 4, marks an easy 2-mile popular hike to the Jemez River. From the parking lot, it is a 3.4-mile moderate, dog-friendly hike out and back to **McCauley Hot Springs**, with its flowing waterfall.

At the junction of NM 4 with NM 126, come to **La Cueva**. Go left on NM 126 to reach **Fenton Lake State Park**, only 33 miles northwest of San Ysidro via NM 4. A pretty 28-acre lake is stocked with rainbow trout, plus a natural population of wild German browns tempts fishermen year-round. Ringed with tall evergreens, there is no prettier place to picnic than this little jewel of a lake. It is possible to keep traveling on NM 126 about another half-hour to **Cuba**, to rejoin US 550 and travel on to the Four Corners Region of **Chaco Canyon** and **Farmington**.

In the little crossroads of La Cueva, the gateway to the **Santa Fe National Forest**, find the pleasant Elk Mountain Lodge at 37485 NM 126 (575-829-3159), a rustic-elegant log lodge with access to wildlife viewing, privacy and seclusion. Rooms come with continental breakfast and an in-room whirlpool spa, making it the perfect getaway for the outdoor romantic. This area is especially popular with cross-country skiers, particularly at the **East Fork of the Jemez River**, 10 miles north of La Cueva on NM 4. This trail is also mountain bike-friendly. Good cross-country skiing abounds in the La Cueva area, including **Redondo Campground**, Las Griegos area, and west of La Cueva on NM 126 and Valle San Antonio Road to Upper San Antonio

NM 126

One of the prettiest, and most challenging, backroads New Mexico has to offer is NM 126 between La Cueva and Cuba. This road is impassable in winter and virtually impassable when wet in summer, when the dirt portion turns to slippery clay. From NM 4, heading north at La Cueva, take a left (west) on NM 126 and travel to **Fenton Lake State Park**, 9.6 miles on NM 126, then 1 mile on FS Road 314. NM 126 is unpaved between mile markers 33 and 13.5, and the curves are so sharp it sometimes feels like your wheels are traversing tree limbs. During this stretch, it is necessary to go slower than slow. While the road is not mandatory 4WD, it is a good idea. Large vehicles will not be able to make it through, how-

ever, and bumpy is an understatement. Well-treed curves requiring your full attention appear as you go north past **Seven Springs Hatchery**, remodeled for breeding native Rio Grande cutthroat trout. The road winds through woodlands to Cuba, gateway to the **San Pedro Parks Wilderness**. Near **Fenton Lake** off Hwy 126 is the very beautiful **San Antonio Campground**, which is handicapped-accessible and boasts some great fishing spots. For information, call the Jemez Ranger District office. As you travel toward Cuba, pass by several lovely campgrounds, such as the **Rio de las Vacas** and the **Clear Creek**. This is one road for the adventurous soul.

FISHING AT FENTON LAKE IS ONE OF SUMMER'S SUPERLATIVE PLEASURES

Canyon. **San Antonio Hot Springs** are 4 miles each way and make a popular, challenging cross-country ski trip. (I skied in and out and was revived by a bowl of green chile stew at **Los Ojos Bar.**) In addition, there are a few cafés here. **Las Conchas Trail** provides moderate forested hiking along the East Fork of the Jemez River

Returning to NM 4, climb out of Jemez Canyon and start winding around the narrow two-lane road. As you gain altitude, arrive at the next natural phenomenon, **Valle Grande**, one of the world's largest volcanic calderas (89,000 acres). The explosion that created it launched rock as far away as Kansas when it was formed during the Pleistocene. Known today as the **Valles Caldera National Preserve**, this vast bowl sits at an elevation of 11,253 feet. From the highway viewpoint, it is possible to see some of the 45,000-strong elk herd. The preserve itself is under management of the National Park Service and offers a rich selection of recreational activities, most of which must be made by reservation in advance with fees. Trout fishing on **San Antonio Creek** is legendary, as is hunting, hiking, bicycling and more. The area, once a ranch and before that a land grant known as Baca Location No. 1, has a long history of traditional use including ranching and tribal hunting and ceremonials. All interests are today seeking a balance to serve the many communities that have dwelled on this land over time.

In 16.3 miles, arrive at **Bandelier National Monument.** As of this writing,

VALLES CALDERA NATIONAL PRESERVE IS PARADISE FOR THOSE WHO LOVE THE OUTDOORS

New Mexico Senator Martin Heinrich was working toward getting Bandelier National Monument designated a national park to gain more protection for its natural and cultural resources. It is the most visited New Mexico attraction and a sacred site to six Indian pueblos. Established in 1916, Bandelier shows evidence of human habitation going back over 11,000 years. Here are 35,000 acres, or 50 square miles, of mesa and canyon country, hundreds of petroglyphs, Indian ruins, and cliff dwellings carved into the soft rock, along with over 70 miles of hiking trails. Due to the massive Conchas Fire of 2011, trail access may be limited. It is home to wildlife and endangered species. It is named for the Swiss archaeologist who was among the earliest explorers of Native American cultures. Heavy traffic in summer may make for a wait to get in. The Visitor Center has plenty of interactive, kid-friendly displays, and the video on the Pajarito Plateau is excellent. This is still one of the best places to be touched by the spirit of the ancestors who dwelled here from 1100 to 1500. They are believed to be descendants of the Ancestral Puebloans who inhabited Four Corners Chaco Canyon, and the outliers, who then migrated closer to the Rio Grande to become the ancestors of today's pueblo-dwellers. An hour-long paved loop trail through **Frijoles Canyon** leads through ruins and cliff dwellings. Or you can go much farther afield into the backcountry along miles of trails; backcountry permits may be needed. Ranger-led night walks and night sky programs are available, too.

From **Bandelier,** it's only about 20 minutes via NM 4 west and NM 501 east to Los Alamos, site of the WWII-era **Manhattan Project** that developed the atomic bomb dropped on Hiroshima. Areas of forest along the way have been devastated by recent fires. **Los Alamos**, with its high per-capita rate of PhDs, is still the Los Alamos National Laboratory and the nation's nerve center for defense development and other high-tech activities. The new national park, with noncontiguous locations, yields interpretations of the social and cultural life of those who worked on the Manhattan Project. Two museums of note worth visiting here: the **Los Alamos History Museum** and the **Bradbury**

DETOUR

T'sankawi Ruin Trail

The admission is included in Bandelier admission, otherwise free. The trail is immediately north of White Rock on NM 4. Look for the sign and gate on the west side of NM 4, just south of the Y-shaped stoplight intersection on East Jemez Road. It is an easy walk to unexcavated ruins with panoramic view across the Rio Grande Valley to Santa Fe and the Sangre de Cristo Mountains. The name translates from Tewa as "village between two canyons at the clump of sharp, round cactus." A 1.5-mile loop trail begins at the parking area along NM 4.

Science Museum. A stroll along Bathtub Row shows where early scientists lived, and **Fuller Lodge**, the John Gaw Meem–designed dining hall where scientists socialized, was originally designed to serve the Los Alamos Boys' School. The WWII-era infrastructure of Los Alamos is being preserved by its declaration as the **Manhattan Project National Historic Park**. Guided tours are available by reservation. Los Alamos is a thriving city of 20,000, and there are plenty of places to grab a bite or a brew. From here you can continue on to Espanola and north to Taos or return down the hill to Santa Fe. Or simply reverse course and return to your starting point via NM 4.

IN THE AREA

Accommodations

CASA BLANCA GUEST HOUSE, 17521 NM 4, Jemez Springs. Call 575-829-3579. $$$.

HILLTOP HOUSE, 400 Trinity at Central Avenue, Los Alamos. Call 505-662-244. $$.

TRAILS END RV PARK, 37695 NM 126. Call 575-829-4072. $.

SOAK AWAY STRESS IN JEMEZ SPRINGS' VICTORIAN BATH HOUSE, WHERE GEOTHERMAL MINERAL WATER IS PIPED INTO PRIVATE TUBS

Attractions and Recreation

BRADBURY SCIENCE MUSEUM, 1350 Central Avenue, Los Alamos. Call 505-667-4444.

CORONADO HISTORIC SITE, 485 Kuaua Road, Bernalillo. Call 505-867-5351.

FULLER LODGE ART CENTER, 2131 Central Avenue, Los Alamos. Call 505-662-1635.

JEMEZ HISTORIC SITE, 18160 NM 4, Jemez Springs. Call 575-829-3530.

JEMEZ RANGER DISTRICT, Call 505-829-3535.

LOS ALAMOS HISTORIC MUSEUM & SHOP, 1050 Bathtub Row, Los Alamos. Call 505-662-4493.

SANDOVAL COUNTY VISITOR CENTER, 264 Camino del Pueblo, Bernalillo. Call 505-867-8687.

SANTA FE NATIONAL FOREST, 11 Forest Lane, Santa Fe. Call 505-438-5300.

T'SANKAWI RUINS TRAIL (INCLUDED IN BANDELIER ADMISSION), Call 505-672-3861.

VALLES CALDERA NATIONAL PRESERVE, Call 575 829-4100 x3. Website: www.nps.gov/vall/planyourvisit/permitsandreservations.htm.

WALATOWA VISITOR CENTER, 7413 NM 4, Jemez Pueblo. Call 575-834-7235.

Dining/Drinks

BLUE WINDOW BISTRO, 813 Central Avenue, Los Alamos. Call 505-662-6305. $$$.

HIGHWAY 4 COFFEE, 17502 NM 4, Jemez Springs. Call 575-829-4655. $$.

LOS OJOS RESTAURANT & SALOON, NM 4, Jemez Springs. Call 505-829-3547. $.

PAJARITO PUB, 614 Trinity Drive, Los Alamos. Call 505-662-8877. $$.

PONDEROSA WINERY, 3171 NM 290, Ponderosa. $$–$$$.

THE RANGE CAFÉ, 925 South Camino del Pueblo, Bernalillo. Call 505-867-1700. $$.

Events

SAN LORENZO FIESTAS, held in the second weekend of August, Bernalillo celebrates San Lorenzo Day with matachine dances, processions, and a street fair—a tradition over 350 years old.

LIGHT AMONG THE RUINS, held at Christmas time, Jemez Historic Site. Over 15,000 farolitos are lit for this special event. Check for exact date.

WATCH FRYBREAD MADE TO ORDER FOR YOUR FRESHLY MADE INDIAN TACO ACROSS THE HIGHWAY FROM THE WALATOWA VISITOR CENTER

15

FINDING THE FOUR CORNERS

WORLD OF THE ANCIENTS: ROCK WITH WINGS TO
CHACO'S OUTLIERS

ESTIMATED LENGTH: 115 miles from **Gallup** to **Farmington** via **Shiprock** plus travel to and from Farmington to nearby sites. 78 miles from **Farmington** to **Chaco Canyon** via US 550

ESTIMATED TIME: Anywhere from a weekend to a lifetime

GETTING THERE: For the clearest sense of approaching the Four Corners on a backroad, depart Gallup on US 491 (some older maps may refer to this road as US 666) and drive 94 miles north to Shiprock. Along the way see the Navajo landscape roll out with grazing sheep and cattle, hogans—Navajo octagonal dwellings—and occasional far-flung stores and businesses. Sheep Springs is approximately halfway. You will feel as though you are entering another world, and you are—that of the indigenous. As you head north, you approach this "rock with wings," in Navajo, Tse Bidahi, a dark igneous volcanic remnant, that was once the plug of a volcano, sacred to the Navajo, measuring a height of 7,177 feet. And rising out of the desert floor at 1,583 feet. Two 150-foot-high volcanic dikes radiate out at the sides of the pinnacle. Go about 2 miles on a rough road and pull over as you face Shiprock itself. Be aware this is a sacred site visited mostly by Native Americans and Shiprock is off limits. Best viewed from US 64 and US 491, then Indian Route 13.

HIGHLIGHTS: Chaco Culture National Historical Park, Aztec Ruins, Salmon Ruins, Shiprock Pinnacle, San Juan River Quality Waters

If traveling from **Albuquerque,** go north 20 miles or so to **Bernalillo** and take US 550 all the way to **Farmington,** through **Cuba,** passing Chaco Culture National Historical Park along the way at approximately 140 miles.

This chapter is structured a bit differently from other journeys in this

LEFT: SHIPROCK, THE "ROCK WITH WINGS," IS A SACRED SITE OF THE NAVAJO LANDSCAPE

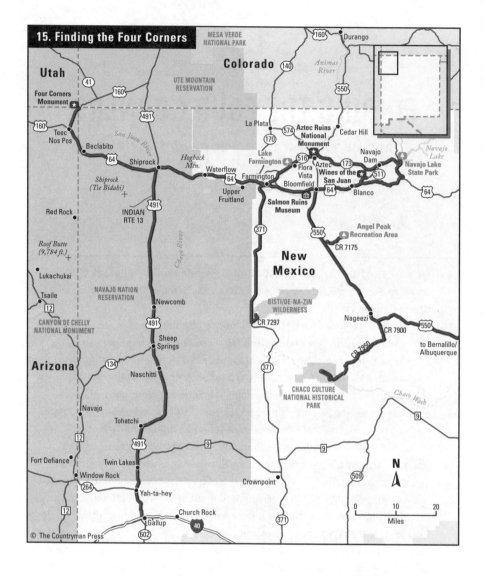

15. Finding the Four Corners

book. There is not one single road to drive; rather, if you are based in Farmington, there are several interesting journeys to take from that central point.

Probably nowhere else in the country has the landscape, the skies, and the cultural heritage, both ancient and living, as the **Four Corners**. The oceanic horizons and time-sculpted sandstone bluffs may appear simple—nature placed exactly where and how it ought to be, at home with herself—but there is a complexity and depth to this arid region that can never be fully deciphered; it is holy ground that evokes the mystery of creation.

Please consider this chapter an invitation to experience this place. More important than knowing its immense geological age is the willingness to open one's eyes and perceptions fully to it and assimilate whatever gift may come. The area where New Mexico borders Colorado, Utah, and Arizona, the only place in the United States where four states meet, is a point of power, and that power emanates throughout the entire area, an area called Dinetah, the Navajo Ancestral Homeland. This Homeland was re-occupied in 1868 on the people's return from incarceration at Bosque Redondo (see Chapter 6). Today, the 17,544,500-acre Navajo Reservation, with a population under 400,000, flows into the Four Corners states. Navajo heritage is Athapascan, from sub-Arctic northwestern Canadian regions and Alaska. They occupied the area by the 15th century CE, and they differ in language, customs, and culture from the Ancestral Puebloans (formerly known as the Anasazi). They are ancestors of today's Pueblo people, who believed their people emerged from an underground opening known as a sipapu; their history is as nomadic Desert People. They slowly migrated from the Four Corners region to the Rio Grande Valley. Their structures, still standing, embody ancient civilizations while retaining strength and mystery. While the World Heritage Site of **Chaco Culture National Historical Park** dominates the Colorado Plateau with its great houses, large structures with numerous dwellings within, and viewing it is a necessary step toward comprehending the people who created it.

A saying among the Dine (the people) is "sheep is life." Traditionally, they lived in widely scattered settlements on the Navajo Reservation, raising sheep for wool and meat, lived off the land, and practiced their ceremonies. They became expert weavers as well as adapting silversmithing from the Spanish. Trading posts mediated between the Reservation and the outside world, provided weaving supplies as well as outlets for native work, both popularizing it and influencing it. In exchange, the Navajo obtained products they could not hunt or grow, such as sugar, coffee, and canned goods. The posts also served as their banking system, where they could pawn their creations and possessions for cash.

The focus for visiting in this chapter is on the outliers, often overlooked, of **Salmon Ruins** in Bloomfield and **Aztec Ruins**, in Aztec, NM, simply because at this point in my personal journey that is where my fascination lies, with the outliers, or satellite communities of Chaco. Outliers—estimates are that 150 to 200 exist—are linked by straight roads, up to 30 feet wide leading from Chaco, built with neither the wheel nor any beast of burden, and stepped through obstacles. These communities of trade and ritual linked not only to one another but remained in relationship to Chaco.

And as Chaco became unsustainable, likely due to drought, the outliers, as colonies, delivered corn and goods. Distant civilizations, such as the Maya of Mesoamerica, shown by the appearance of cacao, feathers, coral, also had a presence. The outliers are more accessible and more intimate. When, as the only visitor to **Salmon Ruins** on a cloudy day last spring, I had the opportunity to walk the paths—silent except for piercing birdcalls—I felt

YOU CAN ALMOST COMMUNE WITH SPIRITS WHO LIVED AT THE SALMON RUINS SITE 1,000 YEARS AGO

the presence of the Ancestrals. I was able to take in, and get my mind around, the archeo-astronomy of an altar that accurately received the solstice light on one of its stone artifacts—astonishing for its placement to catch the light from both solar and lunar events, even as the earth's orbit varied over time. The great houses at Chaco were constructed in precise alignment according to cardinal points to measure and accurately reveal natural cycles such as solstice, equinox, and lunar standstill. This sophisticated technology was transmitted to the outliers; in fact, one theory holds that the Chaco elite migrated to nearby Aztec.

The rivers—the San Juan, the Animas, and the La Plata—shape and define this place, giving it unique beauty and celebrated recreational opportunities, such as fishing the Quality Waters of the San Juan River. No matter how much time is spent here, there will always be an urge toward, and a hunger, for more. **Farmington** makes a fine base to explore the area.

Shiprock, about 30 miles northwest of the rock of that name on US 491, established in 1903 as a northern Navajo Indian agency site, is a center of trading, health care, and energy and tribal business. The Northern Navajo Nation Fair is held here each October and has been since 1903. Do not expect much in the way of amenities in Shiprock, however; it is slim pickings for tourists, but it is possible to make do.

From Shiprock, travel US 64 33 miles to **Teec Nos Pos** to find the Four

Corners Monument, where you can stand in four states at the same time; or, if driving from Farmington, go 60 miles northwest on US 64. A craft market operates there daily.

To get to Farmington, take US 64 26 miles east out of Shiprock. On US 64, come directly to a bridge over the San Juan River. Then, of note is Hogback Mountain on the left, an enormous ridge of upwardly tilted sedimentary rock. This road remains busy with trading posts, including some that are generations old, cafés, car dealerships, pawn shops, and roadside sellers of wood and grilled mutton. Farmington, traditionally a boom-and-bust energy economy, is a center of oil and gas development in the region, coal mining, and electric power generation, a region that consequently suffers from poor air quality. Known among the Navajo as Tohta (among the rivers), is where the La Plata empties into the San Juan and the Animas also runs through it. A fruit industry of "farming-town" began in 1879, and it became a place of thriving orchards. Farmington is today a shopping center for people from the Navajo Reservation, a city of shopping malls and car lots, a medical center, a tourist base, and in many ways the capital of the Four Corners economy. It is a place, judging from the outstanding public library and other amenities, that values quality of life for its citizens. The city of approximately 40,000 sprawls; however, it has many cultural and recreational amenities, in particular, the 8-mile riverwalk green space along the Animas River in the center of town, where eagles fish in one of the last remaining undammed rivers in the west. The 8 miles of trails may be accessed off Browning Parkway, Animas Park, and at Scott Avenue and San Juan Boulevard. The area is popular for jogging, skating, walking, biking, birding. A much-used and well-loved urban oasis. The Riverside Nature Center on Browning Parkway, overlooking a wetlands, provides a special place for bird watching and learn about local plant and animal life.

Farmington, in addition to being close to the Navajo Reservation, also offers access to the Jicarilla Apache, Southern Ute, Ute Mountain Ute and Hopi Native American communities, as well as Mesa Verde National

DETOUR

Navajo Lake State Park

The second largest lake in New Mexico, Navajo Lake State Park, nourished by the Pine and San Juan Rivers, has 150 miles of shoreline and some of the prettiest hiking trails, particularly in the fall when the cottonwoods turn gold along the San Juan River. The lake is 25 miles long. It's a wonderful place for camping, boating, and water skiing, and ideal place to take advantage of the special trout waters of the San Juan River. It is also rich fishing for kokanee salmon, large northern pike, has boat rentals and three full-service marinas.

HISTORIC BUILDINGS AND CONTEMPORARY GALLERIES AND CAFÉS COEXIST HARMONIOUSLY ALONG AZTEC'S MAIN STREET

Park and Canyon de Chelly National Monument.

The Farmington Museum is a regional history and cultural center with a full schedule of lectures and activities. Since 1965, Farmington has hosted the Connie Mack World Series. Connie Mack World Series teams are comprised of highly talented players ages 16 to 18 from across the United States. 12 teams will compete for the championship as pro-scouts and college officials join friends, family and fans at the award-winning Ricketts Park in Farmington. Events are usually late July-early August and kick off with a parade.

San Juan River Quality Waters (505-632-2194; www.sanjuanriver.com) is 26 miles northeast of Aztec off NM 173 and NM 511, with year-round fishing in 12 miles of open water for trophy trout. It is considered one of America's top 10 trout waters. A section of the river for 6 miles south of the dam flows through scenic sandstone canyon and there are four wheelchair accessible piers along the river and an easy hiking trail 1.5 miles on the north side of river. Considered one of the nation's top fisheries, the 4.5-mile section below Navajo Dam is where to find the Quality Waters.

AZTEC

Located on the east side of the Animas River, the town took its name from the nearby ruins. This charming small town, named an All-American City has many Victorian homes and a bustling main street with galleries, Friday night art openings, cafés, and cute little shops. As housing prices in Durango have continued to rise, **Aztec**, with its short commute, is evolving into a bedroom community for that nearby resort.

Within Aztec is the Aztec Museum & Pioneer Village, mainly collections illustrating the way of life of the 19th-century pioneers. The Pioneer Village is composed of 12 original and replicated structures of the 1880s.

And Aztec purportedly had a UFO incident nearby in 1948, with a crashed flying saucer complete with witnesses, recovered alien bodies, and a military cover-up. You decide.

AZTEC RUINS NATIONAL MONUMENT

A UNESCO World Heritage Site, found 14 miles east of Farmington off NM 516 on Ruins Road, **Aztec Ruins** is best known for its reconstructed Great Kiva. Occupied from CE 1050 to 1300, this Animas riverside outlier complex served as a trade and ceremonial center. The 0.5-mile self-guided trail brings visitors through a large Great House. One's imagination wanders through time here, from the Basketmakers, those who preceded the Ancestral Puebloans. During the 10th century CE, the indigenous began moving from their underground pit houses to above ground villages, eventually concentrating their building in a 500-room development of multistoried structures. They built with mortar and stones carried from miles away. Yet they abandoned the site, it is surmised because of drought. In about 1225 CE, people of the Mesa Verde culture to the north moved in and remodeled, building two large kivas. Much of the site remains unexcavated. The small museum and video add dimension. At the time of its discovery in the late 19th century, it was believed to have been built by Indians related to the Aztecs.

AZTEC RUINS NATIONAL MONUMENT IS ONE OF THE MOST COMPLEX AND INTRIGUING CHACOAN OUTLIERS

SALMON RUINS & HERITAGE PARK/SAN JUAN COUNTY ARCHAEOLOGICAL RESEARCH CENTER AND LIBRARY

Named for homesteader Peter Milton Salmon who settled here in 1877 and protected by him and his descendants, the ruins complex includes an interactive museum focused on archaeological techniques and Chacoan prehistory. And Heritage Park is an outdoor display like none other, with examples of regional dwellings from the Paleo Indians through homesteader. Located on the north bank of the San Juan River, it was at one time home to 200 to 300 people. The largest Chacoan outlier, there were at least 150 rooms on the ground floor. Built of Chacoan-style veneer it shows skilled masonry in the precisely cut sandstone blocks and wood, capable of supporting as much as three stories.

LAKE FARMINGTON

This 250-acre lake is open year-round for shore fishing, trout, bass, catfish, and pike, and offers seasonal non-motorized and electric boating and swimming, paddle boats, and kayaks, from Memorial Day to Labor Day. Camping, grills, and picnic tables are available. The lake can be found east of Farmington on Main Street/NM 516. The turn off for Lake Farmington is accessed from NM 516/Main Street, across the street from the Farmington Flea Market.

Angel Peak Recreation Area (505-564-7600) is located 30 miles southeast

---

SIDE TRIP

Bisti/De-Na-Zin Wilderness

Only 37 miles south of Farmington on NM 371, 2 miles on CR 7297, 1 mile north on CR 7290. On Pinon Street at the confluence of the San Juan and Animas rivers, head south to the Bisti/De-Na-Zin Wilderness. Run by the Bureau of Land Management, the wilderness has no services, but there is primitive camping. Bring your own food and water. It is possible to walk among the 42,000 acres of fantastic formations that make this place a moonscape in color where dinosaurs once roamed. The remains of two ancient eras are found here: the end of the age of dinosaurs, 130 to 65 million years ago, and the rise of mammals, 63 to 54 million years ago, making this a fossil treasure chest. Leashed pets are permitted. Some of the best formations are found 2 miles east of the parking lot. Motorized vehicles not permitted. Be aware that cell phone service is sketchy. Compass suggested.

of Farmington on US 550; take 6-mile gravel road northeast into the site. The area does not offer water or services, however camping and picnic areas available. Hiking and wildlife viewing are abundant on this 40-million-year-old, 7,000-foot-high geologic formation that crowns the 10,000 acres of rugged wilderness emerging from an ancient seabed. Not recommended for RVs.

CHACO CULTURE NATIONAL HISTORICAL PARK

A designated UNESCO World Heritage Site, this area was the center of Ancestral Puebloan life from 850 to 1200 CE but was deserted by 1300 CE. This vast trade and ceremonial center is a must-see. Many questions remain: how did these ancient people create their remarkable astronomical alignments, their superbly crafted masonry buildings, and their straight roads to the outliers? Was this a dwelling place, trade center, or spiritual gathering site? Why did they choose to build in this almost inaccessible spot? We will continue to contemplate these mysteries. An international Dark Sky Park, there are night sky programs offered Friday and Saturday evenings from May through October. The park also offers hiking trails, camping, and 9-mile self-guided driving route; a moderate hike to the top of mesas gives a view of the entire complex. The park is located 75 miles south of Farmington on US 550, right on CR 7900, go 4 miles and turn on to CR 7950; go 16 additional miles (8 on gravel, 4 on dirt). Roads may become impassable in wet or icy weather. Always check weather closely when planning a trip here.

DETOUR

Wines of the San Juan Vineyard Winery & Tasting Room

This winery is located at 689 Oso Ride Route, 6 miles below Navajo Lake State Park on NM 511 at Turley. This is the ideal microclimate to produce rich, fruity wines.

Like discovering an enchanted cottage in the midst of the forest, finding Wines of the San Juan is like stumbling on a piece of unexpected magic. Driving past the vineyards and finding the rustic tasting room and shady courtyard, and a pour of your choice of their excellent vintages. Bring some good cheese or a picnic to enjoy. Definitely worth the drive! Thirty miles east of Farmington through the San Juan River Valley.

IN THE AREA

Accommodations

ABE'S MOTEL & FLY SHOP, 1791 NM 173, Navajo Dam. Call 505-632-2194. Website: www.sanjuanriver.com. $.

CASA BLANCA INN & SUITES, 505 East La Plata Street, Farmington. Call 505-327-6503. Website: casablancanm.com. $$.

KOKOPELLI'S CAVE BED & BREAKFAST, 5800 Hogan Avenue, Farmington. Call 505-860-3812. Website: www.kokoscave.us. $$$.

SILVER RIVER ADOBE INN B&B, 3151 West Main Street, Farmington. Call 505-325-8219. Website: silveradobe.com. $$.

STEP BACK INN, 123 West Aztec Boulevard, Aztec. Call 505-334-1200. Website: www.stepbackinn.com. $$.

Attractions and Recreation

ANGEL PEAK RECREATION AREA, 30 miles southeast of Farmington on US 550, take 6-mile gravel road northeast into the site. Call 505-564-7600.

ANIMAS RIVER TRAILS, Berg Park, River Corridor Riverside Nature Center, 1651 San Juan Boulevard, Farmington. Call 505-599-1197.

AZTEC MOUNTAIN BIKING & HIKING TRAILS, includes three main trails: Aztec Trails, Mountain View Trails, and Alien Run, adding up to approximately 30 miles of trails. The system starts at the Aztec city limits and leads to Hart Canyon, site of the alleged 1948 UFO Crash. Call 505-334-9511.

AZTEC MUSEUM & PIONEER VILLAGE, 125 North Main Street, Aztec. Call 505-334-9829. Website: aztecmuseum.org.

AZTEC RUINS NATIONAL MONUMENT, 725 Ruins Road, Aztec. Call 505-334-6174. Website: nps.gov/azru.

BISTI/DE-NA-ZIN WILDERNESS, NM 371 and CR 7297. Call 505-564-7600. Website: blm.gov/nm.

CHACO CULTURE NATIONAL HISTORICAL PARK, 1808 CR 7950, Nageezi. Call 505-786-7014, ext. 221. Website: nps.gov/chcu.

E3 CHILDREN'S MUSEUM & SCIENCE CENTER, 302 North Orchard, Farmington. Call 505-599-1425. Website: farmingtonmuseum.org.

FARMINGTON MUSEUM, 3041 East Main Street, Farmington. Call 505-599-1174. Website: farmingtonmuseum.org.

FOUR CORNERS MONUMENT, NM 160. Call 928-871-6647. Website: navajonationparks.org.

LAKE FARMINGTON, Main Street/NM 516. Call 505-599-1197.

MUSEUM OF NAVAJO ART & CULTURE, 301 West Main Street, Farmington. Call 505-278-8225. Website: farmingtonmuseum.org.

NAVAJO LAKE MARINA, 42 CR 4110, Navajo Dam. Call 505-632-3245.

NAVAHO LAKE STATE PARK/NAVAJO DAM, 45 miles northwest of Farmington on NM 173, 550, and 511. Call 505-632-2278. Website: emnrd .state.nm.us/SPD; navajolakestatepark.html.

NAVAJO TOURISM, NM 264, 100 Taylor Road Street, Michaels, AZ. Call 928-810-8501. Website: discovernavajo.com.

OUTDOOR SUMMER THEATER, at Lions Wilderness Park, 5800 College Boulevard, Farmington. Call 877-599-3331. Website: fmtn.org.

SALMON RUINS & HERITAGE PARK, 6131 NM 64, Bloomfield. Call 505-632-2013. Website: salmonruins.com.

SAN JUAN COLLEGE OUTDOOR EQUIPMENT RENTAL, 4601 College Boulevard, Farmington. Call 505-566-3221. Website: outdoor@sanjuan college.edu.

SAN JUAN RIVER AQUATIC CENTER, 1151 North Sullivan Avenue, Farmington. Call 505-599-1167.

SHIPROCK PINNACLE, NM 491, Indian Route 13, Shiprock. Call 928-810-8501. Website: discovernavajo.com.

STUDIO 116, 116 West Main Street, Farmington. Call 505-801-5889.

TOTAH THEATER, 315 W Main Street, Farmington. Call 505-327-4145.

Dining and Drinks

DAD'S DINER, 4395 Largo Street, Farmington. Call 505-564-2516. $.

LOS HERMINITOS, 2400 W. Main Street, Farmington. Call 505-327-1919. $.

ST. CLAIR WINERY & BISTRO, 5150 E. Main Street, Farmington. Call 505-325-0711. Website: www.lescombeswinery.com. $$$.

SPARERIB BBQ COMPANY, 1700 E. Main Street, Farmington. Call 505-325-4800. Website: www.thespareribbbq.com. $.

THREE RIVERS BREWERY, 101 E. Main Street, Farmington. Call 505-324-2187. Website: www.threeriversbrewery.com. $$.

WINES OF THE SAN JUAN, 233 NM 511, Blanco. Call 505-632-0879. Website: winesofthesanjuan.com.

FARMINGTON'S THREE RIVERS BREWERY SERVES EXCELLENT FOOD ALONG WITH A BIG SELECTION OF MICROBREWS AND HOUSE-BREWED ROOT BEER

Events

FARMINGTON RIVERFEST, May.

SUMMER SOLSTICE, observations held at Aztec Ruins and Salmon Ruin.

AZTEC FIESTA DAYS, June.

CONNIE MACK WORLD SERIES, August.

TOTAH FESTIVAL INDIAN MARKET & POWWOW, September.

NORTHERN NAVAJO NATION SHIPROCK NAVAJO FAIR, October.

Acknowledgments

My thanks and appreciation to the editorial and design staff of The Countryman Press. This book is the culmination of our many projects together. Each book has given me a new revelation of New Mexico's depth and beauty. Thanks to the encouragement of my many friends along the byways. And thanks to my husband, Charles Henry, for his time behind the wheel as I observe and take notes, his insights, and his patience with my need to find the best shot, then stop for it. And thanks especially for his insistence on never driving the same road the same way twice. I am grateful for the memory of our dear dogs, Samantha and Buckley, who always wanted to get in the car and go. And now we have Kelsey, our dear traveling companion, who loves sightseeing from the back seat.

LEFT: LOCAL LORE HAS IT THAT, IN 1947, THE VIRGIN OF GUADALUPE APPEARED ON GUADALUPE MESA ALONG NM 4

Index